Research in Criminology

Series Editors
Alfred Blumstein
David P. Farrington

Research in Criminology

continued on page 225

M. Tonry   L.E. Ohlin   D.P. Farrington

Human Development and Criminal Behavior

New Ways of Advancing Knowledge

With contributions by:
Kenneth Adams
Felton Earls
David C. Rowe
Robert J. Sampson
Richard E. Tremblay

Springer-Verlag
New York Berlin Heidelberg London
Paris Tokyo Hong Kong Barcelona

Michael Tonry
  University of Minnesota Law School, Minneapolis, Minnesota 55455, USA
Lloyd E. Ohlin
  Harvard Law School, Emeritus, Cambridge, Massachusetts 02138, USA
David P. Farrington
  Institute of Criminology, University of Cambridge, Cambridge CB3 9DT, England
Kenneth Adams
  Center for the Study of Crime, Delinquency, and Corrections, Southern Illinois University at Carbondale, Carbondale, Illinois 62901, USA
Felton Earls
  School of Public Health, Harvard University, Boston, Massachusetts 02115, USA
David C. Rowe
  Division of Family Studies, University of Arizona, Tucson, Arizona 85721, USA
Robert J. Sampson
  Department of Sociology, University of Illinois at Urbana-Champaign, Urbana-Champaign, Illinois 61801, USA
Richard E. Tremblay
  School of Psycho-Education, University of Montreal, Montreal H3C 3J8, Canada

Series Editors
Alfred Blumstein, School of Urban and Public Affairs, Carnegie-Mellon University, Pittsburgh, Pennsylvania 15213, USA
David P. Farrington, Institute of Criminology, University of Cambridge, Cambridge CB3 9DT, England

Library of Congress Cataloging-in-Publication Data
Tonry, Michael H.
  Human development and criminal behavior : new ways of advancing
knowledge / Michael Tonry, Lloyd E. Ohlin, David P. Farrington ; with
contributions by Kenneth Adams . . . [et al.].
    p. cm.— (Research in criminology)
  Includes bibliographical references.
  ISBN 0-387-97360-5
  1. Criminal behavior—United States—Longitudinal studies.
2. Juvenile delinquency—United States—Longitudinal studies.
I. Ohlin, Lloyd E. II. Farrington, David P. III. Series.
HV6789.T66   1991
364.2′4—dc20   90-39022

Printed on acid-free paper.

Typeset by Publishers Service of Montana, Bozeman, Montana.
Printed and bound by Edwards Brothers, Inc., Ann Arbor, Michigan.
Printed in the United States of America.

9 8 7 6 5 4 3 2 1

ISBN 0-387-97360-5 Springer-Verlag New York Berlin Heidelberg
ISBN 3-540-97360-5 Springer-Verlag Berlin Heidelberg New York

Preface

This book presents the conclusions and recommendations of the first two years' work of the Program on Human Development and Criminal Behavior. Jointly sponsored by the John D. and Catherine T. MacArthur Foundation and the National Institute of Justice, U.S. Department of Justice, the program was created to design and launch an integrated series of longitudinal studies of human development from birth to age 25 focusing on conduct disorder, delinquency, criminality, and other antisocial behaviors. This book is a sequel to *Understanding and Controlling Crime* by David P. Farrington, Lloyd E. Ohlin, and James Q. Wilson, which was also published by Springer-Verlag, and to some extent represents a further development and elaboration of the ideas first presented then.

The program began in February 1988. During its first phase, which lasted roughly one year, three working groups were created to focus separately on "pathways to the onset of conduct disorder," "the onset of delinquency and criminality," and "continuation of criminality and desistance from it." These working groups were chaired, respectively, by Felton Earls, David Farrington, and Lloyd Ohlin. The working groups were charged to survey theory, knowledge, instruments and measures, promising interventions and experiments, and existing studies in relation to the age groups and developmental stages with which each was centrally concerned. Their reports were completed in December 1988. During the second phase of the program, two working groups were appointed and charged with building on the work of their predecessors to develop a comprehensive design for longitudinal research. These groups were concerned with issues of "research design" (jointly chaired by Felton Earls, David Farrington, and Lloyd Ohlin) and "research administration and organization" (chaired by Albert Reiss). The members of all these working groups are listed in Appendix III. This book is based on the report of the research design working group, which was completed in December 1989.

Each agency has now agreed to support a third phase of developmental work, and the headquarters of the program has been transferred from Castine Research Corporation to the School of Public Health, Harvard University, under the joint direction of Felton Earls and Albert Reiss. After a third phase of continued development of instruments and measures, execution of pilot and methodological studies, completion of plans for data analyses, and selection of research teams and sites, it is hoped that longitudinal projects will be fielded in one or more major metropolitan areas in a fourth phase. We anticipate that much of the data collection and other field work in the fourth phase will be carried out by scholars who are not now associated with the program and who will be selected through competitive processes.

During the first two phases of the program's activity, Lloyd Ohlin and Michael Tonry have served as codirectors and David Farrington as research director. We have benefited from the advice and wisdom of a research advisory board consisting of Albert Reiss (chair), Alfred Blumstein, Felton Earls, Norman Garmezy, Malcolm Klein, Norval Morris, Lee Robins, and James Q. Wilson, in addition to ourselves. We would like to acknowledge especially the unstinting support over many years of Alfred Blumstein, Norval Morris, and James Q. Wilson, which has been crucial in establishing and maintaining this program.

The research agenda set out in this book proposes a series of studies which, if they are carried out, will be the most ambitious and important research on crime, delinquency, and antisocial behavior that has ever been undertaken. We have had the good fortune that both sponsoring agencies were prepared to provide funds for extensive planning and consultation with scholars from a wide array of fields. The product, we believe, is the most genuinely interdisciplinary proposal for research that has ever been devised in criminology. We hope that readers of this book will agree that the fruits of this planning have been worth the expense, time, and effort that they required.

James Stewart, director of the National Institute of Justice, has offered patience and support for our efforts and, in a policy world in which answers are usually wanted yesterday, has appreciated the value of careful step-by-step planning. Richard Linster, Joel Garner, and Carol Petrie have offered advice but never intrusion, and our work is the better for their help. Joel Garner made a special contribution through his stimulating analyses of issues arising in longitudinal-experimental designs. At the MacArthur Foundation, William Bevan and Denis Prager, the successive directors of the Health Program, have consistently encouraged and supported the interdisciplinary thrust of the entire planning effort. We are also grateful for the support provided by James Furman who, in his former capacity as executive vice president of the MacArthur Foundation, fostered the work of the predecessor Justice Program Study Group from 1982 to 1986 and the development of this program.

Michael Tonry, Lloyd Ohlin, and David Farrington are listed as the primary authors of this book because of their role in directing the program during its first two phases. They and the five contributing authors collaborated in preparing initial drafts of separate chapters and in preparing successive revised versions. The final versions reflect the views of many people, including members of the program's research advisory board. Michael Tonry was the primary writer of Chapter 1. Felton Earls was the primary writer of Chapter 2 on "Overview of Theories and Hypotheses," and of Appendix II on "Issues in the Use of Biomedical Measures." David Farrington was the primary writer of Chapter 3 on "Accelerated

Longitudinal Design," Chapter 4 on "Longitudinal-Experimental Combinations," and Chapter 13 on "Young Adolescent Cohorts." Robert Sampson was the primary writer of Chapter 5 on "Community Sampling" and Chapter 8 on "Site Selection." Robert Sampson and David Rowe were the primary writers of Chapter 6 on "Household and Individual Sampling." Kenneth Adams was the primary writer of Chapter 7 on "Sampling Yield," Chapter 9 on "Common Variables," Chapter 10 on "Measurement Issues," Chapter 11 on "Statistical Methods and Analysis," and Appendix I on "Preparatory Field Work and Supplemental Studies." Felton Earls and Richard Tremblay were the primary writers of Chapter 12 on "Prenatal and Preschool Cohorts." Kenneth Adams, Lloyd Ohlin, and Robert Sampson were the primary writers of Chapter 14 on "Young Adult Cohorts," and David Rowe was the primary writer of Chapter 15 on the "Sibling Study."

Our roles in this venture have provided wonderful opportunities for intellectual growth and a sense of satisfaction in being involved in what, we hope, will prove to be one of the most important research initiatives ever undertaken in criminology. The enthusiasm, sense of accomplishment, and intellectual excitement expressed by participants in this planning process have heightened our belief in the potential value of the research proposed in this book. We are grateful for the commitment and unstinting contributions of thought, time, and energy made by every scholar involved in the first two phases of this program.

Michael Tonry
Lloyd E. Ohlin
David P. Farrington

Contents

1
Introduction

The Program on Human Development and Criminal Behavior (the "Program") has developed a sophisticated, interdisciplinary, and intellectually ambitious agenda for research on the causes and prevention of crime. The agenda includes a series of overlapping longitudinal studies in a single site of seven cohorts of individuals ranging in age at the outset from birth to age 18; one or more full or partial replications of the study in other sites; a linked series of experimental assessments of promising interventions directed at different age groups; and a series of related methodological, statistical, and pilot studies.

Background

This book summarizes the conclusions from the first two years of work on the Program. The proposed research agenda has generated an unusual amount of intellectual excitement, which results partly from the interdisciplinary nature of the effort: Developmentalists and behaviorists have seldom interacted extensively with the sociologists, social psychologists, political scientists, and lawyers who make up the world of academic criminology. In principle, we all know that interdisciplinary work in the behavioral and social sciences can yield richer insights than can work in a single discipline. In practice, the world of scholarship is balkanized, and it is difficult to master even a single field. As our work progressed, it became apparent that each research community had much to learn from others and that genuinely interdisciplinary research would significantly increase our knowledge.

The Program also generated excitement partly because of our ambition to investigate the natural history of conduct disorder, delinquency, and crime from birth to age 25. In principle, we all understand that the child is father to the man. In practice, research on these subjects is segmented by age. Pediatricians, child psychiatrists, and psychologists focus their research on discrete stages of development from infancy and preschool to adolescence. In criminology, with a few important exceptions, no one studies preadolescents; some scholars study delinquency, others study adult crime.

In the first two years' work on the Program, more than 50 leading scholars from a diverse array of disciplines participated in working groups, on the research advisory board, as consultants, and as writers of commissioned papers. During ensuing phases of the Program's activities, comparable efforts will be made to elicit widespread participation from scholars of many disciplines.

Policy Context

Violent crime has long perplexed and frightened Americans, never more so than today. Public opinion polls show crime and drug abuse to be the social problems that most disturb Americans.

These broad-based public concerns are justification enough for focusing resources and attention on the causes, prevention, and sanctioning of serious crime. But there is another equally powerful justification. Victims of crime and violent criminals belong disproportionately to minority and low-income groups. Among black males aged 15 to 44, homicide is the leading cause of death. A black or Hispanic American is six times more likely than a white American to be murdered; four times more likely to be raped; three times more likely to be robbed. Nearly half of the American men in prison are black, and a black American adult male is eight times more likely to be in prison or jail than is a white American adult male. On any given day, according to some estimates, one of every twelve black American males in his 20s is in prison or jail.

These are miserable social facts about modern America. Being an offender and being a victim are too often entangled with the blighted lives of the disadvantaged, particularly disadvantaged members of ethnic and racial groups that have historically been the objects of discrimination. Serious efforts to improve our understanding of the causes and prevention of crime and to design and carry out strategies for reducing crime will be concerned with improving the lives of the least well-off in our society.

Unfortunately, policy makers who wish to put in place new programs to reduce crime or to expand the scope or effectiveness of existing programs quickly discover that the knowledge necessary to do this responsibly does not exist except in fragmentary and unsatisfactory form. We do not know enough to mount a well-conceived set of new programs. In the early 1960s, when crime rates in the United States began a dramatic increase that continued to the early 1980s, we knew even less about how to cope with the problem than we do today. The President's Commission on Law Enforcement and Administration of Justice in 1967 summarized its findings with these words: "What [the Commission] has found to be the greatest need is the need to know." Nonetheless, many in the 1960s were comfortably optimistic about the promise of rehabilitation programs; it took a decade or more of research and writing for them to realize that this optimism was misplaced. Some people were certain that hiring more police officers and having them make more frequent random preventive patrols would cut down on street crime. Again, a decade passed before studies shattered this certainty and suggested that feasible changes in levels of preventive patrol would have few or no demonstrable effects on crime rates. Still others believed that programs which provided job training, more schooling, and reduced racial segregation could address the causes of crime. Job training and job creation programs flourished; the proportion of young people staying in school increased; the most obvious forms of racial segregation were ameliorated. Billions of dollars were spent. Crime continued to rise.

We do not conclude from the experience of the last two decades that crime prevention efforts and rehabilitating offenders are wrong or always doomed to failure; that the police can do nothing about crime; or that efforts to attack the causes of crime are a waste of time. We do conclude that broad-brush, inadequately designed, poorly tested programs are not likely to make much of a difference.

So, in the 20 years since 1969, we have as a nation learned some things about controlling and preventing crime—albeit more of what won't work than of what will. If, however, we want in the next 20 years to know more than we do now and we want to see established improved public policies that both reduce crime and improve the lives of the least well-off among us, we require new research strategies.

Origin of the Program

The Program has since its inception been supported jointly by the John D. and Catherine T. MacArthur Foundation and the National Institute of Justice and builds on earlier initiatives of both sponsors. The Program originated at the MacArthur Foundation in 1982, when the Justice Program Study Group, consisting of Illinois Governor Richard Ogilvie, Daniel Glaser, Norval Morris, Lloyd E. Ohlin, Herbert Wechsler, and James Q. Wilson, was appointed. The study group commissioned the book *Understanding and Controlling Crime* (1986) by David P. Farrington, Lloyd E. Ohlin, and James Q. Wilson, which won the 1988 Award for Distinguished Scholarship of the Criminology Section of the American Sociological Association. That book reviewed current knowledge about the causes and prevention of crime and concluded that major advances in policy-relevant knowledge require a two-pronged research strategy. First, in order to advance the low level of current understanding of the developmental pathways leading to predatory adult criminality, long-term longitudinal studies of human development from birth to age 25 were needed. Second, in order to test the effectiveness of a variety of promising interventions, ranging from providing early childhood services to alternative sanctioning policies, major experimental assessments of intervention programs were needed. The study group recommended that longitudinal and experimental studies be combined or linked to the extent feasible in order to enrich both kinds of research.

Moving in parallel, in 1983 the National Institute of Justice funded the National Academy of Sciences Panel on Research on Criminal Careers (the "NAS Panel"), chaired by Alfred Blumstein. The Panel set out to review knowledge about the causes and prevention of crime, with particular emphasis on predatory street crime. The Panel's 1986 report, *Criminal Careers and "Career Criminals"*

(Blumstein, Cohen, Roth, and Visher 1986), urged initiation of longitudinal and experimental studies like those the MacArthur Study Group proposed.

The case for longitudinal-experimental research of the sort envisioned by the Program's research agenda rests on the following belief: If we are to progress in developing ways to reduce the criminal behavior of high-rate offenders, we must know how early childhood experiences, biological predispositions, peer-group relations, school and family processes, and criminal justice interventions contribute to that behavior. We do not know these things now and cannot learn them save by carefully studying how young people grow up.

For most high-rate adult offenders, criminality is not an isolated behavior; rather, it is one aspect of an array of behavioral disorders that typically manifest themselves early in life and, without factors to counteract them, become worse as children enter adolescence. Understanding criminality thus requires that we be able to explain why only some children and not others display a variety of problems—hyperactivity, weak emotional attachments, short time horizons, an indifference to the feelings of others, attention deficit disorders, and physical aggression. All manner of problems are aggravated by these tendencies—crime and delinquency, family violence, reckless driving, alcohol and drug abuse, sexual precocity, poor performance in school, and poor employment experiences. Careful prospective longitudinal cohort studies coupled with assessments of the effects of experimental interventions can unravel these developmental progressions and suggest useful ways of reducing criminal involvement. Such studies are difficult, expensive, and time-consuming. But the alternative to doing them now is to endorse in the future social policies based on guesswork, political ideology, or academic fashion. Governments will respond to citizen demands for action against crime and delinquency, whether or not they have solid knowledge to base those actions on. Crime and other forms of disorder will always occur, but they may increase in intensity in the 1990s as the number of teenagers again begins to increase. The time to begin the basic research is now.

The Program on Human Development and Criminal Behavior is a direct outgrowth of those earlier MacArthur and NIJ initiatives. It officially began work on February 1, 1988. The Program's aims during its two-year planning phases were to complete a comprehensive research agenda and to deliver to the MacArthur Foundation and NIJ proposals for projects to carry out that research agenda. This book summarizes the first two years' work and proposes a comprehensive integrated agenda for research on human development and criminal behavior.

Program Planning

We have aimed to design a comprehensive research agenda to study the causes and prevention of conduct disorder, delinquency, criminality, and serious antisocial conduct. The major components of that research agenda are described in this book and are briefly summarized in this introduction. The proposed program of research has changed substantially since we began work. *Understanding and Controlling Crime* illustrated its proposed strategy by calling for six-year longitudinal studies of four cohorts of male and female subjects identified at birth, age 6, age 12, and age 18. The data obtained would be combined to generate a set of data covering the period from birth to age 24.

In a variety of ways, our current plans represent substantial elaborations of and alterations to those earlier recommendations. First, the participation of developmentalists and behaviorists in our work has taught us the need to take much fuller account of biological, biomedical, and psychological influences on development. Second, the proposed research would incorporate concern for community and environmental influences on behavior, thus merging three quite separate lines of inquiry—the psychologist's individual differences perspective; the modern sociologist's class, group, and race perspective; and the classical sociologist's community or ecological perspective. Third, the plan to study four successive cohorts for six years has given way to a plan to study seven overlapping cohorts for eight years. Fourth, the plan to include female subjects in each cohort has been replaced by plans to include females in a birth cohort and in some, but not all, of the other cohorts. Fifth, the plan to launch simultaneous longitudinal and experimental studies in a single site now appears too ambitious and likely to complicate the longitudinal study unduly. Instead, current plans call for launching intervention experiments at different sites or at the longitudinal study sites but several years after the longitudinal work begins. The latter strategy makes it possible to formulate intervention hypotheses on the basis of findings from the longitudinal research and then to test the interventions' effects while continuing the longitudinal studies. Other alterations to earlier recommendations that have evolved are described elsewhere in this book.

The Program's activities were planned in four phases.

Phase I: *Review of knowledge*. Examine and summarize the current state of relevant behavioral and social science research on human development and antisocial behavior from birth to age 25 (one year; completed).

Phase II: *Research agenda*. Prepare a comprehensive, integrated interdisciplinary research agenda for study of the causes and prevention of conduct disorder, delinquency, criminality, and serious antisocial behavior (one year; completed).

Phase III: *Pilot and preparatory work*. Complete necessary methodological studies, pilot studies, and development of measures and instrumentation; complete a plan for research administration and oversight; select the research teams and sites (three years).

Phase IV: *Field work*. Carry out the eight years of data collection followed by two subsequent years of data analysis (ten years).

Phase I

The Program's first public act, in February 1988, was to convene a meeting in Dallas of 40 leading social and behavioral scientists. We had three aims. First, we wanted to solicit the attendees' reactions to the recommendations of the MacArthur Study Group and of the National Academy of Sciences panel.

Second, we wanted to elicit recommendations on how best to design and carry out longitudinal-experimental studies. Third, we hoped to identify people who could contribute needed insights or disciplinary perspectives to our work.

It was apparent before the Dallas meeting, and became clearer afterward, that the Program's contemplated research designs, analyses, and data required interdisciplinary working groups. Accordingly, such teams were formed to cover the periods from birth to school entry, school entry to middle adolescence, and middle adolescence to adulthood. The groups were chaired, respectively, by Felton Earls of the Harvard School of Public Health, David Farrington of Cambridge University, and Lloyd Ohlin, Harvard Law School emeritus. The identities, affiliations, and disciplinary specialties of the members of the three groups (and of all other Program participants) are shown in Appendix III of this book. Each group contained about six to eight members; half were established senior scholars and half were promising younger scholars.

The working groups met regularly throughout 1988 and produced exhaustive reports to a common charge: summarize the current state of knowledge; survey the current state of theory; survey and identify relevant variables, measures, methods, and instruments; survey and identify promising interventions for experimental assessment; identify promising ongoing studies for possible augmentation or collaboration and completed studies for analysis or reanalysis. Their reports were completed in December 1988. Critical assessments of the reports were solicited from scholars not involved in the Program.

Phase II

Two working groups were organized during Phase II. A research design group, jointly chaired by Lloyd Ohlin, Felton Earls, and David Farrington, was charged to prepare a comprehensive research agenda that incorporated the findings of Phase I. This interdisciplinary group also included Kenneth Adams (Castine Research Corporation), David Rowe (University of Arizona), Robert Sampson (University of Illinois), and Richard Tremblay (University of Montreal). They met seven times over an eight-month period; each member prepared written papers or draft report sections for each meeting. A preliminary version of their report was completed by early June and was discussed in detail at a meeting of the Program's research advisory board. During the remainder of 1989, major sections of the design group's report were rewritten, and critical reactions, especially on the overall design and on data analysis, were sought from methodological and statistical specialists on longitudinal research. This book is based on the report of this design group.

A second working group on research administration and organization, chaired by Albert Reiss (Yale), met several times and prepared detailed lists of organizational and administrative issues to be addressed in carrying out the proposed research agenda. We expect that most of those issues will be addressed and policies will be proposed during Phase III of the Program's work. The research administration issues include development and standardization of instruments and measures; mechanics for coordination and oversight of research teams at different sites; plans for archiving, analyzing, and sharing data; and processes for addressing human subjects and other ethical issues. The research organization issues include the logistics and arrangements for selecting research teams and sites; coordinating projects at different sites and projects funded by different sponsors; assuring quality control; and assuring that plans for data archiving, analysis, and sharing are carried out. To learn from the experience of existing ambitious, multisite data collection projects, a series of case studies were undertaken. These included the Robert Wood Johnson Foundation's eight-site Infant Health and Development Project, the National Institute of Justice's six-site Spouse Assault Replication Project, and the Office of Juvenile Justice and Delinquency Prevention's three-site program of longitudinal studies on the causes and correlates of delinquency. We expect that these and additional case studies will be completed during the Program's next phase of activity.

Proposed Program of Research on Human Development and Criminal Behavior

The Program's aim is to advance understanding of the developmental paths that lead to conduct disorder, delinquency, and crime in order to inform public policies concerned with preventing violent and predatory crime and enhancing the lives of the disadvantaged.

Goals and Rationale

The Program plans to investigate human development from birth to age 25 to learn why some people with particular characteristics or who undergo particular experiences become deviant predators and others do not. We know, for example, that hyperactivity at age 2 is predictive of conduct disorder at age 8, which in turn is predictive of shoplifting at age 13, which is predictive of robbery at age 19, which is predictive of family violence, alcohol abuse, and predatory crime in the 20s and 30s. Of course, not all adult predatory criminals were at earlier ages robbers, shoplifters, or were diagnosed with conduct disorders or hyperactivity. Many, however, did pass through some or all of those earlier stages. By tracking the lives of many individuals of various ages from birth to 25, we want to learn much more than we now know about two overriding questions: What distinguishes antisocial individuals who move on to higher, more serious stages of antisocial conduct from those who do not? And at what ages and developmental stages can intervention programs significantly decrease the proportion of individuals at one antisocial stage who pass on to the next?

One of the Program's premises is that significant advances in understanding these matters will not occur until substantial investments are made in prospective longitudinal studies of antisocial development. Although there have been a few previous longitudinal studies of crime and delinquency, most can offer no more than weak evidence of developmental progressions and causal influences and few or no insights about promising interventions. By studying individuals from birth to 25 in a research design that simultaneously incorporates concern for biological factors, individual differences, social and group processes, and community and environmental influences, the Program's research plans move several steps beyond anything that precedes them. The reports from the three Phase I working groups and this book describe in detail the theoretical, conceptual, methodological, and empirical foundations of our research agenda and set out a variety of developmental and criminal career hypotheses for examination.

Many criminologists agree that, to be broadly useful, theories of antisocial conduct must be integrative. No theory applicable to particular age groups applies convincingly to the life span from birth to age 25. In early childhood, for example, temperament and attachment theories loom large, but their applicability to teenagers or adults is much less certain. For adolescents, control, strain, differential association, and subcultural theories have predominated. Each has merit; none appears broadly persuasive. Social learning, social control, rational-choice, and network theories are commonly invoked to explain adult crime. Thus, our research plan, although informed by awareness of all the modern theoretical explanations of behavior, subscribes narrowly to no single theory or set of theories. Instead, we focus on known developmental patterns and problems, illustrated by the following seven sets of issues our research agenda promises to shed important new light on. These issues are illustrative, not exhaustive, and risk oversimplification. They attempt to identify some likely public policy implications of the Program's research agenda.

1. *Individual differences*. Much longitudinal criminological research has been guided by an interest in social influences on behavior. Relatively little attention has been paid to the biological, biomedical, and psychological characteristics that constitute risk factors present from the beginning of life. Insofar as biological differences and early childhood experiences set children on the early rungs of developmental ladders leading to delinquency and criminality, understanding those influences and how they operate can better inform public policy on socially desirable early life interventions.

2. *Family influences*. A variety of family characteristics, such as poor parenting, are strongly associated with conduct disorder and delinquency. We do not know, however, to what extent these associations are due to family characteristics in themselves or to underlying causes. For example, do poor but manipulable child-rearing practices increase probabilities of conduct disorder, or do inherited temperaments of both parents and children explain both the parents' child-rearing practices and the child's unruliness? If the former, then the case for social investment in programs in parenting skills is enhanced. If the latter, other interventions must be developed that structure opportunities and reward the constructive expression of temperamental differences.

3. *School influences.* Some delinquents fail in elementary school. Others have behavior problems but no achievement problems. Still others suffer neither achievement nor behavior problems. A longitudinal study beginning at birth and obtaining information on behavior and abilities prior to school entry will better inform efforts to understand the interactions among preschool abilities, school failure, behavior problems, and later delinquency, in order better to develop intervention policies.

4. *Peer influences.* We know that delinquent adolescent boys associate with delinquent peers and that male delinquents were often rejected by conventional peers in preschool or early elementary school. What we do not know are the links between early rejection by conventional peers and later association with delinquent peers. Those links would help us decide to what extent intervention to prevent rejection by peers and to facilitate entry into normative peer groups might prevent adolescents from associating with delinquent peers.

5. *Onset of, continuation in, and desistance from crime.* Only over the last ten years have serious attempts been made to apply quantitative research methods and advanced statistical techniques to the understanding of the natural course of criminality. Much more needs to be known about the onset, continuation, variation, and termination of criminal careers. Considerable evidence has now accumulated—based mostly on cross-sectional analyses of official criminal record data and offenders' reports—that has permitted the beginnings of systematic understanding of lifelong involvement in crime.

   One important question the Program's research must investigate is how we can best understand why most individuals are not actively criminal and why only a small percentage of active offenders commit grossly disproportionate numbers of predatory crimes. Other important questions are when and why people begin to offend and what childhood antisocial behaviors provide early indications that a later criminal career is likely. Nearly all criminal career research to date has studied adults and older teenagers. By these ages, however, intervention may be too late. To what extent are prenatal and perinatal influences, biomedical differences, and other individual, social, and community influences related to understanding who, among the mass of offenders, ultimately comprise that small percentage of chronic predators? Only by identifying and charting out a variety of different developmental paths or sequences from birth onwards can we begin to understand criminal careers so that humane and effective public policies against crime can be successful.

6. *Prediction of dangerousness.* Between 6 and 8 percent of active offenders commit as many as half of all crimes reported. Yet ethical and scientific efforts to identify high-rate offenders accurately have failed. A high percentage of delinquent children desist from crime at relatively young ages. Marriage, military service, leaving school, and full-time employment are often associated with delinquent youths' desistance from crime. There is a pressing social need to identify those individuals who are the poorest prospects for desistance, both to design early intervention programs to improve those poor

prospects and to design public policies to protect communities from their criminal predilections.

7. *Community influences.* Although some of the earliest sociological research on delinquency and crime, associated with the Chicago School of sociologists in the 1920s, paid special heed to the influence of community characteristics and structure on delinquency, that perspective went into decline for many years and is only recently undergoing revival. Yet we know that some communities have much higher crime rates than do others despite similar population composition and poverty levels. We know that some neighborhoods provide much more attractive opportunities for criminal activity than others do. What we do not know, however, is whether community and neighborhood characteristics influence participation in delinquency and crime independently of other social and individual differences, and to what degree. The Program's research design incorporates a variety of individual, social, and community variables and, if implemented, will be the most ambitious effort ever made to understand the interactions among these three kinds of influences.

These seven sets of issues are merely illustrations of the empirical and public policy issues the Program's research agenda addresses. The agenda's overriding goal is to increase our understanding of the developmental pathways leading to the onset of delinquency and, ultimately, of serious predatory adult crime and, derivatively, to identify promising interventions for disrupting progression down those developmental paths.

Summary of Research Agenda

The Program is simultaneously an interdisciplinary research agenda on the natural history of conduct disorder, delinquency, and criminality from birth to age 25 and a proposal for a comprehensive set of integrated research projects.

The Cohort Design

The research agenda envisions a series of interdisciplinary studies of antisocial behavior that integrate biological, behavioral, and sociological perspectives in a way that has never before been attempted. We propose launching in two or more urban areas a set of accelerated longitudinal studies of seven cohorts of subjects, starting prenatally and at ages 3, 6, 9, 12, 15, and 18. Male cohorts would be obtained by household sampling of mothers and their children (who may be unborn). Ideally, each cohort will be followed for eight years and will yield nine waves of data. At the initial interview, subjects would be questioned about the preceding year; for example, the oldest cohort would be first interviewed soon after their 18th birthdays and would be asked about their behavior while aged 17. We envisage that some of the youngest cohort would have data collected prenatally from their mothers, who would be first contacted in the second trimester of pregnancy. This design ensures a five-year overlap in age between each adjacent cohort and three years of data collection before and after any given age (except for the youngest and oldest ages).

The prenatal cohort would contain 1,000 boys and 1,000 girls. The other cohorts as now planned would each contain 500 boys, except the 18-year-old cohort, which would contain 1,000 boys. There may in addition be supplemental samples of male and female siblings, females alone, and high crime-risk offenders (such as people arrested for violent crimes or released from prison).

The major focus on males follows from a concern with having a sufficient number of predatory and violent offenders in the study population and our belief that 500 males in each age group would be the minimum required. For some purposes, adjacent cohorts could be amalgamated, thereby providing 1,000, 1,500, or 2,000 males at a given age. We have proposed larger samples of 1,000 males in the birth and age-18 cohorts because amalgamation is not possible at the oldest and youngest ages. We also wish to study the development of 1,000 females in the birth cohort, in the hope that the birth cohort can eventually be followed beyond the initial eight-year project period to advance knowledge about both male and female development over longer periods.

Before discussing the research agenda in greater detail, a few paragraphs should be devoted to its character as a series of prospective accelerated longitudinal studies. Longitudinal studies attempt to learn about the experiences of a group of subjects over time. They are often contrasted with cross-sectional studies, which examine a group of subjects at one time. Cross-sectional studies can be likened to snapshots that depict offenders and their attributes and past experiences at single moments. Like snapshots, cross-sectional studies can describe things and permit observers to know what is correlated with what, but they cannot reliably tell what precedes what. A longitudinal study, by contrast, can be likened to a videotape that, as it unwinds, can show whether children who fail in school then become delinquents, whether they first exhibit problem behaviors and then fail in school, or whether some children follow one developmental path and others follow another.

Long-term longitudinal studies have one serious disadvantage: They take a long time to be carried out. As a result, our research agenda features an *accelerated longitudinal design* in which seven groups of subjects of different ages separated by three-year intervals are followed for eight years. Because of the three-year interval, at the end of three years the research will generate data roughly equivalent to that gained by a single study of a group of subjects from birth to age 21. This is because the original group of 3-year-olds will have been followed to age 6, the 6-year-olds to age 9, the 9-year-olds to age 12, and so on. Assuming the groups of subjects are comparable except for their starting ages, the resulting data can be combined to yield a single data set covering the period from birth to age 21. The validity of these conclusions and of the methods of linking data might be established by later follow-up data. If the research is carried out for eight years, the combined data will cover the lifespan from birth to age 26, and the benefits of the accelerated longitudinal design will for a variety of reasons be much greater.

An accelerated longitudinal study of this kind has never before been undertaken in research on delinquency or criminality, although in principle there is no reason why it should not be. Leading statistical analysts of longitudinal data sets have been consulted and advise that the plan is indeed path-breaking, exciting, and feasible.

Table 1.1 shows a simplified schematic version of the proposed seven-cohort study of male subjects. By showing the number of subjects studied at each age during the course of each cohort study, the table shows that data will be obtained on different cohorts at common ages. At ages 6, 9, and 12, for example, data will be collected on three different cohorts. This has two major advantages. First, for some purposes, data from three cohorts can be aggregated to yield combined samples of 1,500 or 2,000 subjects. Second, data from different cohorts at the same age can be compared, thereby providing an opportunity to disentangle characteristics and behavior that result from the subjects' ages and maturation and those that result from the cultural or social influences of a particular period.

The cohorts also cover critical transition periods in developmental histories, such as preschool, school entry, puberty, school dropout, school completion, entry into employment, transition from juvenile to adult court, marriage, and military service. Older cohorts can be analyzed to predict the experience of younger cohorts. Cross-sectional samples can be drawn from all seven cohorts.

Community Design

At the core of our plan stands a proposal to sample individuals from 30 or more communities, classified according to community characteristics, including crime rates, within a given city. There would be oversampling in high crime communities. Information would be collected from the cohort members and their families about the communities they are living in. Changes in communities over time would be monitored, as would changes in individuals, in order to investigate how patterns of individual development varied with community context. Individuals would also be followed as they moved between communities, to disentangle individual and community influences on crime. This has never been done before in criminology.

As a practical matter, the sampling plan must identify enough conduct-disordered children, delinquents, and adult criminals for study. By selectively choosing individuals from neighborhoods with high crime rates, we can increase the chances of locating offenders and of including them in the sample. Our preliminary judgment, based on analyses of existing data sets, is that this strategy should provide a sufficient number of active criminals and other people with serious behavior problems to permit meaningful statistical analyses. Without more information, however, we cannot be certain that our assessment is correct. For this reason, we recommend that Phase III include a pilot screening study to gauge the effectiveness of the sampling plan. This project should study the desirability and added benefits of supplementing a community sampling procedure with individual-level risk assessments as a way of increasing the yield of offenders.

TABLE 1.1. Numbers of male subjects at each age, prenatal to 25 years.

Age of study	Ages of cohorts at time of sampling							Total subjects at age
	Prenatal	3	6	9	12	15	18	
Prenatal	1000*							1000
0	1000							1000
1	1000							1000
2	1000	500						1500
3	1000	500						1500
4	1000	500						1500
5	1000	500	500					2000
6	1000	500	500					2000
7	1000	500	500					2000
8		500	500	500				1500
9		500	500	500				1500
10		500	500	500				1500
11			500	500	500**			1500
12			500	500	500			1500
13			500	500	500			1500
14				500	500	500		1500
15				500	500	500		1500
16				500	500	500		1500
17					500	500	1000	2000
18					500	500	1000	2000
19					500	500	1000	2000
20						500	1000	1500
21						500	1000	1500
22						500	1000	1500
23							1000	1000
24							1000	1000
25							1000	1000

*There will in addition be 1,000 female subjects in the birth cohort.
**Male and female sibling samples may augment the 12-year-old cohort.

From a theoretical perspective, it is critical to learn how individual development is influenced by the environment—neighborhoods and communities people reside in. A community-level plan assures that samples will include offenders and nonoffenders who come from high- and low-risk areas. Thus, we would be in a position to identify aspects of community organization and structure pertaining to schools, social services, families, and the criminal justice system that could direct people along desirable and undesirable developmental paths. We recommend a series of community surveys to collect important neighborhood information that researchers generally ignore.

Siblings and Female Subjects

In addition to the seven male cohorts, the Program's research agenda calls for studies of a female birth cohort and for other longitudinal studies of females and siblings. Under current plans, as noted earlier, the birth cohort should include

1,000 males and 1,000 females, and the 12-year-old cohort should be supplemented to contain siblings. The sibling component, while a familiar design feature of behavioral genetic studies, is unprecedented in criminological research and requires substantial elaboration in the Program's next phase. By incorporating pairs of siblings in the sample, we could compare the behaviors and experiences of children in the same family to those of children in other families and thereby identify common and unique aspects of family life that shape childhood development in different directions.

Female deviance and crime is an understudied topic, partly because males are the predominant perpetrators of serious and predatory crime. However, our concern with human development and with interrelationships among a variety of problem behaviors requires that we give serious attention to gender differences in antisocial tendencies. In our research plan, females hold prominent roles in the birth cohort, which will be followed into childhood and possibly longer, and in a sibling cohort, which will straddle adolescence and the transitions to parenting and other adult family roles. We are at present undecided whether more or less attention than is now contemplated should be devoted to female subjects and to gender differences in development. One issue that remains unresolved is the extent to which information collected on females should differ from that on males. We recommend that in Phase III developmental specialists be consulted on all of these issues.

Drugs and Crime

Proposals to study drug use and especially the interactions between drug use and criminality appear throughout this report. For example, the proposed research agenda offers anew an opportunity to explore the issue of whether drug use precedes criminality or vice versa. We know, however, that criminal offenders commonly use illicit substances. The National Institute of Justice's Drug Use Forecasting program indicates that between 40 and 85 percent of people arrested on felony charges in U.S. cities test positive for drug use. Other research consistently shows that active criminal offenders tend to be active drug users and that periods of high-rate criminality tend also to be periods of high-rate drug use among drug-using offenders. Measures of drug use would be used throughout the cohort studies on various samples ranging from the mothers of the birth cohort to the members of the cohorts and their peers. During Phase III, a comprehensive strategy should be devised for learning more about the relations among drug use, antisocial behavior, and criminality.

The Longitudinal-Experimental Combination

Where feasible, we recommend that experimental interventions be included in the longitudinal studies to investigate the effectiveness of methods of interrupting the development of offending and antisocial behavior. To some extent, longitudinal and experimental studies have complementary strengths and weaknesses. Longitudinal studies are especially useful in advancing knowledge about the natural history of criminal careers, while experiments are especially useful in investigating the impact of specific events on development. Past longitudinal studies tend to have given insufficient attention to such questions. Also, experiments can typically examine the influence of only one or two independent variables, while longitudinal projects can study literally thousands of variables, but with lower internal validity. It is more economical to carry out both longitudinal and experimental studies with the same individuals than with different individuals, providing that the two studies do not seriously interfere with each other. In order to link the initial three years of follow-up data with no possible interference and to build a picture of development from birth to age 21, we envision no intervention experiments in the main series of cohort studies until after three years of initial data collection.

We recommend at least yearly data collection directly from the subjects themselves, from other informants such as mothers and teachers, and from a variety of institutional records (schools, juvenile courts, police). Other measures could be employed less frequently or only at pertinent ages.

No criminological experiment has ever had several years of face-to-face data collected both before and after an intervention. However, there are a number of reasons why experiments would be strengthened by such longitudinal data collection. The impact of interventions can be better understood in the context of preexisting trends or developmental sequences. Longitudinal data can establish baseline measures to verify the equivalence of people in different experimental conditions, to study the interactions between types of people and types of treatments, and to estimate the impact of attrition from different experimental conditions. Subsequent longitudinal data can be used to assess the impact of the intervention in changing people and to investigate both short-term and long-term effects. It is difficult to estimate in advance the likely time delay between causes and effects or the likely persistence of the effects of interventions; these can be investigated in the follow-up data.

The Cohorts

Little existing research relates factors measured prenatally, soon after birth, or in early childhood to later criminal careers. In the birth and early childhood cohorts (ages 3 and 6), the main aim would be to study the development of conduct disorder. Individual factors such as impulsivity and intelligence should be measured, together with peer interactions, family experiences, school achievement, and physical health and growth. Biological measures might include birth weight, resting pulse rate, and testosterone levels in saliva. The focus should be on risk factors for conduct disorder, on critical periods in development, and on the effect of life transitions (for example from home to preschool to school).

One important theory for this age range suggests that temperamental predispositions (impulsivity, boredom, low empathy, and irritability) are apparent in the first year of life and predict later conduct disorder. Attachment theory emphasizes the significance of the mother-child relationship in the first three years of life, identifying an insecure avoidant relationship as a precursor of conduct disorder. Social learning theory suggests that harsh or inconsistent parenting produces conduct disorder. An important intervention for testing at these ages is a preschool program including good healthcare and nutrition, parent training in child-rearing methods, intellectual stimulation, and social skills training in peer interaction, impulsivity, and low empathy.

In the early adolescent cohorts (ages 9 and 12), the main focus should be on the onset of offending, on factors influencing onset, on links between onsets of different kinds of acts, and on the implications of onset features for the development of later criminality. The aim should be to identify developmental sequences that begin with conduct disorder or minor offending and escalate into more serious crime, and to identify manipulable factors present before antisocial behavior is stabilized. Numerous criminological theories apply to the teenage years, but they usually aim to explain differences between offenders and nonoffenders rather than to predict the developmental course of offending. Individual factors such as impulsivity and intelligence should be measured, together with biological factors such as the onset of puberty, family life, peer relationships, school achievement, drug use, interactions with the juvenile justice system, and employment. One possible experimental intervention would be to train adolescents to resist deviant peer influences.

The older cohorts (ages 15 and 18) should focus on persistence in or desistance from criminal careers and on the development of frequent or serious offenders. Attempts should be made to investigate the effects of the transition from school to work, of settling down with a wife or cohabitee, of alcohol and drug use, and of the transition from juvenile to criminal justice sanctions. There should be a special focus on social control or bonding to school, marriage, and work, on the development and persistence of peer networks and co-offending, and on links between offending and community disorganization.

Costs

Although cost estimates for various components of the proposed research were developed during Phases I and II of the Program, detailed estimates cannot be prepared until Phase III is under way. To this point, preparation of detailed cost estimates has been premature. As development of measures and instruments proceeds, hard choices must be made between cost effectiveness and scientific importance. Use of some biological measures or of observational methods, for example, can be exceedingly expensive. Their importance for realizing the benefits of the research may make them necessary, but until final decisions are made about the precise measures and methods to be employed, and for what samples or subsamples, it is impossible to estimate realistically the costs that will be involved. At a more mundane level, decisions must be made about the frequency of measures: Semiannual interviews with subjects will, for example, inevitably cost substantially more than will annual interviews. As these and other decisions are made, their cost implications will become clear and detailed cost estimates can be made.

The Future

Both the challenges and the likely benefits of the proposed program of research are great. Earlier in this report, the origins of the Program, its first two phases, and its research agenda are described. Phases III and IV, we hope, will be carried out in the coming years and will respectively encompass the development of detailed research plans and protocols and the execution of the research design.

Phase III: The Intermediate Period

We propose that eight major objectives be accomplished in Phase III. First, pilot studies of a number of measures, including biomedical and alternate measures of temperament, should be conducted to determine whether they meet the research needs. Second, development activities should be completed to screen existing research instruments to assess their suitability for this project, and to develop and test new instruments. Third, a series of methodological projects should be launched to reduce attrition of sample subjects; to identify, trace, and elicit cooperation from fathers of research subjects; to compare the reliability of offenders' reports and official records; to study reliability and cooperation problems associated with frequency of measurements; and to study other properties of alternative data collection methods. Fourth, to obtain subjects, it may be necessary to screen between 75,000 and 100,000 households; a pilot study should screen a limited number of households in an eligible research site to determine whether the yield of subjects at high risk of conduct disorder, delinquency, and crime, depending on their ages, can be realized from a single household screening or whether subsequent screenings of individuals are required.

Fifth, the standards and processes for selecting research sites and teams should be completed, those selections should be carried out, and research teams should start work. Sixth, a variety of organizational and administrative decisions should be made to establish protocols and procedures for assuring standardization of instruments and measures; for controlling the quality of the execution of the research; for following rules on data sharing and archiving; for complying with rules and regulations regarding human subjects; and for analyzing and disseminating the findings. Seventh, alternative data analytic methods for analysis of longitudinal data should be surveyed and a data analysis plan developed in time for its elements to be incorporated in development of instruments and measures. Eighth, plans for standardization, delivery, analysis, and archiving of data generated by the entire complex of projects should be completed and arrangements made for the personnel and mechanics to oversee and to carry out those responsibilities.

Phase IV: Field Work

Field work would be carried out in this phase. The mechanisms and processes established during Phase III for assuring quality control, coordinating ongoing projects, assuring compliance with rules on standardization of instruments and measures, data access and sharing, and human subjects would be carried out. Finally, analysis of the data and dissemination of the findings would be undertaken at various intervals, as expeditiously as possible, throughout Phase IV.

The chapters of this book identify tasks to be accomplished and issues to be addressed. The Program on Human Development and Criminal Behavior's research agenda is an ambitious set of closely linked proposals, because that is what is needed to address the complex web of influences that generate criminal careers and deviant behavior. The task ahead is to do what has not yet been done: to launch research enterprises of sufficient scope, intensity, and duration to create a new understanding of the processes leading to conduct disorder, delinquency, and criminality and to develop improved public policies for their prevention and control. This book outlines the research strategies that the Program, at this stage in its development, deems essential to accomplish that end.

2
Overview of Theories and Hypotheses

Theories should provide cogent explanations of natural phenomena. The mechanisms and processes a theory embraces should also provide a compelling structure for discerning causality, prediction, and change. Existing theories of delinquency fall short of these requirements in several ways. Some of the most durable correlates of delinquency, such as age and sex, are not explained by any theory. Moreover, contemporary theories compartmentalize thinking and focus attention on a limited domain within a complex web of information about delinquency. This approach encourages investigators to design studies by emphasizing one narrow set of constructs over another, which may be just as plausible. Other factors that encourage constriction of interest are the limits of existing statistical models used to explore causal pathways. Many causal modeling techniques can only accommodate a few variables at a time, forcing investigators to select probable candidates from a much larger array.

This is not to say that theories are unimportant or uninformative. They play a role and are given considerable attention in this project's design. They do not, however, occupy a predominant role. The primary guide for this project has been the empirical and inductive thinking reflected in decades of research on the correlates of delinquency (Conger and Miller 1966; West and Farrington 1977; Wilson and Herrnstein 1985). Yet, theories provide ways to think deductively about the causes of delinquency and thereby offer valuable ideas for experimental tests. The most important contribution of existing theories to this project may turn out not to be in guiding the longitudinal study but in providing hypotheses that can be formally tested in experiments.

In this chapter we outline key questions, briefly review major theoretical headings, and pose a set of hypotheses as a framework for the proposed research design. These areas will be covered again in the section of the report describing unique aspects of each of the seven cohorts. The purpose here is to introduce the reader in a general way to the overarching conceptual and theoretical issues.

Key Issues

There are five key issues to be resolved by the proposed program of research. The first issue is to identify factors that place children at risk of becoming delinquent. Once children become delinquent, the task is to identify factors responsible for persistence in or desistance from antisocial behavior. The second is to chart developmental sequences that lead from early conduct disorder to delinquent and criminal behavior. The third addresses the interrelationships among individual characteristics, family environments, and community structures as they relate to criminal behavior. The fourth is concerned with identifying opportunities during development when interventions are likely to be most effective. The final issue is to select the most promising strategies for experimental intervention.

These issues make clear the challenge of conducting research that encompasses many intellectual and operational demands. The issues also point to, again, the limited contribution that any one theory can make to the overall research program. Yet, a review of theories can be instructive in suggesting ways to think about developmental relationships. Although the review that follows is age-graded because the theories covered are the products of investigators from different fields with different interests, part of our interdisciplinary effort has been to think about ways of extrapolating the implications of a theory on behavior at one age to behavior at another age.

Theories Covering the Period from Infancy to Middle Childhood

In early childhood, before conduct disorder is typically established, attachment, temperament, and social learning theories represent the major theoretical perspectives. Attachment theory places fundamental importance on a child's emotional tie to a primary caregiving figure, usually the mother, during the first and second years of life (Bowlby 1969). An insecure attachment during this critical period confers a vulnerability on an infant for developing diminished self-esteem and inadequate social skills, which in turn place the child at high risk for conduct disorder and delinquency (Sroufe 1979). Classifying and measuring secure and insecure attachment have become more sophisticated in the past decade, making this one of the most important areas of research in developmental psychology (Ainsworth et al. 1978).

Temperament theory stresses the significance of behavioral predispositions or traits as the basis for healthy or deviant development (Thomas et al. 1963). Traits can be distinguished in infants and are believed to have a lasting influence on a child's interpersonal relationships and on shaping and maintaining the child's interests (Scarr and McCarthey 1983). Certain temperamental traits, such as impulsivity and low sociability, appear to be similar to personality characteristics commonly identified in delinquents. Because the theory of temperament argues for stability of traits, the way is open to investigate the predictive power of traits observed in infants for later conduct disorder and delinquency.

Temperament and attachment theories emphasize different aspects of individual development, and researchers have tended to structure their work around one or the other theory. Scientists who prefer to give primacy to features of the intimate social bonds that characterize an infant's life favor attachment theory, and those who prefer to emphasize biological, and particularly genetic, approaches favor temperament. The relationship between these two major developmental influences has not been thoroughly investigated (Sroufe 1985; Belsky and Rovine 1987). Some have argued, for example, that difficult temperaments may adversely affect the type of emotional bond infants establish with their mothers. Alternatively, insecure attachments may encourage the development of difficult temperaments. The theory of gene-environment interaction (Plomin et al. 1988) provides an important contribution to the potential resolution of this controversy. Assuming that a genetic basis for temperament exists, this theory predicts a strengthening of the temperament-environment relationship over time. Behaviors such as impulsivity, shyness, and activity level, presumed to be genetically determined, directly influence how other people respond to an individual. Since interpersonal relationships among family members tend to be intense and prolonged, it is thus likely that a child's behavioral characteristics in early life will have a strong and lasting impact on the response of parents and siblings to the child. Outside of family settings, the correlation between temperament and environment may be largely determined by the degree to which people actively seek friends and contexts that support or tolerate their behavioral predispositions.

Social learning theory emphasizes the family environment as a setting in which children may learn to be delinquent (Gough 1948; Patterson et al. 1975), either through parents' use of rewards and penalties (behavior modification theory) or through exposure to discordant relationships and deviant behavior (observational learning theory). Distinguishing the influence of social learning from that of temperament and attachment may be difficult, however, given the covariance between them.

While no unique theories characterize risk conditions for antisocial behavior associated with middle childhood, all three theories carry implications for the types of underlying factors (or latent traits) that may be important in mediating behavioral, social, and academic competence during this period.

Theories Covering the Period from Early Adolescence to Young Adulthood

The rate of delinquency peaks during adolescence, and several theories explain the developmental processes that bring about and sustain delinquent behavior. The three theories that have gained the widest attention are social control theory, social learning or differential association theory, and social disorganization theory.

Social control theory emphasizes patterns of relationships in people and social institutions that tie individuals to society (Hirschi 1969). An individual's social bond is characterized by four attributes: attachment to parents, friends, and teachers; commitment to the conventional social order; a belief in shared values; and involvement in law-biding activities. The theory posits that delinquency results when an individual's bond to society is weak or broken.

One of the strongest predictors of delinquency is the delinquency of a person's friends, a fact that fits well with differential association and other learning theories of crime. Although the empirical association is well established, it is fair to say that no one has been able to establish the causal influence of peer networks. As a result, researchers disagree over the meaning of the peer-delinquency correlation. More generally, we have little information on the ways that peer networks recruit people into criminal careers and influence their continuation in or desistance from such careers (Reiss 1988). For these reasons, network analysis adds an important perspective to the longitudinal research design we are advocating.

Social disorganization theory refers to the inability of a community to maintain effective social controls that protect the common values of its residents. Shaw and McKay (1942) argued that three structural factors led to the disruption of community social organization: low economic status, ethnic heterogeneity, and residential mobility. In turn, these factors are related to community variations in crime and delinquency. This model has recently been extended to include a number of other community-level variables such as friendship ties, organizational participation, opportunity structures for crime, and the strength of local services to help explain the relationship of social disorganization to delinquency (Byrne and Sampson 1986). Social disorganization theory is compatible with aspects of theoretical perspectives on networks, subcultural development (Cloward and Ohlin 1960; Schwendinger and Schwendinger 1985), opportunity structures and rational choice (Clarke and Cornish 1985), and behavioral strategies (Cohen and Machalek 1988).

One of our goals in reviewing existing theories is to lay the groundwork for an interdisciplinary perspective, the most important aspect of which is integrating theories that address individual variation in delinquency and criminal behavior with those that explain community variation. For both types of theories a number of cross-cutting issues can be identified. For example, the theory of infant attachment is similar in many ways to the theory of social control. Temperament theory can be studied not only in relation to the early appearance of stable behavioral predispositions but also in relation to conduct disorder, delinquency, and adult criminal careers. Theories of social disorganization and peer networks are as applicable to young children and their families as they are to adolescents and young adults. While we are not ready to articulate a comprehensive theory that integrates biological and social mechanisms during earlier and later developmental periods, we do recognize the importance of an interdisciplinary perspective in preparing the way for a new research agenda.

Hypotheses

In formulating specific hypotheses for our research agenda, we realized that most theories do not encompass all the constructs and processes that have been proven important in decades of research on delinquency and criminal behavior. Moreover, behavioral genetics and neurobiology offer interesting new directions in studying how individuals become delinquent. Yet, existing theories do not encompass these areas of knowledge, nor are they sufficiently elaborated so as to be considered theories themselves. Our hypotheses, then, are partly guided by theories and partly by a large body of empirical research. In the process, we have kept an open mind toward new areas of research and technical developments that may permit us to address questions that could not feasibly be answered in the past. The hypotheses that follow adhere to a developmental perspective in which individual and community factors are assumed to have cumulative effects on the probability of antisocial behavior.

Three alternative hypotheses are advanced in relation to risk mechanisms operating over the first five years of life. These hypotheses describe and predict the onset of conduct disorder or delinquent behavior in middle childhood. Each hypothesis builds on the premise that a latent trait for antisocial behavior develops and can be measured during these first few years of life. The trait is characterized by impulsivity or uninhibited behavior, irritability, low empathy, impatience, and easy boredom.

Hypothesis 1. Genotypic differences among individuals are the primary deter- minant of a latent trait for antisocial behavior. This hypothesis assumes that parent-child relationships can reflect children's influences on parental behavior or hereditary influences that are shared by parents and children. A subsidiary hypothesis predicts that the latent trait is more frequently and more completely expressed in males than in females.

Hypothesis 2. The sensitivity and consistency of primary caregivers to the emo- tional needs of infants determine the type of relationship formed. Insecurely attached infants are more likely to develop a latent trait for antisocial behavior than securely attached ones. This hypothesis presumes that during a sensitive period between the ages of 6 and 24 months the attachment relationship exerts an enduring effect on personality.

Hypothesis 3. Parents' inconsistent and insensitive disciplinary practices even- tually result in the development of conduct disorder and delinquency. This hypothesis suggests that neither early temperament nor attachment (as a stage-specific risk factor) cause such behaviors. Rather, the erratic and in- appropriate use of rewards and punishment teach children to be aggressive and antisocial.

Combinations of the mechanisms reflected in these three hypotheses can also be stated.

Hypothesis 4. Genotypic differences determine a latent trait that is more fully expressed in adverse social environments than in supportive environments. This hypothesis proposes a gene-environment interaction, such that genetic predisposition constitutes a necessary, but not sufficient, condition for the development of the latent trait.

Hypothesis 5. Low verbal intelligence contributes to early risk for conduct disorder and delinquency, but through a different mechanism from the one that produces the latent trait described above. Low verbal intelligence delays the acquisition of social skills needed for effective interactions with parents, teachers, and peers.

Since an experimental component is anticipated in the research design, hypotheses are also needed to guide intervention strategies.

Hypothesis 6. The prevalence of the latent traits for conduct disorder and delinquency and for low verbal intelligence can be reduced by good health practices, early intellectual and social skills development, and competent caretaking and disciplinary practices. It is unlikely that each of these actions contributes equally to a reduction in risk, even though all may prove important in reducing risk appreciably.

The longitudinal design of the proposed study permits testing of hypotheses derived from social control, network, and social disorganization theories in a more rigorous way than in previous cross-sectional studies.

Hypothesis 7. Delinquent and criminal behavior will increase as social control decreases. Measures of social control need to be developmentally and situationally appropriate (attachment to school, work, marriage and family life, sanctions) to test this hypothesis.

Hypothesis 8. Peer rejection from networks of prosocial children during preadolescent years promotes transition to networks of more antisocial adolescents. This process increases the likelihood for delinquent activity and for co-offending.

Hypothesis 9. Once individuals become delinquent, measurable characteristics of peer networks (e.g., numbers and types of friendships) predict their persistence in and desistance from delinquent activity.

Hypothesis 10. Community structure has contextual effects on criminal behavior that are independent of individual characteristics and peer networks.

Hypothesis 11. Individual characteristics, family process, and life course transitions interact with community characteristics to explain patterns of criminal behavior over time.

Even if we are only partially successful in testing these various hypotheses, the project should be able to make a significant contribution to the development of a unified and comprehensive theory of criminal behavior.

Design and Sampling Issues

3
Accelerated Longitudinal Design

The natural history of offending and antisocial behavior can be studied with either longitudinal or cross-sectional data, a distinction first made in the 1920s (see Baltes 1968). Longitudinal data involve repeated measures of the same people, while cross-sectional data involve measures at one time only. For example, in a longitudinal study we might follow a sample of individuals from birth to age 25 with yearly data collection. Comparable cross-sectional data over the same age span would require 26 different samples of individuals, one group at each age from just after birth to age 25, all studied at the same time.

Longitudinal and cross-sectional data can be distinguished from longitudinal and cross-sectional surveys. In particular, longitudinal data can be collected retrospectively in a cross-sectional survey, such as by asking people to report on offending in each of the last five years. To the extent that retrospective data are inadequate or invalid (e.g., because of faulty memory, retrospective bias, or destruction of old records), a prospective longitudinal survey is needed to collect longitudinal data.

The distinction between cross-sectional and longitudinal data can be quite subtle. For example, if people are asked to report on the number of offenses committed in the previous year, the data would be regarded as cross-sectional, since it referred to one time period only. However, if people are asked to report on the number of offenses committed in each month of the previous year, the data would constitute repeated measurements and thus be regarded as longitudinal. As in this example, most cross-sectional data (and indeed most prospective data) refer to some previous time period, rather than to the present (e.g., current feelings or attitudes).

Strengths of the Longitudinal Design

In the interests of clarity, we will contrast a longitudinal survey of one sample of individuals followed from birth to age 25 with a comparable cross-sectional survey of 26 different samples of individuals (see also Farrington, Ohlin, and Wilson 1986). Both surveys can provide information on the prevalence of offending at each age, on the frequency of offending at each age, and hence on the peak ages for prevalence and frequency. However, only the longitudinal survey can provide information on other key features of criminal careers, most notably age of onset of different types of offending, age of termination, and length of criminal careers (e.g., Blumstein et al. 1986). This is because in order to establish the timing of onset and termination we must show that the behavior did not occur before or after specified ages.

Only a longitudinal survey can provide information on cumulative phenomena, such as the cumulative prevalence of offending up to a certain age or the percentage of total crimes committed by chronic offenders (e.g., Wolfgang, Figlio, and Sellin 1972). Similarly, only a longitudinal survey can provide information on sequential patterns of criminal careers, such as escalation in seriousness or specialization in types of offending over time (e.g., Farrington, Snyder, and Finnegan 1988). A longitudinal survey also is needed to investigate stability and continuity over time. For example, the relative ranking of individuals in the frequency or seriousness of offending, or the absolute values of offense frequency or seriousness, may be consistent over time. A longitudinal survey facilitates the study of developmental sequences, such as when we find that smoking cigarettes is followed by marijuana use and later by other illegal drug use (e.g., Yamaguchi and Kandel 1984) and can throw light on different manifestations of the same underlying theoretical construct (e.g., antisocial personality) at different ages. Another distinctive use of a longitudinal survey is to investigate how well later events can be predicted by earlier ones. Information on predictive ability and on event sequences can help determine the most effective time to intervene in order to interrupt the development of criminal careers.

Longitudinal surveys are also needed in situations where aggregate trends differ from individual trends over time. For example, the prepubertal growth spurt is often seen in individual growth curves but not in aggregate curves, because it occurs at different ages for different individuals (Bell 1954). Similarly, the age-crime curve is very different when illustrated by individual and aggregate data. Aggregate offending rates show a marked peak in the teenage years, but studies of individuals show that offending rates stay tolerably constant throughout the period of active offending (Farrington 1986). Hence, the marked peak in criminal activity found in aggregate data seems to reflect a peak in the number of offenders, not in the frequency of offending. More generally, it is often difficult to know whether changes over time found in aggregate data reflect changes within individuals or changes in the population at risk (e.g., due to mortality). These competing hypotheses can be separated by carrying out longitudinal analyses restricted to those individuals at risk for the entire study period.

Perhaps the greatest advantage of the longitudinal survey is its ability to study the same person at different points in time and hence to permit within-individual analyses of individual change. The cross-sectional survey allows only the study of variations between individuals, whereas the longitudinal survey allows the study of both changes within individuals and variations between individuals (see Farrington 1988b).

Causal effects are often inferred from variations between individuals. To illustrate, a study might demonstrate that unemployed males are more likely to be convicted offenders than employed ones and that this relationship holds after controlling statistically for other measured variables. Many researchers would conclude from these findings that unemployment is a cause of offending. However, drawing conclusions about causality—or in other words about the effects of changes within individuals—on the basis of variations between individuals involves a conceptual leap that may not be justifiable. Differences between individuals do not necessarily correspond to changes in the same individual over time. Also, the cross-sectional (between-individual) study inevitably has low internal validity, because it is impossible to measure and control for all factors that might influence the dependent variable.

Longitudinal surveys are superior to cross-sectional ones in establishing an order of events. Longitudinal data can demonstrate causal effects by showing that changes in one factor are followed by changes in another, or in demonstrating the effects of a specific event by tracking the course of development before and after that event. The impact of specific events can sometimes be investigated in randomized experiments. In other situations, quasi-experimental analyses of longitudinal data are desirable to draw causal conclusions with high internal validity by eliminating plausible alternative hypotheses such as maturation, regression, selection, history, instrumentation, mortality, and testing (p. 35). Almost all existing studies of the causes of offending rely on between-individual variation. Reorienting criminology to within-individual data and analyses, and comparing results from within-individual analyses to those obtained from between-individual analyses, would be significant contributions of our project. Information about within-individual changes is also needed to draw valid implications from causal analyses about prevention and treatment programs that are likely to be successful, when success implies that offenders have changed over time.

Accelerated Longitudinal Design

The single longitudinal survey of one sample followed from birth to age 25 has many advantages over the comparable cross-sectional survey of 26 different samples of individuals. However, a single long-term longitudinal survey also has a number of problems.

One problem centers on the distinction between aging, period, and cohort effects. In developmental research, a *cohort* is defined as a group of people experiencing the same event (often birth) during the same time period (often one year). *Cohort effects* follow from membership in one cohort rather than another; for example, people born at the peak of a baby bulge might suffer more intense competition for resources at all ages and in all periods. *Period effects* refer to influences specific to a particular historical period; for example, a period of high unemployment or economic depression might influence the crime rate for people of all ages and all cohorts. *Aging effects* refer to changes that occur with age; for example, aging eventually leads to the physical deterioration of members of all cohorts across all periods.

Cross-sectional data confound aging and cohort effects, while longitudinal data confound aging and period effects. Thus, in cross-sectional data, 10-year-olds may differ from 20-year-olds in terms of cohort composition (e.g., because of immigration, emigration, or death) and in terms of changes that can be attributed to age. In longitudinal data people at age 10 in 1980 may differ at age 20 in 1990 because of historical developments over that time and because of changes that accompany aging. Hence, in order to draw conclusions from longitudinal data about changes with age, we must devise some method of disentangling aging and period effects.

There are other difficulties with long-term longitudinal surveys. Key results may be long delayed, creating a danger that theories, methods, instrumentation, and policy concerns may be out of date by the time results become available. It is usually difficult for researchers to obtain continued funding for a long enough period to encourage long-range planning. Also, it may be difficult to persuade leading researchers to devote many years to one project and to keep research teams together. Unfortunately, researchers age at the same rate as subjects; in long-term surveys they often must arrange to transfer direction from one generation of researchers to the next.

Problems of attrition (losses of subjects from refusal, tracing difficulties, etc.) increase over the course of a longitudinal survey, and the likelihood of community resistance to continued study also increases. Also, the long-term survey may be prone to cumulative testing effects caused by repeated contacts with subjects. Fortunately, previous studies of testing effects in longitudinal surveys on crime suggest that these effects are negligible (Bachman, O'Malley, and Johnston 1978; Douglas 1970). However, further methodological research on minimizing attrition and testing effects would be desirable. Another problem is that it is hard to know the degree to which results specific to one cohort can be generalized to other cohorts.

As a means of advancing knowledge about the development of offending and antisocial behavior from birth to adulthood, the single long-term longitudinal survey has many attractions, but it also has several serious problems. For this reason, Farrington, Ohlin, and Wilson (1986) argued that a preferable research strategy is one intermediate between the single longitudinal survey from birth to age 25 and the cross-sectional survey of 26 samples. They advocated following up several cohorts for several years in order to cover the period from birth into the mid-20s. Specifically, they proposed studying one cohort from birth to age 6, a second from age 6 to age 12, a third from age 12 to age 18, and a fourth from age 18 to age 24. They recommended that all cohort studies be carried out at the same time, so that results could be amalgamated into a picture of development from birth to age 24 after only six years of research. The objective of the proposed design was to maintain the advantages of the longitudinal study and minimize its disadvantages.

The accelerated longitudinal design, such as that advocated by Farrington, Ohlin, and Wilson (1986), was first proposed by Bell (1953), who later provided an empirical example (Bell 1954). Schaie (1965) pointed out that traditional cross-sectional and longitudinal designs were essentially special cases drawn from a general age-period-cohort matrix. He outlined three intermediate follow-up techniques that could be used to achieve at least some success at disentangling aging, period, and cohort effects: (a) cohort-sequential (e.g., beginning with different birth cohorts in different years, such as those born in 1960, 1961, and 1962); (b) cross-sequential (e.g., beginning with different birth cohorts in the same year, such as studying the 1960 to 1962 birth cohorts in 1970); and (c) time-sequential (e.g., following up the same ages in different years, such as ages 10 to 12 in 1970 and ages 10 to 12 in 1971). The Farrington, Ohlin, and Wilson (1986) proposal is termed cross-sequential in this scheme; however, following Bell (1953), we characterize it as an accelerated longitudinal design. (For later discussions of mixed designs, see Schaie and Baltes 1975; Schaie 1977; Labouvie and Nesselroade 1985).

An obvious advantage of the accelerated design over the single-cohort longitudinal survey is that the total follow-up period is shorter. Consequently, the funding period is shorter, results can be produced more quickly, and objections are less likely to be raised about out-of-date theories, methods, instruments, and policy concerns. Problems of ensuring continuity in the research organization are fewer, and a shorter follow-up period reduces problems of cumulative testing effects and attrition. Another advantage is that the follow-up of several cohorts (rather than one) increases confidence in the generalizability of the results.

As already mentioned, a longitudinal survey confounds aging and period effects, whereas a cross-sectional survey confounds aging and cohort effects. Our main interest is in aging effects (i.e., in developmental changes with age). The accelerated design makes it possible to study aging effects independently of period and cohort effects, but only if different cohorts are followed up between the same ages in different periods. This consideration argues for a substantial overlap (of several years) between the follow-up ages of different cohorts. Hence, the Farrington-Ohlin-Wilson (1986) design (birth–6, 6–12, 12–18, 18–24) is inadequate on this criterion because the overlap between different cohorts is only one year.

The main disadvantages of the accelerated design in comparison with the single-cohort longitudinal survey are that within-individual developmental sequences are tracked over shorter periods, and similarly that behavior continuity and prediction are studied over shorter periods. These are consequential disadvantages, especially if there are long-term causal effects (or developmental sequences) that occur without intermediate effects or sequences. Long-term relationships have been demonstrated, for example, between child abuse and later adult violence (e.g., Widom 1989), but there are usually measurable intermediate stages or stepping stones that lead to long-term outcomes.

Long-term causal effects that occur in the absence of identifiable intermediate influences have been called sleeper effects. For example, some argued that the long-term effects of the Perry preschool intellectual enrichment program on offending (Berrueta-Clement et al. 1984) reflect such sleeper effects. It seems more plausible, however, to argue that there was a long chain of shorter-term causal influences rather than a long-delayed effect (Woodhead 1985). In contrast, long-delayed effects may be more common in the case of illnesses such as cancer. The possibility of sleeper effects, however, suggests that the longest possible follow-up period is desirable.

Farrington, Ohlin, and Wilson (1986, pp. 154–155) argued that the accelerated longitudinal design might permit conclusions about long-term effects:

Imagine that in the survey from birth to age 6, a preschool intellectual enrichment program at ages 3–4 produced an improvement in school behavior at age 6. The survey from 6 to 12 may well show how school behavior at 6 predicts school behavior at 12, while the survey from 12 to 18 may show how school behavior at 12 predicts delinquency by 18, and the survey from 18 to 24 may show how delinquency by 18 predicts adult offending by 24. Would it not be reasonable to conclude from this chain of evidence that a preschool intellectual enrichment program has a long-term-crime-reducing effect?

The accelerated design, in comparison with the single-cohort survey, makes it harder to draw conclusions about criminal career features such as onset and termination and about cumulative phenomena such as cumulative prevalence. However, some of these problems might be overcome by asking retrospective questions. For example, in the first interview, subjects could be asked if they had ever committed specified offenses and, if so, at what age they had first committed them. This information could be used, together with later prospective data, in plotting distributions of ages of onset.

The disadvantages of the accelerated design could be overcome if individuals in the different cohorts could be linked to build up a picture of development from the prenatal years to adulthood. Bell (1954) linked up different cohorts essentially by matching individuals at overlapping ages. A key question is whether the advantages of this linkage strategy outweigh the known disadvantages of matching. More sophisticated methods of linkage could also be used. For example, following Rogosa and Willett (1985), individual growth curves could be developed (e.g., for the frequency of offending) for overlapping ages, and individuals (or groups of individuals) could be matched on growth curve parameters. The development of methods for linking different cohorts could be an important methodological contribution of our project. Provided that the total follow-up period is considerably longer than the period of overlap, the validity of any linkage method could be tested in later follow-up data.

In order for different cohorts to be linked, subjects should be as comparable as possible. Unfortunately, problems associated with cross-sectional aspects of the accelerated design can make it difficult to achieve comparability. In general, a representative cohort of 18-year-olds in a city will differ from a representative birth cohort because of immigration, emigration, and deaths in the past 18 years. There is clearly a tension between comparability and representativeness of cohorts that cannot be resolved by interviewing a cohort of individuals born in the same city 18 years ago, even if this were a feasible starting point for a longitudinal survey. The tension between comparability and representativeness, however, might possibly be resolved by linking up only subsamples of each cohort.

Retrospective data covering the intercohort interval might also be used in linking up cohorts. For example, the first interview with a cohort of 18-year-olds could include questions about development since age 12 that might be used in linking up these subjects with those in the 12-year-old cohort. It then becomes important to assess the validity of such retrospective data by asking retrospective questions of the 12-year-old cohort at the end of the 6-year follow-up period and by comparing the retrospective information with data collected prospectively during the follow-up period.

Between the single-cohort longitudinal survey from birth to age 25 and the cross-sectional survey of 26 samples, there are many intermediate possibilities, and the four-cohort scheme proposed by Farrington, Ohlin, and Wilson (1986) is not necessarily the best choice. In choosing among possibilities, an important consideration is that the follow-up period should be quite long (more than five years) in order to gain some of the key advantages of longitudinal research. However, in order to minimize problems of continuity in funding and in research organization, the total project period should be limited to about ten years, thus permitting a maximum follow-up period of seven or eight years.

The next consideration is that the number of different cohorts should not be too great. Each cohort will have to be analyzed separately for some purposes, and hence each must contain a minimum number of people (about 500, as argued elsewhere) in order to draw conclusions about effects and to estimate population parameters within relatively small confidence intervals. It would be prohibitively expensive to have one cohort beginning at every age from birth onwards, and likewise it would be prohibitively expensive to have a two-year intercohort interval. Hence, the minimum possible intercohort interval is three years.

Another consideration is that, to facilitate disentangling of aging effects and linkage of different cohorts, the period of overlap between cohorts should be as long as possible. The period of overlap is the total follow-up period minus the intercohort interval. Given a maximum follow-up period of eight years and a minimum intercohort interval of three years, the maximum period of overlap is five years.

The final consideration relates to the importance of being able to assess the impact of important events, life transitions, and experimental interventions on the course of development by studying periods before and after such events. The follow-up period needs to be long enough before and after the event (arguably at least two or three years in each case) to establish effects on development.

In a multiple cohort study, the length of the follow-up period in years and the interval in years between each cohort determine the minimum follow-up time before and after any given age, assuming that the event and its causal impact occur at a particular age. Table 3.1 shows the minimum follow-up period in years before and after any given age for combinations of various intercohort intervals and follow-up periods. It is convenient to assume that data will be collected at least once a year.

TABLE 3.1. Minimum follow-up periods (in years) before and after any age.

Intercohort interval (in years)	Total follow-up period (in years)				Minimum no. of cohorts to cover starting ages from prenatal to 18
	5	6	7	8	
1	2	3	3	4	19
2	2	2	3	3	10
3	1	2	2	3	7
4	1	1	2	2	6
5	0	1	1	2	5
6	*	0	1	1	4

* = No overlap between cohorts.

All these considerations suggest that the optimal design involves a three-year intercohort interval, an eight-year total follow-up period, and a five-year overlap period. This design requires seven cohorts with starting ages from prenatal to age 18 (prenatal, 3, 6, 9, 12, 15, and 18), to cover the period from the prenatal time to age 26. It also ensures three years of follow-up data before and after any age (excluding the earliest and the latest ages).

One advantage of this design is that a one-year overlap between cohorts is achieved after three years of follow-up, thus allowing early publication (five years after the start of the project) of preliminary conclusions about development from the prenatal time to age 21. Subsequent follow-up data could then validate and extend these early conclusions, and early analyses could guide later follow-up data collection. Insofar as experimental interventions are feasible, they should be delayed until after the initial three-year follow-up period, so that the synthetic cohort can be built from non-experimental data.

4
Longitudinal-Experimental Combinations

An experiment is a systematic attempt to investigate the effect of variations in one factor, the independent variable, on another, the dependent variable. The independent variable is under the control of the experimenter; in other words, the experimenter decides which people receive which treatment, using the word *treatment* very widely to include all kinds of interventions. The focus here is on randomized experiments in which people are assigned at random to different treatments. Given a large number of people, randomization ensures that subjects in experimental and control groups on average are equivalent on all possible extraneous variables, within the limits of small statistical fluctuations. This feature of randomization makes it possible to isolate and disentangle the effect of the independent variable from the effect of all other extraneous variables (see e.g., Farrington 1983).

Experiments are either explanatory or pragmatic; they are designed to test causal hypotheses or to evaluate the impact of different treatments. The two aims are not necessarily incompatible, but in practice most experiments fall into one or the other category. Because randomized experiments are difficult to mount and carry out successfully, they are often conducted when there is good reason from prior nonexperimental research to believe that the hypothesis to be tested is correct or the treatment will be effective. Conversely, experiments rarely are carried out without an explicit hypothesis about the effect of an independent variable on a dependent one.

Technically, a randomized experiment is the best method of testing and eliminating alternative explanations of apparent causal effects or threats to internal validity (see Campbell and Stanley 1966; Cook and Campbell 1979). The major alternative explanations are: (1) history—the observed effect is caused by other independent variables; (2) maturation—the observed effect is part of a preexisting trend; (3) testing—the observed effect is caused by prior testing of research subjects; (4) instrumentation—the observed effect is caused by changes in measurement techniques; (5) regression—the observed effect is caused by statistical regression of extreme scorers to the mean; (6) selection—the observed effect is caused by preexisting differences among the groups being compared; (7) mortality—the observed effect is caused by differential loss of subjects from comparison and experimental groups; (8) instability—the observed effect reflects random variation; and (9) causal order—the true causal order is opposite to that hypothesized.

The alternative explanation that is typically a problem in randomized experiments is mortality, or the differential loss of subjects from different experimental conditions. One way of dealing with this problem is to randomize treatments within matched pairs of subjects. This strategy allows the researcher to drop both members of a pair from the experiment if one member is lost for any reason. This example assumes a simple experiment with one independent variable and two experimental conditions; more complex experiments are, of course, possible, but the basic arguments are essentially unaffected by the increase in complexity.

In contrast, threats to valid causal inference are a great problem in nonexperimental research projects. In particular, in correlational research it is impossible to measure all possible extraneous variables that might influence the presumed dependent variable, and hence it is impossible to isolate and disentangle fully the causal effect of the independent variable of interest. The impact of extraneous variables is typically controlled by statistical adjustments, but this procedure can never be as satisfactory as experimental control, partly because of the limited number of variables included in most causal analyses. Hence, correlational research projects inevitably have low internal validity and a poor ability to demonstrate causal effects unambiguously.

Problems of Experiments

The major problems arising in experiments often involve the legal, ethical, and practical difficulties of mounting an experiment and carrying it through successfully. There are many examples in the literature of implementation failures and randomization designs that broke down (e.g., Conner 1977). Randomized experiments are more difficult and riskier than, for example, correlational research projects.

Typically, it is only possible to study the effect of one or two independent variables at two or three different levels (different experimental conditions) in a randomized experiment in the field (as opposed to the laboratory). For example, very few of the possible causes of offending could in practice be studied experimentally, and it would be extremely difficult to build up something approximating a dose-response curve using randomized experiments. Hence, a theory of offending limited to results obtained in experiments would be extremely inadequate.

Many thorny methodological problems arise in randomized experiments in criminology. For example, it is hard to ensure that all subjects in a treatment group actually receive the treatment and that all those in a control group do not. Consequently, the distinction between treatment and control groups often blurs, leading to an underestimation of the treatment's effect. Also, as already mentioned, differential attrition from treatment and control groups can lead to problems. Another difficulty is that subjects and treatment professionals rarely can be kept blind to the status of research subjects, and knowledge about participation in the experiment may bias the measurement of outcomes. Other common design problems are that experiments have insufficient statistical power to detect effects and that they are rarely designed to study possible interactions between types of people and types of treatments. These methodological problems can be overcome by high-quality design and implementation.

Typically, experiments are designed to investigate only immediate or short-term causal effects. Subjects are rarely followed for more than one year after an experiment. However, some experimental interventions may have long-term effects, and in some cases these effects have been found to differ from short-term ones (e.g., Waldo and Griswold 1979). More fundamentally, researchers rarely know the typical time delay between a cause and an effect, suggesting that measurements at several different intervals are desirable. This is one reason for proposing a longitudinal-experimental study in which experimental interventions are investigated during a long-term longitudinal study with repeated measurement points.

Advantages of the Longitudinal-Experimental Study

Strictly speaking, every experiment is prospective and longitudinal in nature, since it involves a minimum of two contacts with the experimental subjects: one contact for experimental intervention (the independent variable) and one for measuring an outcome (the dependent variable). However, as already indicated, the time interval between contacts for the typical experiment is relatively short. The type of longitudinal-experimental study proposed here has three sequential stages: (1) several data collection efforts over several years; (2) the experimental intervention; and (3) several more data collection efforts for several years afterwards. No study of this kind has ever been carried out in criminology (excluding studies collecting data only from official statistics).

The advantages of longitudinal studies are reviewed at length in Chapter 3. However, as Farrington, Ohlin, and Wilson (1986, p. 61) succinctly point out:

The most important limitation of existing longitudinal studies is the lack of attention to impact questions. We have learned a great deal about the natural history of criminal careers but little about the effects of specific events on the course of development of these careers. From the point of view of explanation, prevention, and treatment, more experimental and quasi-experimental research is needed within longitudinal studies.

Economy is an important advantage that a combined longitudinal-experimental study has over separate longitudinal and experimental studies, because it is cheaper to carry out both studies with a single group of individuals. Other things being equal, the number of subjects and separate data collections (e.g., interviews) is greater in two separate studies than in one combined study.

More fundamentally, experiments and longitudinal studies have different strengths and weaknesses, and a combined project can build on the strengths of both. For example, a longitudinal study can provide information on the natural history of development, while an experimental study can yield knowledge about the impact of interventions on development. Even if the experiment is not carried through successfully, the longitudinal-experimental study will provide valuable knowledge about the natural history of development, and quasi-experimental research on the impact of specific events will still be possible.

Experiments are for testing hypotheses. In a combined project, causal hypotheses can be generated in the longitudinal component and then tested on the same individuals in the experimental component. An experiment is the best method for studying the effects of variations in an independent variable on outcomes, whereas a longitudinal study investigates the effects of changes in an independent variable. Hence, a combined project can compare the effects of both variation and change in the independent variable to see if the same results are obtained. This is an important issue because most criminological findings essentially concern variations between individuals, whereas most theories and interventions refer to changes within individuals. The longitudinal and experimental elements are also complementary in that the experiment can investigate (with high internal validity) the effect of only a few independent variables, whereas the longitudinal study can investigate (with somewhat lower internal validity using quasi-experimental analyses) the effect of many independent variables.

It might be thought that an experimental study with both pretest and posttest measurements would have many of the advantages of the combined longitudinal-experimental study—for example, in permitting the comparison of changes within individuals and variation between individuals. However, Figure 4.1 illustrates some of the advantages of the longitudinal-experimental study in comparison with the simple pretest-posttest design. In this figure, O_1–O_8 are observation points, and X indicates the experimental intervention. The simple pretest-posttest design would involve only observation points O_4 and O_5, whereas the longitudinal-experimental study could have O_1–O_8 observations. The lines indicate the values of an outcome variable over time (e.g., rate of offending).

First of all, note that in all cases, except line C, the change between points O_4 and O_5 is the same. Hence, the simple pretest-posttest design would not distinguish cases A, B, D, E, F, and G. However, as the more extended series of observations shows, these cases differ in very important respects. Line A shows an immediate lasting effect of the intervention; line B shows an immediate but short-lived effect; and line C shows a delayed lasting effect. Line D shows an effect of the intervention on a preexisting trend; without a pretest series of observations, cases A and D could not be distinguished. Line E shows no effect of the intervention because of a preexisting trend, and, similarly, line F shows no effect of the intervention because of random oscillation. Finally, line G shows a discontinuity in the preexisting trend that might be attributable to the intervention. Many other illustrations could be given, but the main point is that false conclusions would be drawn from only observations O_4 and O_5 (the pretest and posttest; see also Campbell and Stanley 1966).

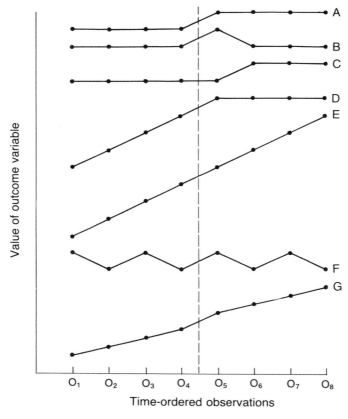

FIGURE 4.1.

Blumstein, Cohen, and Farrington (1988) set out some of the arguments for combining experiments and longitudinal studies. As already indicated, the impact of interventions can be better understood in the context of preexisting trends or developmental sequences, in assessing maturation, instability, and regression effects. Prior information about subjects helps to verify that experimental and comparison groups are equivalent, to set baseline measures, to investigate interactions between types of people (and prior histories) and types of treatments, to establish eligibility for inclusion in the experiment, and to estimate the impact of differential attrition from the experiment. Long-term follow-up information can show the effects of an intervention that are not immediately apparent, making it possible to compare short-term and long-term effects and to investigate the developmental sequences linking them.

Problems of the Longitudinal-Experimental Study

The major problem with combining different research efforts is that an experiment can interfere with a longitudinal study's goals. In a simple experiment, some of the subjects will be ineligible for treatment, some will be selected for the experimental group, and the remainder will be in the control group. Careful thought should be given to the proportions of subjects in these three groups. It would be inadvisable to draw conclusions about the natural history of offending from the experimental group, because this group will have been treated in an unusual way. The experiment may even increase or decrease attrition from the longitudinal study. Hence, in drawing conclusions about the whole sample, results obtained with the groups of ineligibles and controls will have to be weighted appropriately.

It is less clear that experimental subjects have to be eliminated in quasi-experimental analyses. If the experimental intervention could be viewed as another independent variable impinging on the subjects, then investigations of effects of nonmanipulated independent variables could be based on the whole sample. Of course, it might be interesting to investigate whether the impact of an independent variable differs across levels of another independent variable (e.g., in experimental and control groups).

It could be argued that each person should receive only one treatment because of the anticipated effects of treatment in making the experimental subjects different from subjects in the control or ineligible groups. However, there may be good reasons to investigate the interactive effect of two consecutive treatments. If the controls receive a special treatment (e.g., being denied something that is usually available in the community), then it could be argued that they also should not be included in a subsequent experiment. However, it seems unlikely that more than one or two experiments could be conducted with any cohort.

The passage of time will inevitably cause problems. An experiment that was desirable and feasible at one time (e.g., at the start of a longitudinal study) may be less desirable and feasible some years later because of changes in theory or policy concerns, in methodology, or in practical constraints (e.g., a change in a gate-keeper, such as a police chief). Also, some subjects of the longitudinal study will relocate to different areas, and it may be that the experiment can only be conducted in a specific location. Hence, only subjects who stay in the same city may be eligible to participate in the experiment. For a number of reasons, subjects' eligibility might change over time with changes in their personal circumstances.

These considerations suggest that it may be preferable to allow flexibility to include experimental interventions as circumstances permit, which means that specific experimental interventions might be planned after the start of the longitudinal study. It may also be better if the experiment is conducted as an add-on component to the longitudinal study, possibly carried out by independent researchers. Of course, this arrangement makes it necessary to coordinate the longitudinal team and the experimental team.

Prior Longitudinal-Experimental Research in Criminology

Experimental research has been carried out in which subjects have been studied by means of interviews and searches of records over the course of ensuing years. In one of the longest-lasting of these studies, McCord (1978) followed up the boys involved in the Cambridge-Somerville project. In this, the experimental boys received special counseling, typically between the ages of 10 and 15, and data on the experimental and control boys was then collected for at least 30 years. Another famous example of a longitudinal-experimental combination is the Perry Preschool Project, which was carried out in Michigan (Berrueta-Clement et al. 1984). The experimental children attended a daily preschool program, backed up by weekly home visits, at ages 3 and 4, and both experimentals and controls were then followed up to about age 19. More recent longitudinal-experimental studies are being conducted by Richard Tremblay in Montreal (see Tremblay et al. 1989) and David Hawkins in Seattle (see Hawkins, Doueck, and Lishner 1988).

Several other experimental intervention projects have collected information on offending from official records for periods before and after treatment. For example, the Silverlake experiment found that the average number of offenses per person for the community treatment group declined from 2.71 in the year before the intervention to 0.73 in the year after (Empey and Lubeck 1971). The corresponding decline in the institutional treatment group was from 2.66 to 0.74 offenses. The Provo experiment (Empey and Erickson 1972) included information about official offending for four years before and after the experiment.

What is missing from the criminological literature are longitudinal-experimental studies with several years of subject interviews both before and after the experimental intervention. This type of project would greatly advance knowledge, for the reasons outlined above, and this is what is proposed here. The proposed project would be unique in having this design feature.

Conclusions

We recommend that, where feasible, experimental interventions should be included in the proposed longitudinal study. However, such interventions possibly should not be undertaken until longitudinal data has been collected for several years. Planning for experiments should be flexible so that researchers can take advantage of opportunities that are in some sense unique to places and times.

5
Community Sampling

A long tradition of sociological research suggests that crime has a history in particular locales, regardless of the population inhabiting those locales (Reiss 1986). Community influences on crime arguably remain, even when individual-level characteristics are taken into account. Moreover, there are strong theoretical reasons to expect that individual characteristics, family processes, and life transitions interact with community characteristics to explain criminal careers. In particular, trajectories of within-individual longitudinal change may differ by community context. For example, within-individual effects of changes in employment status (e.g., employment to unemployment) on criminal careers might be more salient for youth in socially disorganized areas as compared to youth in socially organized, stable communities. Perhaps more crucially, relations between race and crime may be a product of interactions between community context (e.g., segregation, concentration of family disruption, sparse social networks) and developmental pathways or life transitions.

Unfortunately, these issues rarely have been studied because past research has concentrated on either individual- or community-level effects. Almost no research has examined both types of effects (see Reiss 1986; Sampson 1988). Thus, most individual-level research is inadequate because it neglects variation in community characteristics, while community-level research fails to take account of individual differences. Even when community context is considered, many important characteristics relevant to crime and delinquency have not been measured, especially factors central to early child development (e.g., community variations in quality and access to prenatal health services, child-care facilities, community tolerance of a mother's substance abuse). And past research has been largely cross-sectional, even though communities change as do individuals. As evidence of community change, we offer the simple fact that people may choose to live in neighborhoods with certain attributes. Longitudinal designs that follow the structure, composition, and organization of communities and that follow people as they move between communities are needed to establish the unique contributions of individuals and communities to crime and delinquency (Reiss 1986, p. 29).

These concerns led us to formulate a design that permits the study of contextual factors in the emergence and shaping of antisocial behavior from early childhood to delinquency and adult crime. In the proposed design, local communities are the framework within which other causal influences are examined. Obviously, it is possible to envision influences of larger scope than local communities, such as changes in city, state, federal, and private-sector policies on employment, welfare, health, and criminal justice. But in large part these factors operate at the local community level and can be taken account there. Our basic aim is to include community variations in such key areas as demography, social structure, culture, institutions, and social ties as conditioning environments in studying developmental patterns of antisocial behavior. In other words, only by combining information on both individuals and communities in one longitudinal study, which has never been done, can we be in a position to determine fully the causes of criminal careers. In this regard, the capacity to investigate both change and stability in person-environment interactions is a major innovation of the proposed research.

Initial Sampling Considerations

We recommend that, as a first-stage analysis, between-community variations in crime rates and other aspects of ecological structure should be examined within the research site. Whether at the community, census tract, or block-group level, we should have a quantitative assessment of the major ecological dimensions underlying variations in crime rates.

It is important to understand the structural correlates of delinquency rates for two reasons. The first reason relates to sampling. In designing procedures for collecting data, crime rates and their major predictors can be used to group communities into risk levels. Although we seek a comprehensive sample of communities (including low risk), we recommend oversampling those with high-crime rates or with characteristics associated with crime and delinquency (e.g,. concentration of poverty and family disruption). This strategy ensures sufficient variation in major community-level predictors of crime, thus providing for examination of individual-level developmental transitions across a wide range of community contexts.

The second reason pertains to data analysis. A major substantive issue involves the direct effect of community structures on criminal careers (contextual effects) and interactions between individual development, community context, and criminal-career trajectories. Examining a model of between-community variations first reduces the chance of interpreting residual (unexplained) variation as contextual or interaction effects. Suppose, for example, we find that community residential mobility appears to have an effect on individual delinquency, controlling for individual mobility and other relevant individual factors. We can place increased confidence in substantive interpretations of the contextual effects of residential mobility if we first establish that community mobility explains variation in crime rates across communities independently of other structural characteristics. Put differently, the identification of contextual effects should not be based on arbitrary or ad hoc procedures but instead should be informed by structural analyses of between-community variations (see Sampson 1988).

In short, most delinquency studies fail to pay sufficient attention to community effects and thus by default rule out the possibility of identifying community influences on crime. Examination of community-level variations in crime rates counterbalances this tendency and is thus important not only for stratified sampling, but also for the theoretical interpretation of contextual and interaction effects.

Operational Definitions of Community

The largest useful level of aggregation for research is the metropolitan area, which is usually defined in terms of the Standard Metropolitan Statistical Area (SMSA), county, or city. Census data can be gathered on city and metropolitan characteristics (see items 1 to 4 in the next section) regarding aspects such as population composition, density, criminal justice factors, socioeconomic status (SES), and family structure. These variables are needed for comparisons if research is to be carried out in multiple sites.

Within cities and counties one can usually identify community-based health or city planning areas (or municipalities in areas outside of cities) having reasonable ecological integrity (e.g., recognized boundaries and names) and that can be used as proxies for local communities. In many cities these areas, which are fairly large (containing anywhere from 10,000 to 75,000 people), have well-known names and borders (e.g., freeways, parks, major streets). Chicago has 75 traditional community areas (e.g., Woodlawn, Burnside, South Shore, etc.), whereas New York City has over 300 recognized health areas. As an illustration, Figure 5.1 shows a map of the 63 health areas in the borough of the Bronx, New York City. Many important characteristics related to healthcare, services, schools, and recreation (see items 5 to 10 below) vary over these local community areas (with an average population of 18,555 people). For most cities, census tract data can be aggregated and can be used in conjunction with local government statistics (e.g., city planning and health service data) to provide detailed information on community-area characteristics.

Traditionally, the concept of neighborhood refers to a relatively small and socially homogeneous area of between 2,000 and 5,000 people. Many studies have been able to approximate neighborhoods through use of census tract data on U.S. cities, a strategy made attractive by the fact that census data contain important information on key community characteristics. To be sure, census tract data do not always coincide with sociologically meaningful communities since the former are governmentally defined. One common procedure for circumventing these limitations is to draw a map of neighborhood areas and ask respondents if local neighborhood boundaries correspond to the map. If a respondent's view of a community does not overlap with the census boundaries, that information can be used to reformulate the definition of neighborhoods (i.e., create new maps).

A yet smaller area is what many refer to as a block cluster or block group, which is a two- or three-block area with anywhere from 100 to 1,000 residents.

MAP OF BRONX HEALTH AREAS

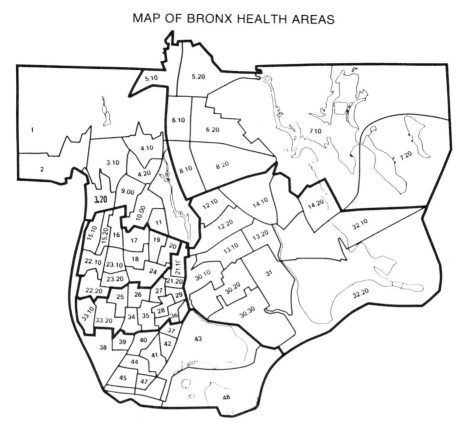

FIGURE 5.1. Map of Bronx health areas. 1980 Bronx population: 1,168,972; average health area population: 18,555. (From: Wallace [1988].) Reprinted with permission.

The density and size of block clusters vary, but our concern is primarily with urban block clusters within relatively large cities (e.g., Cleveland, Pittsburgh, St. Louis, etc.). The census bureau collects data at the block-group level, so it is possible to get desegregated information that can be very useful for sampling frames and enumeration. Census data on potential stratification variables can also be used to generate estimates of the yield of offenders for each area.

Finally, the smallest ecological level usually identified in research is the face-block, or the small cluster of homes and apartments facing the street on one's block. This unit represents the small social world of adjacent neighbors, and is often classified as the micro neighborhood (Fischer 1982, pp. 275–276).

Regardless of which ecological unit is used for sampling, we believe a mul-tilevel approach to community data collection is useful. With regard to causal influences on criminal careers, levels of community aggregation have different importance depending on the characteristic of interest. For example, the quality and quantity of health services vary by larger units (e.g., city districts, health areas), whereas dimensions such as neighborhood ties and attachment are relevant at smaller levels of aggregation (e.g., census tract).

Key Community Characteristics

Theoretical considerations and previous research suggest that it is important to study community characteristics for cohorts of all ages. To provide a broad based assessment of community effects for the full spectrum of childhood, adolescent, and young adult development, we have identified the following community characteristics as reflecting theoretically relevant constructs (see especially Reiss 1986; Sampson and Groves 1989; Byrne and Sampson 1986). Although not exhaustive, the list covers key aspects of demographic structure, economic status, residential housing and mobility patterns, official social control, and several dimensions of informal networks and social control.

1. Demographic structure—e.g., age and sex distributions; racial and ethnic composition; fertility; mortality.
2. Family structure—e.g., prevalence of female-headed families; divorce rate; youth density; life cycle patterns.
3. Residential mobility and net migration patterns.
4. Socioeconomic variables—e.g., income levels, occupational status, concentration of poverty (underclass), unemployment, inequality, welfare participation.
5. School variables—e.g., preschool services, drop-out rates, truancy rates, achievement levels, disciplinary problems, remedial classes, desegregation patterns.
6. Social service resources—e.g., types and extent of day care; family counseling, housing subsidies, drug and alcohol abuse programs; foster and child placement services; job training.
7. Housing structure—e.g., density, crowding, home ownership, public housing, high-rises, defensible space.
8. Recreational resources—e.g., extent and quality of playgrounds, supervised sports, clubs, etc.
9. Formal organizational participation by residents.
10. Existence and strength of community development corporations.
11. Health resources and services—e.g., prenatal care, teen pregnancy counseling and services, early infant care.
12. Information friendship and kinship networks.
13. Religion—types of churches and participation rates.
14. Crime and justice indicators—e.g., police surveillance and response practices (e.g., proactive vs. reactive); structure of police juvenile units, probation and parole case loads; arrest rates and trends; type and rate of reported offenses.

15. Opportunity structures for crime—e.g., density of banks, all-night convenience marts, bars, multiple-dwelling units, etc.
16. Quality of life variables—aspects of the physical environment such as crowding, vacant buildings, graffiti, passerby harassment.
17. Informal control styles and community response to children and youth (e.g., control of teenage street-corner groups).
18. Subcultural and normative climates regarding gangs, crime, drug use, and general antisocial behavior.
19. Underground economy—e.g., drug dealing, fencing, gambling, etc.

Sources of Data and Measurement

Census Data

At least four sources of data on communities can be tapped. The first is government census data on structural characteristics at the city, community, tract, and block level. Many of these community variables might be used for stratification and sampling. For example, variables relating to economic structure, racial composition, welfare, institutionalization (e.g, populations of juvenile homes, prisons, hospitals, etc.), education, housing density, and family disruption are available at the city, tract, and block level. Moreover, planning departments in most local governments have official data on health, fire, and police services by community.

Community Survey

Unfortunately, many community variables of interest to researchers are not represented in census data. To address this shortcoming, survey-based measures of community attributes have recently been developed. Basically, the methodology involves aggregation within defined communities of survey responses on neighborhood conditions. For example, survey items on the respondent's social relationships and values (e.g., social networks, cultural norms, voluntary associations, etc.) can be aggregated to provide community-level measures. This procedure has been used successfully in the past, and the key to success is to have enough people within each area (at least 20), in conjunction with reliable and valid measures of other community-related dimensions.

As a brief illustration of the community variables that can be measured with this methodology, Table 5.1 presents measures designed in the Urban Areas and Youth Project (see Simcha-Fagan and Schwartz 1986). These measures were constructed from a within-area aggregation procedure, with about 50 adult respondents (mother or guardian) per area, in which survey questions were used to create community-based measures. Specifically, each individual's score was subtracted from the overall sum within areas, and the result divided by $N-1$ to eliminate artifactual correlations between community and individual measures in the contextual analysis.

TABLE 5.1. Neighborhood dimensions[†] (extracted from adult survey-reported information).

I	Informal Neighboring ($k = 9$)[a]	($\alpha = .85$)
	1. Number of adults knows in neighborhood.	
	2. Frequency conversation with neighbors.	
	3. Frequency exchange favors.	
II	Neighborhood Attachment ($k = 9$)	($\alpha = .81$)
	1. Plans to stay in neighborhood (length of time).	
	2. Feels "really belongs" in neighborhood.	
	3. If could/unlikely to move out.	
III	Network Size and Breadth ($k = 3$)	($\alpha = .73$)
	1. Number of people considers friends.	
	2. Number close friends.	
	3. Proportion of friends outside neighborhood.	
IV	Neighborhood Level of Organizational Involvement ($k = 4$)	($\alpha = .64$)
	1. Number of organizations in neighborhood adult family members belong to.	
	2. Residents ever organized to solve problems.	
	3. Been asked by local organization to participate.	
V	Neighborhood Anomie ($k = 4$)	($\alpha = .67$)
	1. People around here will take advantage.	
	2. Does not know who can really count on.	
	3. People around here don't care about others.	
VI	Local Personal Ties ($k = 7$)	($\alpha = .73$)
	1. Number of adults knows in neighborhood.	
	2. Proportion of friends in neighborhood.	
	3. Proportion of relatives in neighborhood.	
VII	Social Disorder ($k = 6$)	($\alpha = .87$)
	1. Litter or trash on streets.	
	2. Drug addicts in neighborhood.	
	3. Abandoned houses or stores.	
VIII	Conflict Subculture ($k = 5$)	($\alpha = .84$)
	1. Fights with weapon in neighborhood.	
	2. Youth gang conflicts.	
	3. People badly hurt in a quarrel.	
IX	Illegal Economy ($k = 7$)	($\alpha = .84$)
	People in neighborhood make part/all of their income from:	
	1. A regular 9-to-5 job.	
	2. Selling stolen goods.	
	3. Selling drugs.	

[†] Representative items and Alpha reliability coefficients.
[a] k = total number of items in the factor.
Source: Simcha-Fagan and Schwartz (1986). Reprinted with permission.

Sampson (1988) and Sampson and Groves (1989) also used survey procedures to create community measures from the British Crime Survey ($N = 10,950$) using a sample drawn from 238 relatively small, homogeneous, contiguous neighborhoods. The average size of these sampled areas was roughly 5,000 people. The within-area samples were large enough (an average of 46 respondents), in conjunction with the comprehensiveness of the survey instrument, to permit theoretically derived community variables to be constructed independently of census data. Thus, in addition to traditional variables such as residential stability, family structure (percent divorced or separated), socioeconomic status, age composition (mean number of children under 18), and unemployment rate, it was possible to construct community-level indicators of local friendship networks, control of teenage peer groups, collective attachment, and rates of social participation in various leisure and organizational activities (e.g., Sampson 1988).

The proposed design is even more conducive to measurement of community concepts. If different age cohorts are drawn from the same community sampling, collection of community survey data will produce a relatively large number of respondents in each community. For example, mothers of the prenatal cohort can be asked standardized questions about their community. Similarly, mothers of the age 3 cohort can be asked the same questions, on up through the age 18 cohort. If the total sample size is approximately 5,000 subjects in a city and the sample covers 25 to 50 communities, we would have anywhere from 100 to 200 survey interviews for each community. Given these sample sizes within community areas, the reliability of community measures would be greater than in any previous research. The resulting community-level data derived from the survey could then be averaged and merged back into individual-level files.

In short, pooling information across cohorts in conjunction with the community sampling and survey measurement is a powerful design. Even though the number of individuals in any one cohort within the same community would be small, survey-based community measures would be derived from the entire set of cohorts. This design permits analysis of individual development within cohorts and of interactions with community contexts.

Ethnography

It is not necessary to live in an area for years in order to collect ethnographic data on community characteristics. Relatively short stays and intensive observation can be used to approximate ethnographies. We suggest that this data collection method could be used to supplement census data and surveys.

Informant Interviews

Claude Fischer (1982) used informant interviews (in conjunction with surveys) to collect data on 50 northern California communities. People knowledgeable about the local community were selected from telephone directories, newspapers, names encountered during on-site visits, and names other informants recommended. Questionnaires were sent to people in the following categories: real estate, school officials, churches, city planners, banks, chamber of commerce, police and fire departments, community groups and elected officials. By collecting key information from several informants per area, one can get a good picture of the community, especially regarding institutional resources and organizational participation. Moreover, the informant technique is essential for measuring community change. Even if selective migration away from the community leads to a biased follow-up sample, researchers can still identify a representative core of informants that can be called at regular intervals.

In sum, using the four procedures (census data, community survey, ethnographies, and informant interviews) outlined above, it is possible to collect a rich set of data to profile community characteristics.

Community Sampling and Stratification

We recommend a two-stage sampling procedure whereby communities first are selected and then samples are drawn within them. To the extent possible, geographic sampling units should be defined in terms of socially meaningful areas with at least some natural boundaries or the equivalent (e.g., a main traffic drag) and with low levels of abandonment and vacant housing. In defining sampling units, it is also desirable to avoid crossing school district lines within neighborhoods. Moreover, it is important not to choose an area so small as to capture frequent moves across blocks or block groups and thereby complicate our attempts to demonstrate how individual and structural factors interact. Also, another consideration is that the larger the unit, the higher the probability that we can sample all or most communities in a city, which would be highly desirable. In addition, mobility and tracking become less problematic, because subjects may be moving to other sampled communities within the metropolitan region where community measures are already developed.

Given these concerns, we recommend that census tracts or local health or planning areas be used to define communities for sampling purposes. Census tracts are desirable because they are compact local units with an average population of about 5,000 (larger in some central cities). Moreover, census lines are usually drawn along geographically and socially meaningful boundaries. As noted earlier, many cities also have health areas, which are larger (having an average population of between 10,000 and 30,000 people) than census tracts but which are still relatively compact and geographically distinct and hence approximate the concept of a local community.

Health areas have the additional advantage of overlapping with variations in health services (e.g., prenatal care) that are of central concern in studying young children. As but one example, Figure 5.2 shows the average rate of low birthweight babies across Bronx health areas. The dramatic community-level variations we observe could be used to inform a prenatal sampling design. Community risk factors for birth and younger cohorts will probably be quite similar to those for older cohorts. For example, consider the distribution of violent death across Bronx health areas in Figure 5.3. High-risk areas for violence are virtually the

►

FIGURE 5.2. Map of average annual rate of low birthweight babies (less than 2501 gm.) per 10,000 live births for Bronx health areas, (A) 1969–71, (B) 1979–81. (From: Wallace [1990].) Reprinted with permission.

A

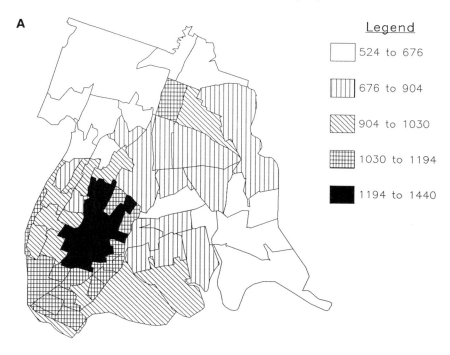

Legend

☐ 524 to 676

▥ 676 to 904

▨ 904 to 1030

▦ 1030 to 1194

■ 1194 to 1440

B

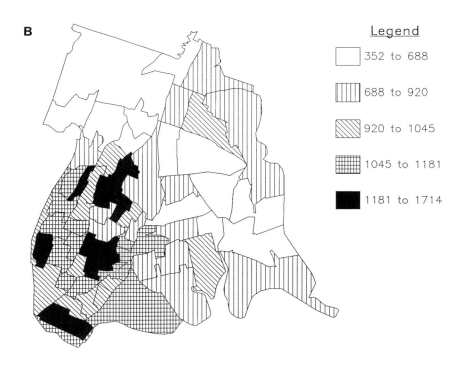

Legend

☐ 352 to 688

▥ 688 to 920

▨ 920 to 1045

▦ 1045 to 1181

■ 1181 to 1714

A

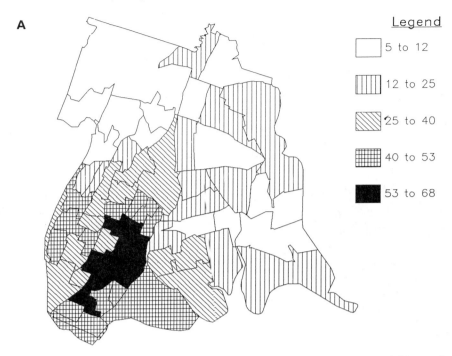

FIGURE 5.3. Map of average annual intentional violent death rate—homicides and suicides—per 100,000 population for Bronx health areas, (**A**) 1970–73, (**B**) 1978–82. (From: Wallace [1990].) Reprinted with permission.

same as for infant mortality and low birthweight babies (cf. Figure 5.2). Indeed, as predicted by social disorganization theory, high rates of poverty, family disruption, infant mortality, child abuse, low birthweight, drug abuse by pregnant women, and crime concentrate in communities, making comparability across cohorts in terms of community risk factors a reasonable goal.

Sampling options will be highly influenced by the city selected. If a small to moderate-sized city (e.g, 100,000 people) with a low population density is selected, census tracts could be operationally defined as communities, and we might be able to draw samples from all such areas. In larger cities of 400,000 to 500,000 people, it is probably desirable to sample as many health (or local community) areas as possible (e.g., 40 health areas with an average of 10,000 residents each).

On the other hand, if a large city such as New York or Los Angeles is selected, it becomes necessary to stratify and to select only a small portion of the communities. For example, the Simcha-Fagan study in New York City employed a two-stage research design in selecting community areas. As part of the first stage, a

B

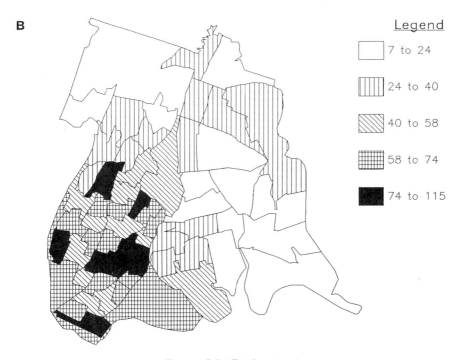

FIGURE 5.3. (**B**) *Continued.*

between-community analysis of crime rates was conducted at the health-area level ($N = 335$), as was a factor analysis of ecological structure at several levels (e.g. health area, tract, block group). The major correlates (using both single indicators and factor scores) of delinquency rates were low-economic status and family disruption, a finding consistent with other ecological research in U.S. cities. Economic status and family disruption also emerged as important factors at the tract and block levels. Thus, on the basis of data on geographic areas, health areas, block-groups, and census-tracts a community selection model that ensured adequate variation on economic status and family disruption was defined. In the second stage of the design, areas representative of each neighborhood type were randomly selected.

Fischer (1982) also used a stratified sampling strategy to study 50 communities in Northern California. If the areas had been selected proportional to population, the sample would have yielded too few small towns and inner-city areas. Consequently, Fischer divided the region into five strata—major center cities, inner suburbs, outer suburbs, other cities, and small towns—and selected ten localities within each stratum. Census data on block groups and on census tracts were used in sampling more urbanized areas, whereas data on municipalities were used in sampling small towns and outlying areas. These procedures underscore the point that the research site will dictate to some extent the level of aggregation in sampling and the need for stratification. However, as a general rule, data on census, health and planning areas, in combination with maps and selected informant interviews, should be sufficient for sampling communities.

Community-level sampling considerations also are relevant for individual-level sampling. Specifically, census data at small levels of aggregation can be used to predict the yield of offenders and inform oversampling of certain groups. For these purposes, it may be most efficient to begin at lower levels of aggregation, most probably the block or block group, and build up to the community level. Several block groups could be selected within a larger community (e.g., census tract, community area) to facilitate the screening and oversampling of high-risk or high-child-density sections of communities. For example, suppose we wished to increase the yield of offenders in a community with a low crime rate. Assuming individual-level data were not available, one possibility would be to divide block groups into strata based on known predictors of crime such as family disruption or poverty. All block groups high on these factors could be selected and combined with a random selection of remaining block groups. In a similar vein, block-group data could be used to oversample areas with above-average densities of male youth in desired age ranges. With appropriate weighting, survey-based responses still could be used to develop representative community-level measures, and the yield of offenders or youths with certain characteristics would be increased.

The sampling design we recommend offers considerable power in terms of separating individual and community effects and establishing individual-community interactions over time. With a large sample size we can study a sufficient number of communities that vary on key dimensions. Simcha-Fagan and Schwartz's (1986) study was cross-sectional and limited to only 12 areas, a design precluding both longitudinal and between-community analyses. Moreover, only two factors (family structure and economic level) were considered in the area-selection model, and many community constructs of interest were not measured in the survey. By contrast, the proposal to sample up to 50 communities allows us to identify risk strata and use an area-selection method that permits consideration and measurement of several important community constructs. Both within-community change and between-community variation, which are important for reasons noted earlier, are also captured in the proposed design. In addition, follow-up of individuals as they move between different communities will enhance the separation of community and individual effects on crime and deviance.

Cost and Time Concerns

The major point to be made with regard to the sampling of communities is that the strategy does not involve the listing or screening of households, and hence conventional cost estimates are not applicable. Rather, the initial selection of communities, from which individual-level samples will be drawn, involves analyses of data such as census, maps, and local health data just discussed. As such, the cost is relatively low; all that is needed is the requisite community data and standard computer analyses.

It is difficult to provide exact cost estimates, because so much depends on the site selected. For example, if a city like New York, Chicago, or Providence (Rhode Island) was selected, data on many community variables are already available. On the other hand, many cities may have little in the way of accessible local data on well-defined community areas. Nevertheless, all cities have census data, so that retrieval of these data, mapping of areas, and analyses of community structure should be feasible within several months. Depending on the city selected, collecting other data to inform sampling (e.g., health data, planning data on services, crime rates) and linking these data to census data could take anywhere from a few weeks to several months. For example, one might have to write new computer programs to match crime incident data to specific community boundaries (e.g., census tracts) and then aggregate to create rates.

Once the major community sampling units are selected, blocks and block groups within communities need to be listed and stratified. The cost of this procedure will depend on the nature of the stratification. Also, once the individual-level sample is selected, costs of administering a survey on community attributes depend on the cost per question and per respondent and on the required number of questions and respondents.

Ethnographic and informant questionnaire studies should be moderate in cost because we have proposed a relatively short observation period and questionnaire. For example, Fischer's (1982) instrument is rather short and could easily be administered to between five and ten key informants per area. The major cost of the procedure is in identifying informants from directories and nominations, which for us would involve identifying anywhere from 125 to 500 informants (25 areas and 5 informants per area minimum; 50 areas and 10 informants per area maximum). Several months' time should be sufficient to execute this task. These and other community-related costs (e.g,. tracking community change) need to be explored in more detail as the design progresses.

Community Change and Mobility

We clearly want to monitor community change over the life of the project. One method is to gather updated census information and ethnographic observations. Community-based interviews can also be administered yearly in each sampled community. As to the survey-based measures, we suggest administering the full set of community questions at the beginning of the study to achieve a baseline of cross-sectional information. These community items could also be repeated at some set interval (e.g., at year four and at the end of the study). The problem, of course, is that the sample in a community may no longer be representative of that community after the first survey if selective migration has occurred. People who move out of an area may be systematically different from those who stay, hence biasing the survey-based community measures at later times. This bias could be counteracted by conducting a short cross-sectional household survey (perhaps by phone) at the end of the study within each of the communities.

There is also the problem of people moving to communities that have no other sample respondents (or only a few). For example, suppose a person moved from Milwaukee, the original site, to Cleveland. Survey data on the Cleveland community would presumably be based on responses from only that one subject. Although individuals moving out of a community present a design problem, if we choose a fairly stable city using census data, most changes in residence will be within the metropolitan area. If so, subjects should be moving into other target communities where information has already been gathered or is currently being gathered. The community-based data file then can be attached to that person for a later time period, and community change measures thus created. As mentioned above, the greater the proportion of communities initially sampled in a city, the more likely it is that mobile subjects will be captured as part of the routine data collection scheme. For those who move into communities not originally sampled, census data on these new areas (e.g., block, census tract) can always be examined to determine changes in major structural characteristics.

As for individuals who do move out of the metropolitan area, they should, of course, be followed, and again, census data are always available for many structural characteristics of communities. A modified version of the community instrument could be administered to capture other variables of interest (e.g., informal networks, community cohesion). Short ethnographic observations and perhaps even informant questionnaires could also be used to provide a general assessment of key changes in environmental contexts. It should be expected, however, that for a certain segment of the original sample, probably 10 percent to 15 percent, follow-up collection of community data will be difficult.

6
Household and Individual Sampling

As detailed in previous chapters, we propose a cross-sequential research design involving seven cohorts—a prenatal cohort and cohorts starting at 3, 6, 9, 12, 15, and 18 years of age. We also recommend that each cohort be tracked for a period of eight years, so that cohorts will overlap with one another in age ranges; that the 12-year-old cohort have a sibling cohort attached to it; and that both the prenatal and 12-year-old cohorts include females, for a total of 2,050 females. Details of the community and sibling designs are presented elsewhere in this report. The purpose of this section is to highlight key issues in the overall sampling plan.

The design objectives of the proposed study are complex. First, the design calls for the investigation of community-level influences and, for this reason, it requires variability in community characteristics. Second, the design allows for the investigation of within-individual changes by following subjects for eight years. Third, the design seeks the advantages of an accelerated longitudinal structure in which overlapping cohorts permit the characterization of developmental curves in less time than a single cohort study from birth to age 25 years. The accelerated design requires equivalent cohorts, insofar as this can be achieved. Fourth, the design targets the separation of family and nonfamily influences. The 12-year-old cohort is slated to include brothers, sisters, and mixed sex siblings (9 to 15 years old), who are studied as intensively as other subjects. Finally, each cohort should be representative of the general population, which means that the initial sampling procedure should be unbiased and well described and that effects of attrition during the longitudinal follow-up must be minimized.

Household Sampling Procedures

We recommend that all cohort samples be drawn using a household sampling procedure. While the possibility of enriching the prenatal cohort with subjects drawn from prenatal care clinics and hospitals was considered, since utilization of prenatal care is very likely correlated with educational level and social class, we concluded that prenatal clinics should not be the preferred sampling frame. A household sampling procedure is more desirable because it yields a more representative sample than the alternatives. For example, samples selected by random-digit dialing omit families that do not have telephones. In addition, a single screening effort on households can produce the subjects needed to satisfy all cohort design requirements. If the number of households that must be screened to detect pregnant women proves to be impractical, we recommend including some very young infants (e.g., up to 3 to 6 months) in the prenatal cohort and collecting retrospective data on pregnancy experiences.

As a first step, the research site, which needs to be a medium to large city, should be divided into community areas based on census characteristics and available local data. Each community should represent a fairly distinct area in terms of geography and demographic traits (e.g., crime rate, percentage of single-family households, and so on). Primary sampling units (PSUs; composed primarily of city blocks) are nested within communities (see Chapter 5 on community sampling).

The second step should be to carry out a stratified random-sampling procedure whereby PSUs are stratified for community sociodemographic characteristics and possibly crime rate. Sampling rates will have to be determined for each PSU so as to yield the desired sample size and composition. Sample characteristics should include a balanced representation of blacks and whites, a full range of community features, and oversampling of areas containing individuals at high risk for antisocial conduct and delinquency (e.g., high crime, poverty areas). Finally, field interviewers should contact household members and enroll children who qualify in the sample.

Sampling Unit

The desirability of having equivalent groups of cohort subjects across all ages suggests that the sampling unit should be the same for all cohorts. The sampling unit can be defined as the mother or guardian along with a child (nonsibling cohort) or two children (sibling cohort). In the prenatal cohort, the sampling unit could be defined as the mother and her unborn child. Whenever possible, the adult sampled should be the biological mother, but children should not be excluded from consideration because they reside with some other adult (biological father, female relative, etc.). Indeed, for populations most relevant to crime research (e.g., mostly lower-income, high-crime, high-risk, etc.) the stability of household structures may be tenuous. The proposed design is easily executed for the traditional American family, but high-risk individuals can be attached to more than one household and can hence be reported as being members of multiple households. For example, in high-risk areas, many children in our older cohorts (i.e., 15 and 18 years) may be runaways with living arrangements that are constantly in flux. A teenager might live two months with friends, several months with an aunt or relative, then with his or her mother, and in some cases then in a jail or a detention center. Where does such a child actually live? Who is going to be the adult reporter? The notion of a biological mother and child living under one roof is not appropriate for many households in socially disorganized communities. Therefore, we strongly recommend establishing rules that explicitly define families and places of residence (e.g., the number of nights a child has spent in a household unit in the past month, the number of days the guardian or mother was in charge of the child's care, etc.).

Another sampling problem can arise from migration into or out of a chosen research site. Families with young children who have resided for a long time in the community and families with older children who have just arrived may be quite different in demographic and personal characteristics. Although younger and older children in the same community will be assigned to different cohorts, the cohorts may be nonequivalent because of differences in family backgrounds.

Sampling a large geographic region such as an SMSA may partly resolve the lack of equivalence. By sampling across communities within a city or metropolitan area, cohorts may be population representative, even though children assigned to different cohorts within a single, local community may be non-equivalent. A substantial change in population characteristics in the total geographic region, however, such as that caused by the influx of a new ethnic group, would tend to make cohorts nonequivalent, despite sampling over a large regional area. The challenge for site selection is to identify sites that minimize historical changes in population composition over the past 18 pears, and our recommendations for choosing a fairly stable metropolitan region are discussed in more detail in Chapter 8.

To recapitulate, we recommend making the mother (or guardian) and the child the sampling unit in all cohorts. For the older cohorts, we expect that a small proportion of eligible subjects will be living alone. These youths should still be included in the sample, even though guardians are in effect absent, as should youths temporarily detained in other settings (e.g., hospital, school for troubled youth). To study older children with more unconventional living arrangements (e.g., adolescents actually residing in detention or prison), special samples may have to be drawn, as described in the section on supplemental studies elsewhere in this book.

Risk Factors for Stratification

The main sampling choices are between a simple random sample and a stratified random sample having an increased proportion of children at risk for later criminal behavior. In Wolfgang's Philadelphia birth cohort (1972), about 35 percent of the individuals experienced an arrest for any offense (see Chapter 7 on sampling yield). Rates of felony arrest were lower, but still, as much as 10 percent of the cohort had such contacts. Unlike psychiatric disorders, the higher base rate of crime makes sampling from the general population feasible. However, chronic offenders and individuals who eventually serve time in prison constitute a much smaller proportion of the population. Given our interests in these groups, it is desirable to enrich the cohorts by including a greater number of high-risk families and youths.

One strategy for increasing the yield of offenders is to stratify the sample by individual-level risk factors (e.g., past arrest experience, early childbearing by mother), but, for several reasons, individual-level stratification is problematic. First of all, optimal risk factors will vary across age cohorts. Second, individual screening questions on sensitive items serve as a red light to potential subjects and may significantly increase refusal rates. For example, it is standard survey practice to ask questions on income at the end of an interview, after establishing rapport with subjects. Asking about items such as arrest history in a short screening interview creates problems because people who cooperate will in all likelihood be systematically different from those who refuse. Also, housing projects and other high crime areas are characterized by pervasive fear and distrust among residents. Simply getting people to answer the door may be difficult. Soliciting responses to questions on sensitive topics may be nearly impossible, especially if people feel they must be cautious with the people they speak to.

Third, we must anticipate that in many situations screening questions will be answered by proxy respondents not heads of households. It is fairly reasonable to assume that whoever (e.g., babysitter, aunt, boyfriend) answers the door can provide some information on children in the household, but this person may not be a valid reporter for risk screening. Again, screening for risk on some factors, such as the mother's age at the birth of the first child, assumes a family structure (e.g., mother at home) that is often inappropriate to high risk areas. Finally, as the section on yield estimates shows, an individual-level screening effort may not be needed to increase the proportion of potential offenders.

Unless reliable, valid, and cost-efficient individual-level screening questions can be identified in pilot work, the least complicated, scientifically defensible method of increasing the proportion of individuals at risk is to oversample children from communities with high crime rates or with characteristics associated with high crime rates. To achieve this objective we recommend that community areas in the site be subdivided into successively smaller units, down to the block level or smaller. Since census statistics at the block level are available, along with local information on housing projects, it is possible to oversample blocks within larger communities on the basis of known structural risk factors (e.g., poverty rate, family disruption, welfare, infant mortality, etc.). A low level of aggregation increases the overlap of community characteristics with individual characteristics, and it might even be possible to get arrest data or child-abuse case load data from city agencies for relatively small community areas.

The complexity of stratified sampling by area presents familiar problems that are easy to handle as long as we know what proportion the strata represent in the overall population. For example, weighting procedures may be used to correct sample statistics (e.g., means, proportions, or correlations) for over- or undersampling of particular groups. For this reason, a multilevel stratified sample by area is an efficient way to increase yield while keeping the design feasible.

Ethnicity

It is desirable to have a balanced representation of subjects by race or ethnicity, and we recommend that cohort samples consist primarily of whites and blacks. For reasons described in Chapter 8 on site selection, a design that targets Hispanics for oversampling (e.g., to achieve 33 percent representation) is in all likelihood not feasible; however, Hispanics should not be systematically excluded. On the other hand, the goal of approximately equal representation of black and white subjects is realistic. To obtain a reasonable balance of whites and blacks in the sample, it is important to select a site in which both races are sufficiently represented and with variation in the socioeconomic level within race groups. In racially mixed communities, it may be desirable to stratify on race using household screening information.

Funneling Sampling Strategies

A funneling sampling process was considered early in our deliberations but was later abandoned. One version of a funneling strategy is to increase the representation of high-risk individuals at each step from the prenatal to the oldest cohort. For example, starting with a prenatal cohort representative of the population, each later cohort can be structured to increase the representation of children with successively more severe criminal outcomes (e.g., resulting in an 18-year-old cohort consisting mostly or exclusively of arrestees).

Problems with this procedure, however, discourage its use. First, funneling strategies boost the representation of more serious or chronic outcomes at each stage, making it increasingly difficult to study the development of other outcomes, such as successful outcomes of high-risk children. Second, the procedures tend to eliminate delinquent youth who have never been officially arrested, a nontrivial segment of the population. Third, if we elect to narrow the sample to those most at risk, we must know the combination of risk factors that is most predictive. However, a major aim of the project is to identify these factors. Fourth, correlational analyses in older cohorts would be limited by lack of variation in the dependent variable, antisocial behavior. In summary, the representation of high-risk individuals can be increased in each cohort through a stratified sampling procedure without sacrificing representativeness.

Screening Interview

The screening interview should contain questions to determine whether a household contains a child or children who qualify by age for a component of the research design (i.e., cohort, sibling sample). In most cases disproportionate sampling on race and risk factors can be handled by adjusting sampling fractions within the primary sampling units. Other features of the household, such as the presence or absence of a father, of stepchildren, and so on, do not restrict a child's eligibility. In the prenatal cohort, the mother and the unborn child qualify if they are contained in the stratified sampling.

Interview Schedules and Follow-up

Major design concerns stemming from the high-risk nature of the sample are tracking and panel decay. Many subjects will change residence, and the complexity of design problems can mushroom because every year the scope of data collection increases as people move about. For example, will we follow a subject who moves from Chicago to Alabama? If so, what about the person's mother or guardian? Will it matter if the mother stays in Chicago? What if the mother moves to Detroit? For the older cohorts tracking problems will be exacerbated, especially because parents and children tend to go their separate ways. Again, our desire to focus on high-risk subjects interacts with design complexity. We thus suggest that special efforts and budgets be set aside for tracking difficult cases, especially older youths.

A further recommendation is that the research team think in terms of continuous data collection as opposed to a static notion of collecting data once or twice a year. Subjects can move one month after a yearly interview or eleven months later. In a longitudinal study it is best to know as quickly as possible about a move, to facilitate tracking. In the past, survey research organizations have attempted to monitor continuously residential moves even though the people were not scheduled for interviews. For instance, monthly telephone calls could be made to those with phones, or postcards requesting address corrections could be mailed out to monitor location. Researchers can also ask for the telephone numbers of relatives and friends so that they can inquires about moves. These strategies will increase the cost of the research, but they are critical if we hope to maintain the integrity of the sample over extended periods of time. As an efficient use of resources, we also recommend interviewing children soon after their birthdays, so that interviewing is a continual process throughout the year.

Sample Size Estimates

Sample size requirements depend partly on assessment of the strength of effects we wish to detect. For example, we might be interested in studying the relationship between criminal parents and arrested sons, a situation that can be illustrated most easily with dichotomous variables (similar conclusions would apply if variables were measured on categorical or continuous scales). Thus, we might compare the proportion of boys with criminal parents who were arrested ($P2$) with the proportion of boys with noncriminal parents who were arrested ($P1$). In general, a difference of less than .10 (10 percent) between these proportions (corresponding to a correlation of .10) is likely to have little practical significance (Farrington and Loeber 1989).

The estimated sample size also depends on our chosen value of:

1. The probability of rejecting the null hypothesis of no effect (e.g., concluding that the two variables are related) when in fact the null hypothesis is correct. This probability is called alpha, or the probability of a Type I error. It is also the P value in a conventional test of statistical significance;
2. The probability of failing to reject the null hypothesis of no effect (e.g., concluding that the two variables are not related) when in fact the null hypothesis is false. This probability is called beta, or the probability of a Type II error. Statistical power is defined to be (1 − beta).

Generally, Type I errors are considered to be more serious than Type II errors, which implies that alpha should be less than beta. The maximum Type I error that is normally tolerated is .05. If a directional prediction can be made, as is often the case (here, that P2 will be greater than P1), a one-tailed test can be used. The minimum statistical power that might be accepted is .75; in other words, the investigator has a 75 percent chance of detecting a real effect that is present.

Fleiss (1981) expounds these ideas in detail and documents the sample sizes for various values of P1, P2, alpha, and statistical power, assuming that the two groups being compared are of equal size. For values of P1 and P2 between .20 and .80, for (P2 − P1) of .10, for alpha of .05 (one-tailed), and for statistical power of .75, the required sample size fluctuates between 440 and 576. Hence, it would be reasonable to aim for an initial sample size of about 500 subjects per cohort. In the next chapter, we provide estimates of the number of offenders we should find in cohorts of this size.

Screening Yield Estimates

Screening yield refers to the number of households that must be canvassed to produce the final cohort and sibling samples, and, clearly, the number of households to be screened is large. For example, in the ongoing OJJDP Denver Study, directed by David Huizinga, about 20,000 households were screened in order to identify about 1,100 eligible ones with children at ages 7, 9, 11, 13 or 15. In this study, the probability of locating an eligible household was about .055. The proposed design calls for subjects across a wider range of age categories (prenatal, 3, 6, 9, 12, 15 and 18 years), which will tend to increase the probability of finding an eligible household. However, we have indicated that it may be difficult to identify enough pregnant women by means of household screening.

For the nonsibling cohorts, only one subject will be selected from a household. If the experience of this project is similar to that in Denver, about 100,000 households will have to be screened to identify 5,500 eligible households (5,500/.055

= 100,000) with a child of cohort age. Assuming a 25 percent margin of error, the screening effort might involve between 75,000 and 125,000 households.

The suggested sibling design (see Chapter 15), which calls for 250 pairs of each sibling type (brothers, sisters, mixed sex), does not pose great additional problems. Brothers and mixed-sex pairs partly derive from the siblings of cohort children (about 100 pairs of each) and partly from additional (150 pairs of each) siblings sampled in the age range of 9 to 15 years. In addition, 250 pairs of sisters are to be found; along with 250 girls of cohort age (12 years). The number of households that must be screened to locate these subjects depends on the proportion of households with children in them. Given the possibility of using census data to enrich sampling frames with households having children, a sampling procedure can be designed to minimize costs. Final cost estimates, however, can only be made after a site is selected and pilot work is carried out.

7
Sampling Yield

An important aspect of sampling yield relates to the number of offenders we are likely to find in a sample. From this perspective, sampling yield is a critical feature of the design because we need to have enough offenders of various types for reliable statistical analyses. In anticipation that simple random sampling procedures may not identify many criminals, even when carried out in a high-crime rate urban area, we propose to use a stratified sampling procedure in which we disproportionately draw from the highest risk groups. We suggest using community characteristics, individual characteristics, or a combination of the two to identify the risk groups.

At this point, we review the findings of major longitudinal studies and, on the basis of these data, estimate the number of offenders we are likely to find in our cohorts. Since no previous study matches exactly the proposed design in terms of sample characteristics and length of follow-up, the estimates offered here are imprecise and can only establish the rough contours of likely yield. Nonetheless, the estimates may prove useful because they demonstrate the viability of the sampling plan and identify areas where sampling procedures need to be refined.

The Philadelphia Cohorts

Marvin Wolfgang and colleagues (1972, 1987) have studied two cohorts of males in Philadelphia—one born in 1945 and the other in 1958. The 1945 cohort study stands as a benchmark against which subsequent research can be compared. In *Delinquency in a Birth Cohort* (Wolfgang, Figlio, and Sellin 1972), findings on police contacts are presented for this cohort and, with a few assumptions, we can use the data to estimate sampling yield. In particular, the proportion (34.9 percent) of the cohort with a police contact for a nontraffic offense between ages 7 (youngest age of contact) and 18 (age at follow-up) can be used as a prevalence estimate over this age span. In the proposed design, the cohort that comes closest to covering this span is the 9-year-old cohort, which is to be followed through age 17. We will assume that the offender prevalence figure for the 1945 cohort applies to the 9-year-old cohort, as well as to the 12-, 15-, and 18-year-old

TABLE 7.1. Estimated number of offenders in the proposed sample based on the Philadelphia 1945 birth cohort data.

Type of offender	Percent of sample	Number for 9, 12, 15, and 18 cohorts ($N = 2,500$)	Number for one cohort ($N = 500$)
One-time offender	16.7	416	83
Nonchronic recidivist (two to four contacts)	15.1	376	75
Chronic recidivist (five or more contacts)	9.8	246	49
Total	41.6	1038	207

Note: Offenders are defined in terms of persons with a police contact for a nontraffic offense. It is assumed that 60 percent of the sample will be high-risk and 40 percent will be low-risk and that the probability of a police contact is .502 for high-risk subjects and .286 for low-risk subjects. Although these probabilities correspond to differences across racial groups in the Philadelphia cohort, other criteria will be used to identify high- and low-risk subjects in the proposed sample.

cohorts. This assumption is a bit generous in that the active offending period for the 1945 cohort is longer than the eight-year follow-up we propose, and the prevalence of offending will probably be lower among the older cohorts.

Analyses by Wolfgang and colleagues (1972) also show that ethnicity is strongly associated with crime, nonwhites being much more likely to become offenders than whites (50.2 percent vs. 28.6 percent). For simplicity, we will assume that our sample is stratified into two risk groups. We also will assume that the high-risk group has the same probability of arrest as the nonwhite subjects in the 1945 cohort and that the low-risk group has the same probability as the white subjects. In effect, this assumption reduces the risk criteria to only one variable (ethnicity), and we can expect that the criteria eventually used to identify high-risk subjects will be different and probably more discriminating. Finally, estimates are based on a sample size of 2,500 (the total number of subjects across the 9-, 12-, 15-, and 18-year-old cohorts), comprising 60 percent high-risk and 40 percent low-risk subjects. Because we are also interested in the yield for a single cohort, we include a comparable estimate for a sample of 500 subjects. If the sample size or the sampling ratios change, estimates will need to be adjusted accordingly. For example, if we increase the proportion of high-risk subjects in the sample, the yield of active offenders will be greater.

Table 7.1 estimates the number of offenders in the proposed sample by level of criminal activity. Over the course of the follow-up period, we estimate that the sample will yield 1,038 offenders, which is approximately 42 percent of the four oldest cohorts. In addition, chronic offenders ($N = 246$), defined in terms of persons with five or more police contacts for nontraffic offenses, should constitute about 10 percent of the sample.

Wolfgang and colleagues (1972) also present data on the number and types of crimes subjects in the 1945 cohort committed. Although the following estimates

TABLE 7.2. Estimated number of offenses in the proposed sample based on the Philadelphia 1945 birth cohort data.

Type of offense	Total for 9, 12, 15, and 18 cohorts ($N = 2,500$)	Total for one cohort ($N = 500$)
Homicide	7	1
Rape	21	4
Robbery	92	18
Aggravated assault	99	20
Burglary	237	47
Larceny	469	94
Auto theft	131	26
Other assault	213	43
Weapons	118	24
Sex offense	52	10
Liquor law	79	16
Drunkenness	75	15
Disorderly conduct	565	113
Other	1447	289
Total	3605	720

differ from those just presented in that they refer to crimes, not criminals, they provide a framework for evaluating the feasibility of analyses directed at specific types of offenses.

We observe in Table 7.2 that the estimated total number of crimes committed by the four oldest cohorts is large ($N = 3,605$), although most of these offenses are relatively minor. With regard to serious offenses, the number of property crimes such as burglary ($N = 237$) and larceny ($N = 469$) is substantial, while the number of violent crimes is much lower. Estimates for aggravated assault ($N = 99$) and robbery ($N = 92$) fall just short of 100 incidents, while minor assaults are more common ($N = 213$). Both homicide ($N = 7$) and rape ($N = 21$) are infrequent events that will be difficult to study.

The 1945 cohort data contrast with contemporary impressions of urban crime in that they describe mostly minor offenses with surprisingly few violent crimes. It may be that as a result of historical changes the 1945 cohort data are no longer representative of offender behavior. Consequently, estimates derived from the data may be too low. We can check this hypothesis by comparing estimates based on data from the 1945 and 1958 Philadelphia cohorts. The following data for the latter cohort come from a study by Neil Weiner (1985) and deal only with violent crimes.

We find in Table 7.3 that the estimated number of violent offenses nearly doubles when using data from the 1958 cohort. Robbery ($N = 268$) accounts for nearly all of the increase, while estimates for other violent offenses remain substantially unchanged. Homicide ($N = 11$) and rape ($N = 21$) continue to be infrequent events, and serious assaults ($N = 111$) marginally exceed a threshold of 100 inci-

TABLE 7.3. Comparison of the estimated number of violent offenses for the 9-, 12-, 15-, and 18-year-old cohorts combined based on 1945 and 1958 Philadelphia birth cohort data.

Type of offense	Estimated number of offenses	
	Based on 1945 cohort data	Based on 1958 cohort data
Homicide	7	11
Rape	21	21
Robbery	92	268
Aggravated assault	99	111
Total	219	411

dents. Thus, estimates based on more recent data indicate that we should be able to study violence in detail, if we are interested in robbery. To the extent that crime rates have continued to rise relative to the experiences of the 1958 cohort, we can expect the number of offenses in the sample to be greater than estimated here.

The data from the 1958 cohort also allow us to estimate the number of subjects who will be arrested for UCR Part I violent offenses. Based on the same assumptions outlined previously, we estimate that 201 high-risk subjects and 25 low-risk subjects will become violent offenders, the total ($N = 226$) representing 9 percent of the four cohorts.

In reviewing these estimates, we should keep in mind that the actual yield of the sampling procedures depends on a number of factors including levels of crime (i.e., base rate) in the research site, outcomes of interest (self-report data capture more offense behavior than official records, police contacts are more common than arrests; violent or chronic offenders represent a small subset of the offender population), discriminating power of the risk criteria, and sampling proportions across degrees of risk (e.g, the proportion that is high and low risk). Finally, while the estimates indicate that the sample should include a substantial number of offenders, we have not taken into account comparisons between subgroups of offenders we might be interested in. For example, data from both the 1945 and 1958 Philadelphia cohorts indicate that we will have a difficult time comparing black and white violent offenders.

In considering how the base rates of risk groups, which are linked to the efficiency of risk criteria, relate to the advantages of a stratified sampling procedure, it may be useful to examine several examples that illustrate the range of sampling yields across different base rates and mixtures of high- and low-risk subjects. The scenarios in Table 7.4 were selected to represent viable sampling strategies given the recommended sample size and the need to have adequate representation of offenders and nonoffenders across all risk groups. Although base rates in the following examples are unrealistically high for outcomes such as chronic or violent offending, they are plausible with regard to police contact for a nontraffic

TABLE 7.4. Illustrative yield of offenders in a cohort of 500 subjects stratified into two risk groups by selected sampling proportions and base rates.

	\multicolumn{8}{c}{Risk group and sampling proportion}							
	H 50%	L 50%	H 60%	L 40%	H 67%	L 33%	H 75%	L 25%
Base rate	.5	.25	.5	.25	.5	.25	.5	.25
Est. yield	125	63	150	50	167	42	188	31
Total yield	188		200		209		219	
Pct. cohort	37.5%		40.0%		41.8%		43.8%	

	\multicolumn{12}{c}{Risk group and sampling proportion}											
	H 33%	M 33%	L 33%	H 40%	M 35%	L 25%	H 50%	M 30%	L 20%	H 60%	M 25%	L 15%
Base rate	.6	.4	.2	.6	.4	.2	.6	.4	.2	.6	.4	.2
Est. yield	99	66	33	120	70	25	150	60	20	180	50	15
Total yield	198			215			230			245		
Pct. cohort	40.0%			43.0%			46.0%			49.0%		

	\multicolumn{12}{c}{Risk group and sampling proportion}											
	H H 25%	H L 25%	L H 25%	L L 25%	H H 35%	H L 30%	L H 20%	L L 15%	H H 40%	H L 25%	L H 20%	L L 15%
Base rate	.6	.5	.4	.2	.6	.5	.4	.2	.6	.5	.4	.2
Est. yield	75	63	50	25	105	75	40	15	120	63	40	15
Total yield	213				235				238			
Pct. cohort	42.6%				47.0%				47.6%			

Note: H = High, M = Medium, L = Low.

offense, at least in light of the Philadelphia cohort data and, as we shall see later, the Racine cohort data.

The illustrations cover use of two, three, and four risk strata. The fourfold risk classification (high/high, high/low, low/high, low/low) comes closest to the proposal that we might stratify subjects on both community and individual risk levels. Given uncertainty as to the advantages of a two-stage risk assessment at the community and individual levels, other schemes are illustrated to demonstrate that comparable yields can be achieved by means of simpler approaches.

The illustrations in Table 7.4 show how the sampling yield increases as the difference in base rates across risk groups increases, which means using more discriminating risk criteria, and as the proportion of the sample from the high-risk group increases. In deciding on specific procedures, the research team will have the option of emphasizing either of these approaches to increase yield, and in reviewing these examples, we can find instances in which use of more dis-criminating risk criteria is attractive. For example, a 60/40 split of high-risk

($P = .6$) and low-risk ($P = .2$) subjects produces an almost identical number of offenders (220 vs. 219) as does a 75/25 split with slightly less discriminating base rates (high $= .5$, low $= .25$). However, the more discriminating risk criteria result in nearly one-third more offenders in the low-risk category (40 vs. 31), an important consideration when it comes to making comparisons across offender groups. Although we cannot say that to increase yield more discriminating risk criteria always should be preferred over adjustments in sampling proportions, the latter approach appears to be a more viable strategy for the proposed design, especially in view of the need for adequate representation across all risk groups given fixed cohort sizes.

Another observation prompted by the above illustrations is that the potential advantages of a stratified over a nonstratified procedure depend in part on the population base rate. In particular, a stratified procedure holds more substantial payoff when dealing with infrequent events. Although some outcomes of interest are clearly low base-rate phenomena, many of our research questions center on outcomes that are neither rare nor common. For example, the Philadelphia data suggest that, in a simple random sample of urban males, 35 percent of subjects can be classified as offenders in terms of police contact. Examples of stratified procedures presented here tend to produce a sample of about 50 percent offenders. The difference in yield (15 percent) represents 75 offenders in a cohort of 500 subjects, which is a consequential increase when it comes to studying the careers of active offenders. Nevertheless, one can legitimately question in this situation whether the stratified approach involves an equitable trade-off given the design and analytic complications introduced. Alternatively, if we are concerned with an outcome having a 5 percent base rate and a stratified sampling procedure can increase the yield to 20 percent, we would probably be more willing to suffer complications to the design and statistical analyses. Thus, in order to derive the maximum benefit from a stratified sampling procedure, risk classifications should discriminate among subjects with regard to the infrequent events of greatest interest.

Although the yield scenarios just reviewed are plausible, they do not exhaust all the base rate and sample proportion combinations that might be used, nor are they relevant to events with low probability such as violence. Table 7.5 gives the yield across a variety of base rate and sampling ratio combinations for a cohort of 500 subjects. To use the table, sampling ratios should sum to 100 percent across all risk groups. The far right column (100 percent) gives estimates for the overall population (i.e., without any risk stratification), while the bottom row (1.0) gives the total number of subjects for each sampling ratio, which can be used to compute yield percentages within risk groups. The chart may be especially useful in thinking about infrequent behaviors. For example, if we have three risk groups with base rates of .15, .10 and .05 and we sample from each group at ratios of 50 percent, 30 percent, and 20 percent respectively, we find that the corresponding yields are 38 (.15, 50 percent), 15 (.10, 30 percent), and 5 (.05, 20 percent), for a total of 58 offenders.

TABLE 7.5. Number of offenders in a cohort of 500 subjects, by base rate and sampling ratio.

										Sampling ratio									
	5%	10	15	20	25	30	35	40	45	50	55	60	65	70	75	80	85	90	95	100%
.05	1	3	4	5	6	8	9	10	11	13	14	15	16	18	19	20	21	23	24	25
.10	3	5	8	10	13	15	18	20	23	25	28	30	33	35	38	40	43	45	48	50
.15	4	8	11	15	19	23	26	30	34	38	41	45	49	53	56	60	64	68	71	75
.20	5	10	15	20	25	30	35	40	45	50	55	60	65	70	75	80	85	90	95	100
.25	6	13	19	25	31	38	44	50	56	63	69	75	81	88	94	100	106	113	119	125
.30	8	15	23	30	38	45	53	60	68	75	83	90	98	105	113	120	128	135	143	150
.35	9	18	26	35	44	53	61	70	79	88	96	105	114	123	131	140	149	158	166	175
.40	10	20	30	40	50	60	70	80	90	100	110	120	130	140	150	160	170	180	190	200
.45	11	23	34	45	56	68	79	90	101	113	124	135	146	158	169	180	191	203	214	225
.50	13	25	38	50	63	75	88	100	113	125	138	150	163	175	188	200	213	225	238	250
.55	14	28	41	55	69	83	96	110	124	138	151	165	179	193	206	220	234	248	261	275
.60	15	30	45	60	75	90	105	120	135	150	165	180	195	210	225	240	255	270	285	300
.65	16	33	49	65	81	98	114	130	146	163	179	195	211	228	244	260	276	293	309	325
.70	18	35	53	70	88	105	123	140	158	175	193	210	228	245	263	280	298	315	333	350
.75	19	38	56	75	94	113	131	150	169	188	206	225	244	263	281	300	319	338	356	375
.80	20	40	60	80	100	120	140	160	180	200	220	240	260	280	300	320	340	360	383	400
.85	21	43	64	85	106	128	149	170	191	213	234	255	276	298	319	340	361	383	404	425
.90	23	45	68	90	113	135	158	180	202	225	248	270	293	315	338	360	383	405	428	450
.95	24	48	71	95	119	143	166	190	214	238	261	285	309	332	356	380	404	428	451	475
1.00	25	50	75	100	125	150	175	200	225	250	275	300	325	350	375	400	425	450	475	500

The Racine Cohorts

In his book *Criminal Career Continuity*, Lyle Shannon (1988) reports data relevant to the first stage of the proposed sampling plan—disproportionate sampling across levels of community risk. Interpolating from graphs in the book, we find that official FBI data for Racine, Wisconsin, in 1978 (the most recent year that was reported) show an average rate of 3.9 arrests (UCR Part I and II offenses) for every 100 persons between ages 6 and 44 years. When comparable arrest rates are computed by census tract, we find that the lowest rate is 1.6 and the highest is 16.0. Averages for the five census tracts with the highest and lowest arrest rates are 2.5 and 9.5, respectively, an almost fourfold difference. This finding is interesting because it provides insight into the efficiency of a stratified sampling procedure at the community level. However, these differences between communities are post-hoc descriptions of the dependent variable, and in order to reproduce these differences in our sampling plan, we would have to identify stratification criteria that are accurate at predicting the rank ordering of communities by arrest rate.

Nonetheless, let us assume that we find ourselves in a situation that resembles Racine, Wisconsin, with high- and low-risk communities having average arrest rates of 9.5 and 2.5. With all high-risk subjects, we can expect to find 47.5 arrests a year in a sample of 500, or 380 arrests over an eight-year follow-up. With all low-risk subjects, there would be about 12.5 arrests per year, for a total of 100 arrests. The number of offenders we would find in a sample of mixed risk levels falls somewhere between these two limits. If we assume that 60 percent of subjects come from high-risk areas and 40 percent from low-risk areas, we would have 33.5 arrests per year, or 268 arrests over the course of the study.

Shannon (1988) also presents individual level data on three birth cohorts— 1942, 1949, 1955—relevant to the issue of sampling yield. Table 7.6 displays the probability of police contact for males with continuous residence in Racine. The data exclude contacts for traffic, status offenses, suspicion, investigation, or information, making them comparable to data on the 1945 Philadelphia cohort. Shannon finds that the probability of police contact ranges from .478 to .573 as the age at follow-up goes from 22 to 33 years. For the 1945 Philadelphia cohort, Wolfgang reports a probability of .349 at age 18 and of .473 at age 30. Thus, concerns that the Philadelphia data are unrepresentative because they overestimate the chances of police encounters do not find support in the Racine data. If anything, the Racine cohort suggest that estimates based on the Philadelphia cohort are conservative. Although not shown in Table 7.6, we also find that conditional probabilities for subsequent offenses are greater in Racine than in Philadelphia, indicating that earlier yield estimates of multiple offenders may fall on the conservative side as well.

Finally, we found that rates of violent offenses increased dramatically in Philadelphia between the 1945 and 1958 cohorts, and the Shannon data indicate that an increase in rates of serious offenses also occurred during this time in Racine. From the 1942 to the 1955 cohort the probability of felony crimes almost

TABLE 7.6. Probability of police contact for a nontraffic offense and for a felony offense as reported for the Philadelphia and Racine birth cohorts.

Birth cohort	Prob. of any contact	Prob. of felony contact	Age at end of follow-up
Racine			
1942	.573	.132	33
1949	.535	.151	26
1955	.478	.219	22
Philadelphia			
1945	.349		18
1945	.473		30

doubled, going from .132 to .219, notwithstanding the fact that the 1942 cohort had a substantially longer follow-up.

The Racine data also confirm that the incidence of serious offenses (felonies) in a sample will be substantially lower than police contacts. For the 1942 cohort, the probability of a felony was about one quarter that of a police contact, while for the 1955 cohort the fraction was about one half. These data on felony contacts give us an opportunity to estimate the cumulative prevalence of serious offending in our sample. Shannon's figures for the 1955 cohort apply to males between ages 6 and 22, and the most closely related of our cohorts are the 9 to 17 and the 12 to 20 year old groups. Since the age ranges of these cohorts fall short of that covered by Shannon's cohort, the estimates will be somewhat generous. With this caveat in mind, we note that the 1955 Racine cohort data suggest that 21.9 percent of our older cohorts, or 110 subjects per cohort, will have a police encounter for a felony offense over the study period. We note, however, that Shannon reports substantially lower felony rates for the 1942 and 1949 cohorts. If we take the lowest figure reported by Shannon as a worst-case scenario, we estimate a yield of 66 felons per cohort (13.2 percent of subjects). These data highlight the important role that base rates, which vary across research sites and across time, will play in determining the yield of the sample.

The New York City Neighborhood Study

The figures in Table 7.7 were provided by Professor Simcha-Fagan in a telephone conversation. The data are based on a sample of 533 boys between ages 11.5 and 17.5 drawn from 12 neighborhoods classified as high- or low-risk on the basis of socioeconomic status and family organization.

Looking first at the overall figures, we see that the average proportion of boys arrested in high-risk communities (19.2 percent) is about twice as large as that in low-risk communities (10.6 percent). The range across all communities is considerable (4 percent to 26 percent), with roughly the same spread within low- (4 percent to 14 percent) and high-risk (15 percent to 26 percent) classifications. Although these proportions are substantially smaller than those Wolfgang and

TABLE 7.7. Community level rates of percent of males between ages 11.5 and 17.5 years with known police contact for New York City.

Racial composition of community	Low-risk communities		High-risk communities	
	Mean	Range	Mean	Range
Predominantly white	13.6%	10–14%	16.5%	15–18%
Predominantly black	7.7%	4–10%	22.0%	18–26%
Overall	10.6%	4–14%	19.2%	15–26%

Shannon reported, the age composition of the Simcha-Fagan sample is much younger. In addition, geographic differences in police practices and record keeping may be at work. Yet, if we take the New York City figures as conservative scenarios, the data suggest that somewhere between 10 percent and 20 percent of the older cohorts will have an official police record.

When we disaggregate communities in terms of the predominant race of the residents (more than 70 percent of one race), a very different picture emerges between white and black communities. The difference in averages between low- (13.6 percent) and high-risk (16.5 percent) white communities is only 3 percent, and ranges within risk groups show relatively little variability (10 percent to 14 percent, 15 percent to 18 percent). In contrast, for black communities the difference between the averages for low- (7.7 percent) and high-risk (22.0 percent) communities is 14 percent, representing a nearly threefold increase across risk levels. The ranges for low- (4 percent to 10 percent) and high-risk (18 percent to 26 percent) black communities show more variability than those for white communities, and the gap between the point where the lower range ends and the higher one starts is substantial.

Thus, we see that the yield ratio between high- and low-risk communities is about two, but when disaggregated by racial composition the ratio is 1.2 for white communities and 2.8 for black communities. These findings demonstrate that the risk criteria used in the Simcha-Fagan study are much more discriminating for black communities. If we encounter a similar situation, we should have little trouble using neighborhood characteristics to identify high-risk blacks, although we may have trouble finding a group of white subjects of sufficiently high risk. The findings also point to problems that may be encountered in studying racially segregated communities, especially if racial composition strongly correlates with economic and social risk factors. In view of these potential difficulties, we suggest that special attention be given to the racial composition of neighborhoods in site selection and perhaps special consideration be given to cities with racially integrated neighborhoods. More generally, however, the issue is one of ensuring an adequate yield of offenders across racial and risk groups (including low-risk groups) to allow for statistical comparisons, working within the constraints imposed by sample size restrictions.

The Columbus, Ohio Cohorts

In *The Violent Few*, Donna Hamparian and colleagues (1978) report on their study of the arrest careers of violent offenders. The sample consisted of all people born in Columbus, Ohio, between 1956 and 1960 who were arrested for a violent offense by January 1, 1976, the end of the follow-up period. The researchers found that the 1956 to 1958 cohorts contained 811 violent youth, while the 1959 and 1960 cohorts contained 377 violent youth. It is not clear whether the difference in the numbers of violent youth across cohorts is a function of length of follow-up, the distribution of the peak age of violent offending, the numbers of cohort subjects, or other cohort differences. Unfortunately, the study contains little data on nonviolent or noncriminal youth in the birth cohorts, limiting the utility of the findings for our purposes.

Not surprisingly, violent offenders were mostly males (84.3 percent). Blacks were overrepresented among the violent offenders; blacks constituted 15.4 percent of all five birth cohorts (based on census data) but represented 54.8 percent of the violent sample. At the community level, the authors found that the ten census tracts with the largest numbers of violent offenders represented 7.8 percent of the cohort populations but contributed 32.4 percent to the sample. Furthermore, they report that 26.3 percent of census tracts (54 out of 205) had no violent youth over the years studied. In general, these data indicate that the efficiency of disproportionate sampling strategies based on race or on census tract are comparable.

Among the violent youth, the authors report that 16.5 percent had committed multiple violent offenses and that 31.0 percent could be classified as chronic offenders who had committed a total of five or more offenses (nonviolent and violent). Although offense chronicity is associated with violence, we also see that the proportion of repeatedly violent offenders is low.

In studying the offense behavior of the 1956 to 1958 cohorts, the authors found that 811 violent youth committed 3,373 total offenses and 1,091 violent offenses. More significantly, only 270 of the violent offenses were classified as major crimes against the person. These findings hold serious implications if one of the primary objectives of the proposed research is to study extremely violent offenders. For example, if a research team had elected to follow from birth every person born in Columbus, Ohio, in 1956, 1957, and 1958, a sample that would quickly bankrupt most research budgets, only 270 serious violent offenders, comprising roughly 100 robbers and 100 assaulters, would have been identified after 20 years of research.

However, we must recognize that sample yield is influenced greatly by how violent offenders are defined. Thus, by using more generous criteria than arrest (for example, by looking to self-report data), many more violent offenders should be identified than in the Columbus, Ohio, cohorts.

The Connecticut Juvenile Institution Cohort

The Columbus findings of Hamparian and colleagues (1978) stand in sharp contrast to the situation Otnow-Lewis and colleagues (1989) described in Connec-

TABLE 7.8. Estimated number of delinquent onsets by type of offense and by age of cohort.

Age range of cohort subjects	Estimated number and proportion of delinquency onsets for 500 cohort subjects			
	Felony assault	Felony theft	General delinquency	Illicit drug use
12 to 20 years	167 (33%)	165 (33%)	280 (56%)	215 (43%)
15 to 23 years	95 (19%)	125 (25%)	130 (26%)	225 (45%)
18 to 26 years	50 (10%)	65 (13%)	50 (10%)	150 (30%)

Note: These estimates are based on annual initiation rates derived from the National Youth Survey, which comprises a nationally representative sample of males and females. The estimates were computed by adding the initiation rates at each age as reported in the NYS over the age range for the appropriate cohort and multiplying the resulting fraction by the number of subjects ($N = 500$).

ticut. In her study, Otnow-Lewis tracked for seven years a sample of 95 youth released from a juvenile institution in Connecticut. Over the course of the study, 89 of the juveniles had a subsequent adult criminal record. On average, the group was arrested 11.6 times (median = 9), with nearly half of the boys ($N = 45$) arrested for a class A or B felony. Within a relatively short time, this small group of delinquents logged arrests for 9 murders, 12 sexual assaults, 9 kidnappings, 58 nonsexual assaults, and 44 robberies. The total of these violent offenses is 132, which is roughly half the number of violent offenses committed by three successive birth cohorts in Columbus, Ohio.

The difference in the number of violent offenders Hamparian and Otnow-Lewis identify is attributable to a number of factors, not the least of which is geographic variation, because the Columbus data presumably include all cohort members who were institutionalized. Nonetheless, it is clear that by drawing from an institutionalized population we can dramatically increase the yield of chronic or violent offenders in the sample. The increase in yield, however, probably comes at the expense of representativeness, because all but 15 of the Connecticut institutionalized juveniles came from abusive or violent families and 59 percent of them had multiple neurological, psychotic, and cognitive disabilities.

The National Youth Survey

We have suggested that self-report data will produce a higher yield of offenders than official data, and the National Youth Survey (NYS), a longitudinal study of adolescent youth that includes self-reported delinquency items, can help to confirm this point. The NYS sample consists of a nationally representative group of males and females between 11 and 17 years of age when the sample was chosen in 1976. The sample covers urban, suburban, and rural geographic areas. Unfortunately, the published data most relevant for our purposes are not broken down by individual risk factors (e.g., ethnicity or sex). Since our sample will come largely from high-risk urban areas and will consist mostly of males, estimates based on the NYS national data will be conservative.

TABLE 7.9. Cumulative percent of sample in the National Youth Survey involved in problem behaviors from 1976 to 1986 and corresponding estimates of the cumulative number of persons and acts for a cohort of 500 subjects.

Behavior category	Cumulative percent reported in NYS survey	Estimate for cohort of 500 subjects	
		Cumulative number of persons	Cumulative number of acts
Delinquency			
general delinquency	87.3%	437	54,370
index offenses	41.5	208	3,330
serious violent offenses	35.7	179	2,315
felony assault	32.5	163	1,525
felony theft	31.4	157	2,269
Illicit drug use			
alcohol	94.1	471	124,146
marijuana	65.3	327	84,770
polydrug use	37.1	186	17,065
cocaine	23.7	119	3,913
Mental health			
mental health problems	24.4	122	N/A
depression	13.3	67	N/A
mental health service use	13.8	69	1,020

Note: The National Youth Survey involves a national sample of 740 males and 687 females (total = 1427) followed between 1976 and 1986. The estimates for a cohort of 500 subjects were derived by multiplying the cumulative percent figure shown in the table by 500 and by multiplying the cumulative number of acts (not shown in table) by 500/1427.

In one of their reports, Delbert Elliott and colleagues (1985) constructed a synthetic cohort covering ages 11 to 24 and estimated the initiation rates for a single cohort across this age range. This information can be used to estimate the number of onsets of delinquency we can expect to find in our cohorts. The estimates in Table 7.8 indicate that the younger cohorts will capture most of the onsets. For subjects in the 12-year-old cohort, we estimate that 56 percent ($N = 280$) will embark on a delinquent career during the follow-up period. In addition, we predict that 33 percent ($N = 167$) of cohort members will commit their first felony assault and 33 percent ($N = 165$) will commit their first felony theft. In comparison, we estimate that 26 percent ($N = 130$) of the 15-year-old cohort subjects and 10 percent ($N = 50$) or the 18-year-old cohort subjects will begin their offending careers during the follow-up.

The National Youth Survey data also contain cumulative prevalence estimates for specific problem behaviors, including types of delinquency, illicit drug use, and mental health difficulties (Menard, Elliott, and Huizinga 1988). The data can be used to estimate the number of people in a cohort engaging in specific acts as well as the total number of acts likely to be observed. These estimates are presented in Table 7.9.

Before reviewing the estimates, we should mention again that the data are based on a ten-year follow-up of a national sample of males and females between ages 11 and 17 at the start of the study. The sample we are recommending will be drawn from an urban area and will comprise mostly males, differences that will tend to increase the yield of delinquent acts. However, an eight-year follow-up is planned, which will work to decrease the yield. Finally, unlike the NYS cohorts, our cohorts will contain subjects of the same age, suggesting that the estimates represent a general expectation pooled across several cohorts.

We see that general delinquency, which encompasses many less serious acts, is a nearly universal phenomenon. In the NYS, 87 percent of the sample engaged in at least one delinquent act. Applying this proportion to a cohort of 500 subjects translates into 437 individuals. We also estimate that a cohort of 500 subjects will commit 54,370 delinquent acts, an astonishingly high figure, probably because relatively trivial acts are included under the heading of general delinquency. If we limit our focus to relatively serious offenses, we see that 41.5 percent of the NYS youth engaged in at least one UCR Index offense, and 35.7 percent in at least one UCR Part I violent offense. When felony theft and felony assault are isolated, the proportions do not change much. On the basis of these findings, we estimate that, among 500 cohort subjects, 208 will commit an Index offense and 179 will commit a serious violent offense. The estimated number of acts committed by violent and serious offenders also is large. The data suggest that, over the course of study for one cohort, we will observe 3,330 Index offenses and 2,315 serious violent offenses.

Illicit drug use occurs very frequently in the NYS cohort. On the basis of the NYS proportions we estimate that over an eight-year period 471 out of 500 cohort subjects will use alcohol a total of 124,146 times and 327 subjects will use marijuana a total of 84,770 times. We predict also that there will be 186 users who take more than one drug and who report using drugs on 17,065 occasions and 119 people who use cocaine a total of 3,913 times.

Finally, we note that the sample should include a fair representation of people with mental health difficulties who are treated for their problems. Specifically, we estimate that 122 cohort subjects will report mental health problems and that 69 will become clients of mental health services, with 1,020 service contacts.

The data from the NYS confirm that the number of offenders in the sample will be much greater when using self-report data as a criterion measure rather than official records. In fact, self-report data reveal the almost universal prevalence of some problem behaviors, such as general delinquency and alcohol use. Self-report methods also identify more violent offenders, although we can expect that a substantial portion of the self-reported violence spectrum involves less serious acts than those reflected in police or court data. Nonetheless, even when we restrict our scope to UCR Part I violent offenses, the estimated yield of offenders from self-report data is substantial.

Conclusions

We have reviewed several different research projects and on the basis of these findings have attempted to estimate the yield of the proposed sampling procedures. The range of estimates is considerable, reflecting the fact that many different factors work to produce any set of research findings. It is difficult to summarize the particulars of such divergent predictions, but we can identify some general issues and principles to guide us through steps we must take to bring the research plans to fruition. First, we should restate the obvious facts that site selection will have a lot to do with the number of offenders identified and that more generous definitions of outcomes in terms of degree of seriousness or nature of contact (self-report, police contact, arrest, etc.) would produce greater yields for a given sample.

Among the conclusions this review suggests is that stratification at either the individual or community level produces an increase in yield of about the same magnitude. Across communities we find that the ratio of offenders between high- and low-risk communities is 4:1 in Racine and 3:1 for black communities in New York City. Differences across individual characteristics, most notably race, produce a similar ratio. A central issue is whether combining individual- and community-level risk factors results in a greater yield than either approach individually, and we do not have data that address this question. For this reason, we suggest that this issue be addressed as part of the preparatory field work. However, assuming for the moment that the answer to this question is no, we can use either individual- or community-level risk factors if sampling yield is our only concern.

In addition, we have identified some difficulties that are likely to be encountered and that need to be addressed more directly. The issues are:

1. It is difficult to identify a large number of seriously violent or chronic offenders because their numbers are low. Thus, it is difficult to guarantee that the proposed research design will allow for the study of these offenders in great detail. There are several strategies for dealing with low base rates. The approaches include expanding the sampling frame to include more offenders who have been identified by the criminal justice system, especially offenders who have spent time in juvenile and adult correctional facilities. Various other supplemental sampling strategies may also prove useful.
2. The problem of low base rates will be exacerbated by subgroup analyses, such as those focusing on certain types of offenses or offenders.
3. The association between race and crime presents difficulties at both the individual and community level. If communities are stratified into risk groups, attention must be given to racial homogeneity across communities. If stratification takes place at the individual level, it is important to have enough subjects in both racial groups to allow for reliable comparisons. The problem is not only that race is a strong correlate of criminality, but also that developmental paths are known to differ by race. It is important to be able to study differ-

ences in developmental patterns by race, which requires sufficient numbers of offenders and nonoffenders across racial groups.

4. It is challenging, given a fixed sample size and a relatively limited set of risk factors, to balance yield considerations with the need to have some minimum number of offenders across all combinations of sampling strata. In particular, it is important to ensure that there are enough low-risk offenders (e.g., low-risk individuals in low-risk areas) for reliable comparisons.

An important offsetting consideration is not given much attention in this review—that to the extent we can combine cohorts in the analyses, we can multiply by several times our yield of offenders. In Chapter 11 on statistical methods, we discuss strategies and procedures for amalgamating cohorts. Finally, the estimates of sampling yield are for juvenile delinquency and adult crime, which are outcome behaviors central only to older cohorts in the design, not to younger cohorts. Again, we suggest that these issues be confronted when the project moves into the prepraratory field work stage.

8
Site Selection

Site selection is one of the most crucial aspects of the study. In discussing possible criteria for choosing sites, it quickly became apparent to us that numerous variables must be considered. We therefore narrowed the focus to a small set of key factors. The list includes population stability, quality of and access to official and historical records (e.g., school, police, courts, community and medical organizations, etc.), ethnic composition, ecological integrity of local communities, experimental intervention contingencies (e.g., existing apparatus; cooperation, etc.), and size of the city in relation to the wider metropolitan area.

Perhaps the most important criterion in site selection is population stability. We recommend that the chosen sites be fairly stable cities that are not undergoing rapid change. A city with extreme turnover presents formidable problems in terms of sampling, cooperation, interviewing, follow-up, and measurement of community characteristics, among other things. We do not recommend the selection of deviant outliers or cities with extremely stable populations. Rather, the challenge is to find cities with relatively stable residential mobility patterns within the metropolitan area that also meet other design needs (e.g., sufficient yield of crime; ethnic mix, etc.).

To facilitate site selection decisions, we suggest that census data on population mobility be examined. Such data are presented on key migration patterns in the 55 largest cities for 1975 to 1980 (data for 1985 to 1990 are not yet available) in Table 8.1. The 1970s were characterized by significant out-migration from central cities. Recent trends suggest much more stability so the following is almost a worst-case scenario.

The data in Table 8.1 can be broken down by race, and various percentages on population movement among households, cities, and counties also can be calculated. Thus, census data, preferably 1990 data, can be used to develop baseline information on characteristics of residential mobility for cities under consideration.

Population mobility data can be combined with other census data on important social characteristics. In particular, we might want to contrast cities with fairly stable populations that vary on other key dimensions such as race, income,

TABLE 8.1. Population mobility in 55 largest U.S. cities: 1975–1980.

Variable	Mean	Std. dev.	Minimum	Maximum
In-migrants from city				
from same SMSA	33,892	39,700	3,716	217,750
In-migrants to city				
from other SMSA	119,899	136,591	19,657	631,826
Out-migrants from city				
to same SMSA	88,525	76,659	6,471	371,995
Out-migrants from city				
to other SMSA	123,895	137,924	12,396	902,752
1970 population	761,104	1,135,723	251,817	7,894,851
1980 population	728,113	1,030,997	223,532	7,071,639

family structure, and perhaps crime levels. For example, Sampson (1987) conducted a city-level analysis of the correlates of robbery and homicide in U.S. cities using numerous social, demographic, economic, and family variables. As an illustration, Table 8.2 presents the mean levels of some key variables (including crime) for the 171 U.S. cities with a population greater than 100,000 people. Some variables are related to area racial composition, and these relationships may be useful in identifying cities as potential sites.

A possibility we considered is that of selecting a city in which Hispanics could comprise a significant portion (e.g., 33 percent) of the sample. However, that objective is difficult to achieve because the mean level of Hispanics across all U.S. cities with a population over 100,000 in 1980 was only 3 percent. In fact, as of 1980 no city had an officially recorded Hispanic population over 25 percent. However, we note that the Hispanic population is growing rapidly and has been undercounted by the census in the past; we also note that the fertility rate is especially high among Hispanics. Yet, given potential problems in data collection with regard to language barriers, high levels of illegal immigration and mobility, we do not recommend oversampling for Hispanics in the design. This recommendation does not imply that Hispanics should be excluded in household sampling; rather, our review of the evidence suggests that it is probably not feasible to choose sites or to stratify communities on the basis of the Hispanic population. By contrast, it should be relatively easy to choose sites and communities within cities that will provide a balanced sample of black and nonblack (white plus Hispanic) subjects. In any case, use of 1985 or 1990 census data appears essential for decisions regarding the ethnic composition of the sample.

Another criterion that can be examined with census data is the ratio of the central city to the wider metropolitan area. The smaller this ratio, the harder data collection becomes. For example, if a city represents only a small proportion of the metropolitan area, there is greater potential for movement out of the city into surrounding communities. Furthermore, there will be more within-SMSA police departments, courts, schools, and hospitals that cross jurisdictions, which will

TABLE 8.2. Descriptive statistics of structural characteristics and racially disaggregated offending rates, U.S. cities, 1980.

Variable	Mean	Std. dev.
Employed men per 100 women:		
black	52.95	14.36
white	62.26	7.72
Mean public assistance income:		
black	2,565.4	666.3
white	2,418.4	367.1
Per-capita income:		
black	3,767.8	708.8
white	6,356.4	998.9
Median age:		
black	24.48	1.78
white	31.81	3.48
Percentage of households headed by females:		
black	26.42	6.13
white	9.26	1.68
Percentage of households with children headed by females:		
black	43.58	9.52
white	17.69	3.70
Percentage of families on welfare:		
black	22.10	7.57
white	6.46	3.16
Region:		
north	.36	.48
west	.26	.44
Percentage black	19.21	16.63
Structural density of rental housing (% units in 5 + unit structures)	48.42	11.42
Homicide offending*:		
black juvenile	16.25	24.48
black adult	91.67	67.94
Robbery offending*:		
black juvenile	1,870.8	2,607.4
white juvenile	330.2	305.1
black adult	2,371.8	1,910.9
white adult	308.3	261.8

Source: Sampson (1987). *per 100,000. Reprinted with permission.

greatly increase logistical problems in collecting follow-up data, not to mention variations in data quality. For these reasons, it will be convenient if the city is the dominant ecological unit in the metropolitan area.

To explore this recommendation, we computed the ratio of the city population to the surrounding county and SMSA for 171 cities with a 1980 population greater than 100,000. The city-to-SMSA ratio averages .35, with a standard deviation of .22, a minimum of .01, and maximum of 1.0. In comparison, the city-to-county ratio averages .52, with a standard deviation of .31, a minimum of .02 and a maximum of 1.0. These data show wide variation in the ecological dominance of cities. Although cities constitute on average a third of the surrounding SMSA and half of the surrounding county, some cities represent only 1 or 2 percent of the metropolitan area. We recommend that to the extent possible cities be selected that are near or above the mean on ecological dominance. This strategy will substantially reduce problems of tracking subjects and improve the quality of and access to official records. In addition, it will be easier to measure community characteristics and track community change in areas where the city dominates the metropolitan area because there is an increased probability that within-SMSA residential moves will involve other sampled communities.

For several reasons, it is desirable to choose sites that have recognized community areas with reasonable ecological integrity. First, the substantive interpretation of community effects is facilitated if the data describe socially meaningful areas. Second, collection of data is easier if recognized areas overlap with city planning and healthcare boundaries. For example, Buka (1989) reports that data are available on 35 health areas and over 213 census tracts in Rhode Island. The same is also true of cities like New York and Chicago. Third, it is often necessary to obtain help from community institutions in securing local cooperation with interview studies. Once it is known in an area that researchers are collecting sensitive data on individuals, collective suspicions get raised and refusal rates may increase. To the extent that we can enlist community groups for support, we increase the chances of high response rates.

Finally, it is desirable to have some historical data on patterns of community structure and crime in the research site. For example, Chicago has 75 community areas that have been studied intensively for many decades, producing rich historical data on patterns of community structure and crime rates. Cities with similar historical data should be considered for the study of criminal careers in ecological context.

In short, we recommend that sites be examined on crucial dimensions before selection. As an example of the types of information that can be evaluated, Table 8.3 describes characteristics of cities and surrounding areas that are potential research sites. Although these eight cities were chosen for illustrative purposes only, they vary on such dimensions as region (e.g., rustbelt vs. sunbelt), population size, ethnic composition, and residential mobility. In general, we see that the population in jail or detention is quite small compared to the total juvenile population. Consequently, we should not face major problems regarding institutionalization of potential subjects for the older cohorts. In any case, these and many other characteristics (e.g., quality of official records, nature of community boundaries within a city) can and should be assessed in selecting sites.

Multiple Sites

Our proposal calls for implementation of the core research design in at least two research sites. Arguments for conducting identical or similar projects in more than one location stem from the requirement that theories embody generalizable

Table 8.3. Selected demographic and ecological characteristics of eight U.S. cities.

	Pittsburgh	St. Louis	Milwaukee	Chicago	Los Angeles	Atlanta	New York	San Antonio
1980 city population	423,938	453,085	636,212	3,005,078	2,966,850	425,022	7,071,639	785,109
1980 SMSA population	2,231,253	1,812,340	1,383,069	7,154,948	7,417,125	2,023,914	8,319,575	1,075,492
In-migrants to city from same SMSA, 1975 to 1980	17,995	26,878	33,724	78,611	217,750	24,196	31,158	9,883
In-migrants to city from other SMSA, 1975 to 1980	35,967	25,498	63,965	219,120	596,321	58,594	631,826	111,991
Out-migrants from city to same SMSA, 1975 to 1980	88,989	80,660	79,329	286,572	371,995	91,419	119,735	43,147
Out-migrants from city to other SMSA, 1975 to 1980	87,729	74,568	81,685	286,788	464,541	82,651	902,752	128,105
% of persons in 1980 residing in a different county than in 1975	10	12	13	8	19	21	16	16
% persons in 1980 residing in same house as in 1975	64	60	53	58	45	53	60	55
City to SMSA population ratio	.19	.25	.46	.42	.40	.21	.85	.73
% Black	24	46	23	40	17	67	25	7
% Hispanic	<1	<1	1	6	4	<1	9	11
W-B segregation index	86	90	88	93	90	92	77	90
% of persons in poverty	17	22	14	20	16	28	20	21
% of white female-headed families	11	11	10	10	9	8	10	12
% of black female-headed families	30	31	37	31	26	32	30	24
% of vacant housing units	7	12	5	7	5	9	5	7
Fertility (# children born per female between ages 15 to 44 years)	.98	1.33	1.23	1.34	1.15	1.21	1.13	1.42
Death rate per 1,000 population	15.50	11.40	9.20	9.40	8.20	9.70	10.50	7.20
# of white juveniles	57,148	45,559	99,674	304,267	383,307	18,456	838,615	192,795
# of black juveniles	31,913	71,636	62,690	432,426	152,951	94,407	582,212	18,486
1983 county adult jail population	647	731	974	6,343	12,500	2,079	9,220	832
1982 county juvenile detention population	85	111	43	381	3,945	159	324	72

differences, which makes it important to know if findings hold across different conditions of research. Hence, we need to know which findings reflect influences unique to a particular location or project, which are conditional on theoretically relevant features of sites or subjects, and which are robust and universal enough to be regarded as core theoretical propositions. Multiple research sites in which important findings can be replicated allow us to address many of these issues.

In emphasizing the issue of replicability, we do not mean to imply that this is the sole argument for multiple sites or that projects in these sites must be identical in every way. Indeed, resources for research are scarce, and every large-scale venture should make important and unique contributions to knowledge. How can we reconcile the need for replication with a call for unique research design features? One approach is to provide carefully for variations in site and sample selection criteria and in aspects of data collection. For example, it may be possible in a second site to use risk criteria that increase the yield of active or chronic offenders while maintaining important requirements of sampling, such as that samples be representative of the general population and that subjects be comparable across cohorts. Similarly, data collection instruments might vary to accommodate different research interests while still including a core set of common variables across sites. For example, it might be desirable in a second site to target a group of subjects (i.e., violent offenders) or a theory (e.g., deterrence) for special research efforts. Also, opportunities for experiments and interventions will vary across sites as might the appropriateness of subjects for a treatment regimen.

There are also advantages in delaying the start of research in a second site so as to capitalize on experience gained in the first project. In this way, researchers learn the best ways to organize, implement, and manage a large-scale research effort. If the interval between projects is long enough (e.g., two or three years after first data collection), the results of preliminary analyses from the first site might be available before the start of the second project. These results could be used to modify instruments or data collection strategies in the second site so as to target critical issues and hypotheses identified in the preliminary analyses. However, in varying instrumentation or sample selection across multiple sites, care must be taken not to jeopardize replication efforts by introducing extraneous factors into the design that could produce differences in findings between sites.

Measurement and Analysis

9
Common Variables

Some lives show remarkable consistency. The unruly, obstreperous child, whose parents have a hard time managing, may develop into the hard-core juvenile delinquent that even specialized schools cannot handle, and later may become the adult criminal who, eventually incarcerated, spends the better part of a prison career sequestered in punitive segregation for chronic disciplinary problems. Sometimes consistency can be found at a more general level, as when different problem behaviors show transitions and apparent substitutions. The difficult child, incapable of making friends at school, may turn to drugs at an early age, move into drug dealing and theft, and then land in a psychiatric hospital. Other lives show dramatic changes, sometimes for the better and sometimes not. The rebellious adolescent may find a girlfriend and settle down into a more conventional life-style, while the otherwise well-adjusted adult may take up heavy drinking after a divorce, an addiction that results in the loss of a job and enrollment in Alcoholics Anonymous.

We are interested in tracing patterns of problem behaviors over time. Where there is chronic behavior, we suspect that a continuity of causal influences operates. For example, among highly recidivistic offenders, distinctive features of psychological orientation, such as those reflected in personality and temperament styles, may work to shape and organize behavior into consistent patterns over time. Similarly, when we locate abrupt behavior changes, we suspect that discrete shifts in important causal influences have occurred, such as those represented by puberty, school entry, or other key life transitions that may lead to the onset of delinquency.

A longitudinal study allows us to examine behavior patterns over extended times, but, in order to investigate developmental processes, we need to measure important factors throughout the period they operate. As a key feature of the accelerated longitudinal design, we propose the use of a set of common measures that tap into key developmental life processes. We use the term *common* generously in that the variables so designated need only apply to a majority of cohorts. The domains covered by the common variables are outlined in Table 9.1, which also lists suggestions on frequency of measurement by cohort. The domains include antisocial and deviant behavior, experiences with the criminal justice

TABLE 9.1. Interviewing strategies for proposed variables by cohort age group.

			Cohort starting ages				
	Prenatal	3	6	9	12	15	18
Variables: Outcome							
Conduct disorder	PS (5–8)	PS (5–11)	PA (6–12)	R,PA (9–12)	R	R	R
Delinquency			PA (9–14)	PA	R,PA (9–17)	R,PA (15–17)	R
Criminality					R,PA (18–20)	R,PA (18–23)	R,PA
Alcohol/drug			PA	PA	R,PA	R,PA	R,PA
Sexual activity			PA	PA	R,PA	R,PA	R,PA
Biological							
Height	PS	PS	PA	PA	PA	PB	PB
Weight	PS	PS	PA	PA	PA	PB	PB
Body mass	PS	PS	PA	PA	PA	PB	PB
Strength, agility	PS	PA	PA	PA	PA	PA	PB
Physical condition at birth	P	R	R	R	R	R	R
Hormone levels	PS	PA	PA	PS	PS	PA	PA
Physical stigmata	IF	IF	IF	IF	IF	IF	IF
Vagal tone	PS	PA	PA	PA	PA	PA	PA
Archive-physical samples	IF	IF	IF	IF	IF	IF	IF
Family							
Structure	PA	R,PA	R,PA	R,PA	R,PA	R,PA	R,PA
Deviance history	IF	IF	IF	IF	IF	IF	IF
Marital relationship:							
parent	PA	R,PA	R,PA	R,PA	R,PA	R,PA	R
subject					PA (16–20)	PA (16–23)	PA
Parent-child relationship	PS	R,PS	R,PA	R,PA	R,PA	R,PA	R
Child abuse	PA	R,PA	R,PA	R,PA	R,PA (12–18)	R,PA (15–18)	R,PA (18)
Quality of environment	PA	PA	PA	PA	PA	PA	PA
Employment/Work history							
Parent	PA	PA	PA	PA	PA (12–18)	PA (15–18)	PA (18)
Subject					PA (16–20)	PA (16–23)	PA

Social service resources							
Parent	PA (18)	PA (15–18)	PA (12–18)	PA	PA	PA	PA
Subject	PA	PA (16–22)	PA (16–19)	PA	PA	PA	IF
Education/school							
Parents' level	IF	IF	IF	IF	IF	IF	IF
Subject:							
achievement	R,PA (18)	R,PA (15–18)	R,PA (12–18)	R,PA	PA	PA (5–10)	PA (5–8)
misbehavior	R,PA (18)	R,PA (15–18)	R,PA (12–18)	R,PA	PA	PA (5–10)	PA (5–8)
truancy	R,PA (18)	R,PA (15–18)	R,PA (12–18)	R,PA	PA	PA (5–10)	PA (5–8)
Social networks							
Parent				PA (8–10)	PA (5–10)	PA	PA
Subject	PA	PA	PA	PA	PA	PA (5–10)	PA (5–10)
Psychological							
Temperament	IF	IF	IF	IF	IF	PB	PA
Attachment style	IF	IF	IF	IF	IF	PB	PA
Cognitive function	IF	IF	IF	PB	PB	PB	PA
Personality traits	IF	IF	IF	PB	PB	PB	PA
Emotional disorders	R,IF	R,IF	R,IF	R,IF	R,IF	R,IF	IF
Neurological function	IF	IF	IF	IF	IF	PB	PA
Stressful life events							
Parent	R,PA	R,PA	R,PA	R,PA	R,PA	R,PA	PA
Subject	R,PA	R,PA	R,PA	R,PA	R,PA	R,PA	PA

R – retrospective
PA – prospective, annual
PS – prospective, semiannual
PB – prospective, biennial
IF – initial assessment with possible follow-up to detect change
$(y_1 - y_2)$ – age range over which data are to be collected

Gender, ethnicity and age (date of birth) will be collected on all subjects at the initial review, as will assessment of first and second degree relatives regarding criminality, alcohol/drug abuse and mental illness. Data on the parents' marital relationship will be collected if the subject is still living at home.

system, biological measures, psychological measures, school measures, peer and network measures, measures of economic and social service resources, stressful life events, and community measures. We discuss each of these sets of variables in turn, mentioning as examples instruments that might be used.

Measures of Antisocial and Deviant Behavior

Although the ultimate focus of the proposed research is on criminal behavior (acts that pose serious threats to the physical and material well-being of the citizenry), a developmental perspective requires that we investigate a variety of other behaviors along the way. The behaviors we wish to predict or explain vary by age and by stage of criminal career development, but the correspondence is less than perfect. Research interests do not conveniently equate with the age or criminal history of subjects, and neat schemes for mapping out research agendas necessarily reflect a simplified approach to real-world situations. In general, we can say that, for the childhood cohorts, the primary outcome variable is conduct disorder; among adolescents, it is the onset of juvenile delinquency; and with young adults the emphasis turns to the development of a criminal career and to desistance from crime. In addition, we are strongly interested in studying drug use, including cigarettes, alcohol, marijuana, and hard drugs, given the well-documented connections between drug use and crime. Finally, we have interests in studying other forms of deviance such as precocious or promiscuous sexual behavior, mental illness, and school failure and dropout, both in terms of the relations these behaviors have to crime and as outcome variables worthy of study in their own right.

Conduct disorder, the major outcome variable for the youngest cohorts, is a psychiatric disorder involving antisocial behavior among children. The diagnostic criteria for the disorder are shown in Table 9.2. Children qualify as conduct disordered if they demonstrate at least three of thirteen different behaviors throughout a six-month period. The list of behaviors is: stealing, running away from home, lying, setting fires, truancy, breaking and entering, destroying property, physical cruelty to animals, forcing others into sexual activity, weapon use, initiating fights, forcible theft, and physical cruelty to people. Conduct disorders also are ranked as mild, moderate, or severe, based on the number of conduct problems observed. Aside from use of clinical interviews, the Diagnostic Interview Schedule for Children (DISC) is the primary survey instrument for assessing psychiatric problems, including conduct disorders, among youth.

Conduct disorder is a psychiatric diagnostic category that describes a state or condition of an individual, even though the diagnosis is grounded in specific behavioral observations. For our purposes, there are several limitations with this type of categorical approach to the study of child behavior problems. Specifically, (1) accurate psychiatric diagnoses may require interviews with trained clinicians, which can be expensive and cumbersome; (2) conduct disorder as a diagnostic category encompasses a broad constellation of behaviors, and for

TABLE 9.2. Diagnostic criteria for conduct disorder.

A disturbance of conduct lasting at least six months, during which at least three of the following have been present:

(1) has stolen without confrontation of a victim on more than one occasion (including forgery)

(2) has run away from home overnight at least twice while living in parental or parental surrogate home (or once without returning)

(3) often lies (other than to avoid physical or sexual abuse)

(4) has deliberately engaged in fire-setting

(5) is often truant from school (for older person, absent from work)

(6) has broken into someone else's house, building, or car

(7) has deliberately destroyed others' property (other than by fire-setting)

(8) has been physically cruel to animals

(9) has forced someone into sexual activity with him or her

(10) has used a weapon in more than one fight

(11) often initiates physical fights

(12) has stolen with confrontation of a victim (e.g., mugging, purse-snatching, extortion, armed robbery)

(13) has been physically cruel to people

Criteria for severity of conduct disorder:

Mild: Few if any conduct problems in excess of those required to make the diagnosis, and conduct problems that cause only minor harm to others.

Moderate: Number of conduct problems and effect on others intermediate between mild and severe.

Severe: Many conduct problems in excess of those required to make the diagnosis, or conduct problems that cause considerable harm to others, e.g., serious physical injury to victims, extensive vandalism or theft, prolonged absence from home.

Source: *Diagnostic and Statistical Manual of Mental Disorders*, p. 55. (3rd edition, revised), 1987. Washington, DC: American Psychiatric Association. Reprinted with permission.

some purposes we may be interested in studying specific acts rather than behavioral syndromes; (3) criterion behaviors tend to differ by age of the child in likelihood of occurrence and in face assessments of problem severity (e.g., truancy can occur only after a child reaches school age; lying is typically considered more of a problem at some ages that at others); and (4) the diagnosis requires that the disturbance of conduct endures at least six months, making it difficult to study non-chronic problem behavior. One way to minimize these problems is to collect data on specific behaviors in such a way that they can be reconfigured to represent, either fully or in part, the diagnostic category. For example, the Child Behavior Checklist is often used to describe the problem behavior of children between the ages of 2 and 16 (Achenbach and Edelbrock 1983), and this instrument might be modified in light of diagnostic criteria.

Regarding measures of delinquency and criminality, the research agenda requires a fairly detailed accounting of antisocial behaviors. For example, in order to chart incidence rates, we will need to know the exact number of times an act has occurred over a given period; if we are to study onsets and sequences of behaviors, we will have to record the timing of each event; if we intend to examine patterns of escalation and deescalation, we will have to describe the seriousness of offenses in terms of the amount stolen or the level of personal injury inflicted; finally, in order to test various theoretical propositions, we will need to collect data on the circumstances of the offense, such as drug use, weapon use, or co-offending, and on the offender's motivations and perceptions.

As we review the survey instruments that have been used to study delinquency and crime, we find that none fits our requirements exactly, generally falling short by not providing sufficient detail on events. However, we can, much to our advantage, capitalize on the substantial work that psychologists and criminologists have invested in the development of reliable survey instrumentation by modifying existing questionnaires to fit our purposes. We have already mentioned the Child Behavior Checklist, which covers a substantial portion of the delinquency spectrum and which comes in versions that ask parents as well as teachers to describe the behavior of students (Achenbach and Edelbrock 1983). Other prime candidates for modification include the National Youth Survey developed by Delbert Elliott and colleagues; the instruments developed by David Huizinga, Rolf Loeber, and Terence Thornberry as part of the ongoing Program of Research on the Causes and Correlates of Delinquency sponsored by the Office of Juvenile Justice and Delinquency Prevention; and the instruments used in the various Philadelphia cohort studies conducted by Marvin Wolfgang and colleagues.

In developing instrumentation, we will have to face practical constraints, such as time and budget restrictions, on the amount of data that can be collected. Since researchers' ambitions can easily outstrip their resources it becomes important to identify a core set of items that represent key measures of antisocial behavior. Participation across a comprehensive set of antisocial behaviors is a basic outcome variable, and the survey list of behaviors should vary by the subject's age. However, because we are interested in studying precocious onsets, we should not presume too much by way of behaviors that are developmentally implausible or impossible. Data collection should also include the frequency and timing of incidents (in terms as specific as possible), along with information on a limited set of offense attributes, including a measure of seriousness.

We are interested in many attributes of criminal behavior, and our wide-ranging research agenda is likely to raise special problems when dealing with high-rate offenders, a group that can present researchers with an overwhelming data collection task. One strategy for keeping the amount of data to a manageable level is to collect basic information on all offenses and to limit collection of detailed information to a subset of offenses, such as the most serious or the most recent. Detailed descriptions of criminal incidents might profitably derive from structured or semistructured interviews with offenders in lieu of, or in combination with use of, a more extensive survey questionnaire. In opting for this strategy, supplemental data should be collected systematically, without undesirable bias in the selection of incidents.

High-rate offenders will pose other data-collection problems. We can anticipate that extremely active offenders may find it difficult to count precisely the number of times they have committed an offense, may confuse in their memory the attributes of different incidents, and may be unwilling to tolerate long interviews, with the same questions asked repeatedly on each event. One approach to these problems might be to vary the interview format with the level of criminal activity, something that can be ascertained early in an interview with relatively little effort. Another strategy might be to conduct separate interviews on criminal behavior for very active criminals. These approaches would require some pilot work in order to develop an efficient interview protocol that enhances recall. However, given that extremely chronic offenders are of special theoretical and policy interest, pilot work to develop specialized research methodologies for this group may prove to be a very worthwhile investment.

We are especially interested in substance abuse. Because the use of many drugs is prohibited or regulated by law, no special justification is required for collecting data on illegal drug use in a study of crime. However, some drugs are legal (e.g., cigarettes, alcohol), and in these instances we want to study progressions (or stepping-stone hypotheses), addictions, and specialized motivations to crime. The data should include information on frequency of use of specific drugs, the amount of money spent on drugs, drug-dealing activities, and treatment experiences (under both professional and nonprofessional auspices). It is also important to have information on the timing of drug use so that we can relate levels of criminal activity to periods before, during, and after use of specific drugs.

The complexity of interactions among the many outcome variables we recommend collecting data on can be illustrated most readily in connection with drug use and sale. A major issue that needs to be resolved is that of the temporal order between drug use and various stages of conduct disorder, onset of delinquency, chronicity, and desistance. What is the extent of childhood and adolescent exposure and experimentation with drugs? Does drug use tend to follow or precede onset of delinquency or chronic criminality? How does drug use contribute to persistence in crime? We also need to know more about the dynamics or processes involved in the drug-crime connection. To what extent to drug networks and crime networks overlap or reinforce one another? Are they both part of a general crime subculture? Do crimes vary with type of drug abuse? Does chronic drug use lead to a decline in co-offending and an increase in solitary criminality? Are high crime-rate communities also high drug-rate communities with fairly stable institutional patterns for drug dealing and use? These and similar questions can only be answered if sufficiently detailed descriptions are obtained on a variety of outcome variables and their possible interactions.

Experiences with the Criminal Justice System

As part of the effort to describe offender careers, we must document contact with the criminal justice system. The list of relevant experiences includes contacts with police (arrest), courts (both juvenile and adult), and correctional agencies (probation, parole, community service orders, and prison). These data might conveniently be collected from official records, provided that the records are well maintained and computerized. For each experience with the criminal justice system, we would want to know the date and type of criminal behavior, along with the date, type, and outcome of the system contact. Criminal justice agencies routinely collect most of this information. For example, arrest records usually contain the date and reason for arrest, and as part of offender-based tracking systems operating in most jurisdictions, arrests can be linked to dispositional information such as court charges and adjudications. We may, however, encounter problems in documenting contacts with the juvenile justice system, given the decay of juvenile court records due to court-mandated confidentiality requirements limiting access to (and sometimes requiring destruction of) juvenile records. It is difficult, however, to judge in advance how serious this problem might be, given local variations in juvenile court rules and procedures.

Biomedical Measures

We propose to collect a variety of biomedical measures across cohorts, ranging from basic items such as gender and race to more complicated measures such as hormone levels. Notwithstanding a resurgence of interest in biological causes of crime (Wilson and Herrnstein 1985), biomedical measures have been used only rarely in modern criminological research. Undoubtedly, many criminologists are unacquainted with biomedical data collection techniques, especially those requiring specialized technical competence. We detail in Appendix II some problems and issues that will have to be addressed. At this point, we provide a brief overview of biomedical measures that might be used in the proposed research.

Among subjects' physical characteristics we suggest documenting are height, weight, body mass, and heart rate variability, taking care to ensure that measurement is accurate. For infants and children, these variables can be used to plot physical growth curves, which represent an indirect measure of nutritional status, and for adolescents they can help chart the course of pubertal development. For the oldest subjects, these variables provide a crude measure of level of physical ability and may possibly allow for somatotype (body type) designations.

Important measures around time of birth include birth weight and complications of pregnancy and delivery. Hospitals routinely record these items, and, given access to medical records, it should be possible to collect the information for all cohort subjects. We also suggest collecting data on subjects' hormone levels, a proposal made potentially viable by recent developments in laboratory test procedures that allow hormone levels to be gauged from saliva samples. Because this technology is relatively new, we may find on closer inspection that saliva tests cannot be used. Alternatively, blood tests could be used to measure hormone levels, although the proposal for universal testing would probably then have to be reconsidered.

Given the reliable and substantial differences in crime rates between males and females, hormones of special interest are those that regulate sexual development.

The male sex hormone, testosterone, which, among other things, affects the body's development of muscle mass, has been implicated in aggressive behavior, although the evidence is not entirely convincing. There are two periods of major change in levels of sex hormones—during infancy and adolescence—having important consequences for physical development, and more frequent measurement may be required during these periods to capture important changes. At other ages, when sex hormone levels are relatively stable, we may find that seemingly small variations bring important consequences. Another interesting hormone is cortisol, which may provide a measure of biological reactivity to novel stimuli and thus hold promise as a psychophysical correlate of individual differences in personality and temperament.

The research plan also calls for collecting data on physical stigmata, especially marks that reflect a history of disease or abnormal physical development. Minor stigmata are sometimes considered as soft signs of underlying disturbances in nervous system development. Major stigmata more convincingly suggest the presence of neurological abnormality and also can adversely affect a person's self-concept and degree of social acceptance.

Finally, we recommend that physical specimens, such as hair, deciduous teeth, and blood samples, be collected that can be archived and held for later analyses pending future developments in medical technology. The rationale for this proposal is that breakthroughs in medical testing occur so rapidly that within the not-too-distant future we may have at hand technologies that can add greatly to our understanding of the physiological basis for criminal behavior. Given the substantial investment the project will be making by way of collecting a great variety of data on subjects, it seems prudent to make provisions that will allow researchers to capitalize on future developments in scientific technology.

Psychological Measures

The notion of temperament encompasses many different schemes for classifying individuals in terms of general psychological dispositions that presumably have physiological origins. Temperament schemes are generally built around distinctive styles of behavior and emotion that translate into different types of individuals. The terminology of some of these classification schemes has found its way into conventional discourse. It is not unusual, for example, to speak of introverted, extroverted, sanguine, or melancholic people (Kagan 1989). Temperament provides us with a way of characterizing basic differences in emotional profiles that predate personality development and that persist throughout life. In principle, temperament variables should allow us to characterize the psychological orientation of infants as well as adults.

A variety of instruments has been developed to describe individual temperament differences. Some of the survey instruments that have been widely used are the Dimensions of Temperament Survey (Lerner et al. 1982), the Infant Temperament Scale (Carey and McDevitt 1978), the Toddler Temperament Scale

(Fullard et al. 1984), and the EASI Temperament Survey (Buss and Plomin 1975). Because we recommend that temperament data be collected on subjects across all cohorts, it would be most convenient to have a single instrument that provides comparable measurement at all ages. In this regard, life-span measures that can be used retrospectively are attractive. One such measure, the Dimensions of Temperament Survey (DOTS), comprises scales that describe behavioral patterns in terms of regularity of biological functioning, response to novel experiences, and style of adjustment to the environment (Lerner et al. 1982). Other measures based on different temperament classification schemes might also be used.

Since temperament presumably can be traced to constitutional factors, it should be possible to find physiological correlates of individual differences in temperament. Recent efforts to demonstrate that emotional reactivity underlies differences in infant temperament have pioneered the use of several psychophysiological measures. Three that might be used are cortisol level (a hormone produced by the adrenal cortex), vagal tone (heart rate variability), and regional brain electrical activity (Fox 1989). We discuss in Appendix II collecting data on hormone levels, and information on cortisol can be derived from the assay. Heart rate variability can be linked to functions of the autonomic nervous system, and differences in vagal tone have been shown to distinguish extremely inhibited or shy children. While heart rate variability may prove to be a useful measure of temperamental differences, the measure's stability varies with the age of subjects, and reliable measurement depends heavily on the conditions of testing (Fox 1989). In addition, it is not clear that heart rate variability reflects temperamental differences most relevant to delinquency and crime, because the measure has been used most successfully with shy children. We leave open the possibility of using regional brain activity tests (EEG), because practical constraints may preclude use of this highly specialized and expensive technique. These considerations argue for pilot work on physiological correlates of temperament differences, the results of which can form the basis for deciding which physiological measures are incorporated into the longitudinal study.

Another important psychological variable we have identified is attachment style. The variable derives from attachment theory, which posits that the quality of the mother-infant relationship is a critical factor in the child's subsequent personality development. According to the theory, a child's experience with the mother becomes a prototype for all subsequent interpersonal relationships, so that attachment style becomes an enduring feature of psychological development.

The primary method for gauging attachment style among infants and children is the strange situation technique. The technique involves clinical observations on a series of structured interactions between mother, child, and stranger (Ainsworth et al. 1978). At later ages, attachment style can be assessed by means of the adult attachment interview (George et al. 1984). A limitation of these techniques is that they require a large investment of time and other resources, including use of skilled observers. Unless other, more convenient instruments are identified, attachment style may only be measured in cohort subsamples.

Personality refers to "deeply ingrained patterns of behavior, which include the way one relates to, perceives and thinks about the environment and oneself" (American Psychiatric Association 1987, p. 403). Personality and temperament variables can overlap as descriptions of the psychological orientation of individuals. However, personality differs from temperament in that greater theoretical emphasis is placed on the influence of experience, and taxonomies are organized around sets of traits, which represent propensities to think or behave in certain ways. Personality traits can provide for complex classification of subjects, which can be especially useful in the stages of life beyond childhood, and many standardized personality tests have been developed, each based on a different constellation of traits. Among the more widely used personality tests are the Minnesota Multiphasic Personality Inventory (MMPI) (Graham 1987), the California Psychological Inventory (CPI) (Gough 1975, Megargee 1977), the Omnibus Personality Inventory (Heist and Yonge 1968), the High School Personality Questionnaire (Cattell et al. 1984), the Sixteen Personality Factor Questionnaire (Harrell and Lombardo 1984), the Myers-Briggs Type Indicator (Myers 1985), and the Edwards Personal Preference Schedule (Edwards 1959). An example of an instrument appropriate for young subjects is the California Child Q-Set (Block and Block 1980), which can be used at age 3 and can differentiate between undercontrolled and antisocial children.

An advantage of using a standardized personality test is that we can draw on previous research on normative population scores and psychometric test properties. In deciding on which inventory to use, tests that may yield seemingly tautological explanations of antisocial behavior should be avoided. In this regard, the MMPI is often faulted for revealing that criminals score high on the psychopathic deviate (Pd) scale. For our purposes, aggressivity and impulsivity are important traits to be measured, and personality tests must be scrutinized to ensure that they tap these critical dimensions. In addition, we should be sensitive to the fact that the research will be dealing with minority and lower-class subjects, which means that tests with serious cultural or class biases should be avoided.

Level of cognitive functioning is another important psychological variable, and research consistently demonstrates a significant difference in IQ scores between delinquents and nondelinquents. Although little progress would be made by simply replicating this finding, one of our objectives is to investigate the mechanisms that have been advanced to explain it. The most popular IQ tests are the Wechsler Adult Intelligence Scale (Wechsler 1955, 1981), the Wechsler Intelligence Scale for Children (Wechsler 1949, 1974), and the Stanford-Binet test (Terman and Merrill 1973). For infants, the Bayley Scales of Infant Development can be used to assess intelligence (Bayley 1969). Intelligence tests, however, need to be administered under standardized conditions and are time-consuming. IQ test scores may sometimes be located in school records, but data may be available only sporadically. Given the importance of intelligence constructs to delinquency theory, it is worth the effort to collect IQ data in a more systematic fashion.

Lastly, we recommend collecting data on mental illness and emotional disorders across cohort subjects. Among children, this information is critical given that the

American Psychiatric Association's Diagnostic and Statistical Manual of Mental Disorders (DSM-III-R) cites attention-deficit hyperactivity disorder, oppositional defiant disorder, and specific developmental disorders both as antecedent predisposing factors and as concurrent features of conduct disorder (APA 1987, p. 54). Among adults, institutional and offense careers undoubtedly will differ for seriously disturbed offenders. At a minimum, there is a need to record treatment experiences (psychiatric, psychological, and lay counseling), along with accompanying diagnostic judgments, that occur in the lives of cohort subjects. Since epidemiological research reveals that many of the emotionally ill do not seek treatment, we recommend generating diagnostic information on subjects by means of a clinical instrument such as the Diagnostic Interview Schedule (DIS) or Diagnostic Interview Schedule for Children (DISC). Although standardized diagnostic instruments can be time-consuming, assessments need not be made frequently, and most tests also provide information on lifetime prevalence. In addition, by systematically incorporating data on emotional disorders in the research, we broaden the appeal of the project by creating links to the mental health area. Also, we are in a position to study important research issues on multiproblem individuals, such as those who can be characterized as both mad and bad.

Family Variables

We suggest documenting basic family characteristics, such as size, composition, and housing arrangements, for all subjects. It is also important to know the criminal, mental illness, and drug and alcohol abuse histories of family members and of close relatives, so that we can trace continuities in familial patterns of antisocial and other problem behaviors. Along these lines, experiences of domestic violence and of child abuse are critical elements in the hypothesized intergenerational transmission of violence (Widom 1989), and it therefore would be useful to collect information of both past and current experiences of this nature.

In addition, the nature and quality of the family environment needs to be described, including aspects of family relationships (e.g., husband and wife, parent and child, brother and sister). The Family Environment Scale developed by Moos and Moos (1981) is an example of an instrument that might prove useful in describing domestic situations, since it provides measures of cohesion, expressiveness, conflict, independence, achievement orientation, intellectual-cultural orientation, moral-religious emphasis, organization, and control. Another example of a potentially useful instrument, one that relies on a combination of observations and interviews, is the Home Observation for Measure of the Environment (Bradley et al. 1988). This instrument can be used to assess the quality of cognitive, emotional, and social stimulation provided to children from birth through age twelve.

We have already discussed plans for measuring attachment style, which concerns the nature of the mother-child relationship, and the parental acceptance/rejection questionnaire (Rohner 1984) might be a useful supplement, since it can be used to describe, retrospectively, childhood perceptions of parental receptivity between ages 7 and 12.

Discipline and child supervision are important aspects of parenting that are related to delinquency. The child-rearing practices report, developed by Block (1965), may be a useful measure to have for cohort subjects because it captures a variety of parental behaviors, including child discipline. One version of the instrument can be used for children as young as age 3, while another version is available for children who are 16 years and older.

Marriage and birth are important events that subjects can experience both as child family members and as adult heads of household. Among the various instruments that assess the quality of marital relationships are the Conflict Tactics Scale of Straus (1979); the O'Leary-Porter Scale (Porter and O'Leary 1980), which examines overt disagreements on various issues; and the marital satisfaction measure of Huston (1983), which describes a spouse's subjective perceptions of the relationship.

School Measures

Schools play a critical role in modern society, making it important to study in considerable depth the experiences of students who participate as research subjects. In terms of an agenda of common variables, we recommend use of primary measures of school achievement and of academic and disciplinary problems. Levels of achievement can be documented by school grades (and by standardized test scores, if available), which should be relatively easy to view, given cooperative administrators and adequate record-keeping systems. Other items include significant experiences reflecting academic difficulty, such as placement in special educational programs, failing to progress to the next grade level on schedule, and school dropout. Experiences indicative of behavior problems, such as truancy, official disciplinary reports, suspension, and expulsion, are also critical because they are in some respects measures of delinquency. Finally, another set of important variables refers to the subjective dimensions of school experiences, including attachment to teachers and commitment to institutional goals and values. These items probably will have to be collected via a survey questionnaire, which may require development and pilot work.

Peer and Network Variables

Peer associations hold a central position in contemporary theories of juvenile delinquency. For adolescents, we advise collecting information on social networks that might bring closure to long-standing etiological controversies over the sequencing of antisocial behavior and peer affiliations. Social relationships can be important factors in the development of antisocial behavior across all stages of life, and these issues should also be addressed. For example, while infants do not have important peers, parents are embedded in social relationships that hold consequences for their children, as illustrated by the mother enmeshed in a drug subculture. Similarly, interpersonal associations among adult offenders may influence criminal careers, as when desistance is brought about by a newly established romantic relationship. Among the critical items are the structure and orientation of social networks, as reflected by patterns of associations and by the criminal behavior of associates, along with other important network characteristics, such as the amount of time spent in different types of activities. Finally, in order to test hypotheses on the formation and transmission of habits and values, it is useful to know about the social psychological aspects of network relationships, including the degree of interpersonal attachment or social integration among network participants.

It may be difficult to capture fully in a set of common measures important aspects of social relationships, since network boundaries may be ill-defined and difficult to trace and information may be required of network participants who are not the subjects of the study. Pilot work may be necessary on this topic and might be carried out in conjunction with a specialized study of peer networks.

Economic and Social Resources

Several theories emphasize the relation between levels of economic and social resources and criminal behavior, especially acquisitive crimes. At earlier ages, the effects of economic variables are mediated from parents to children by way of family experiences, while opportunities for more direct influences arise later in life. Employment experiences rank among the critical economic variables for measurement, encompassing income and job characteristics (type of work, percent of time employed, etc.). Given that some criminological theories highlight the disjuncture between economic aspirations and experience, it would be useful to have some measures that allow for a test of these hypotheses. Resources and services governmental and community agencies provide also need to be factored into the economic picture. These economic resources include welfare payments, subsidized housing, aid to families with dependent children, job training and placement services, and assistance from church and local organizations.

Stressful Life Events

Dramatic and significant life changes (e.g., serious illness, accidents, hospitalization, institutionalization, loss of job, divorce, death of a close friend or relative) have been linked to a variety of subsequent pathological conditions, and at least one study shows a connection with delinquency (Novy and Donahue 1985). Although it is a relatively straightforward task to document occurrences of significant life events, in order to make sense of relationships that might be uncovered we need to do more than construct a chronological inventory of personal misfortunes. The theoretical framework most commonly invoked to explain the adverse effects of some events is the stress-adjustment paradigm, which argues that significant life changes create stress that some people mismanage with counterproductive behavior. The stress-adjustment paradigm suggests that individual assessments of the undesirability of life events and of various coping strategies deployed over time in response to adversity should be documented. In so doing, we need to ensure that the events covered are appropriate to the life situations of subjects of different ages. Many self-report instruments are available for assessing life events during adolescence (Williams and Uchiyama 1989), an especially tumultuous phase of life for many people. Some of these instruments provide for assessments over longer periods.

Community Measures

As part of a multidisciplinary approach to the study of crime, we have identified variables that describe the communities subjects live in. Much of the information we recommend collecting will come from official statistics, such as census data that can be used to describe characteristics of geographic locales. The list of officially recorded information on communities is impressive. For example, we can readily access data on community crime rates, poverty rates, age and sex distributions, racial and ethnic composition, residential mobility, and number of female-headed households. For some purposes, however, information that is not available through official statistics will be needed, and, in Chapter 5, we provide details on a community survey that we suggest might be undertaken. Items that might be covered in the survey include social services; health, religious, and recreational resources; quality of life variables; informal friendship and kinship networks; formal organizational participation; subcultural and normative climate; juvenile gangs; access to illegal goods such as drugs and guns; and control styles of youth behavior.

10
Measurement Issues

Throughout this book we identify a number of measurement issues, particularly in the chapters that describe the cohort studies. These comprise two general sets of concerns. First, we must be sure to identify the most appropriate, relevant, and useful concepts for a theoretical perspective on human development and crime covering the first quarter century of life. This issue is perhaps the most critical one to the success of the scientific goals of the proposed research. On the one hand, we need to be eclectic in drawing on existing theories and research. Most important, however, we must continually remind ourselves that technical acuity of measurement is worthless if we measure the wrong concepts. The second set of issues relates to measurement processes and procedures. At a minimum, measures have to be reliable and valid, and data should be collected comprehensively yet efficiently. The statistical aspects of measurement should not be given abbreviated attention, since accurate measures are necessary for testing hypotheses and building inductive theories.

In this chapter we consider each of these broad concerns in relation to a specific example. To begin with, we discuss issues of continuity in theoretical concepts as illustrated by possible relations between conduct disorder and delinquency. We next discuss issues of retrospective data, emphasizing how these data can be used to link cohorts together in the analysis. These discussions clearly do not exhaust all the measurement issues we have raised in this book, and thus continuing attention should be given to these matters as the research plan advances.

Continuities in Constructs

The proposal to assemble data on common measures across all cohorts presupposes that an underlying set of theoretical constructs operates throughout life. Although the notion that a continuity of influences or processes exists is an attractive one, few studies have addressed the challenges such an extended conceptual framework pose. Our preference is to use life-span measures that have already been developed, such as the Dimensions of Temperament Scale; however, few such measures now exist. Thus, before moving into the field with our research, we must resolve a number of issues regarding the selection of specific instruments.

Among the issues to be dealt with is the possibility that a theoretical construct may have different manifestations over time—a situation that, left unattended, can lead to the confounding of measures and concepts. Rutter (1989) points to heterotypic continuity, in which behaviors that appear quite different represent the same underlying phenomenon. This principle can be generalized as a concern that applies throughout our research. In some cases, different instruments may be needed to measure the same construct at different developmental stages. Because our objective is to study development over extended periods, we will have to reconcile these differences. In related fashion, we may find that the most appropriate sources of data to measure a given construct change over time. Finally, we must be sensitive to transitions and continuities in the theoretical abstractions we create as we move across different conceptual levels. As children grow into adults, what were once important family attributes—for example, social class and marital discord—develop counterparts as characteristics of individual subjects.

An example of an important conceptual issue that needs to be addressed is that of the relation between different types of antisocial behavior throughout life. We are especially interested in the sequence from conduct disorder to delinquency to adult crime, a chronic pattern the most obstinate and recalcitrant offenders evidence. At the theoretical level, we must determine whether these behaviors reflect the influence of a single underlying construct or of multiple constructs and whether we can speak of causal relations between types of antisocial behaviors, as, for example, by arguing that conduct disorder causes delinquency. In resolving these issues, we must pay attention to the substantial overlap among conduct disorder, delinquency, and crime in terms of the actual behaviors. Of the 13 behaviors listed as symptoms of conduct disorder, 10 could be prosecuted as crimes, setting aside age of majority considerations (Loeber and Baicker-McKee 1989). Similarly, with the exception of status offenses, nearly all the offenses that the juvenile court handles are crimes if committed by adults, and in many respects the juvenile delinquency label tells us more about the age of the offender and about the agency that responded to the problem than about the offense.

The implications of this redundancy between age-graded categories of antisocial behavior depend on the inferences we want to make. If we simply want to show that conduct disorder predicts delinquency, we should have few problems producing additional evidence to support the proposition that current antisocial behavior predicts similar future behavior. On the other hand, if we want to conclude that conduct disorder causes delinquency, we will have to show that the two behaviors differ in theoretically relevant ways. Otherwise, our causal explanation of delinquency can become tautological.

We can avoid many of these problems by sharpening our hypotheses and our theoretical framework. If, for example, we confirm the hypothesis that conduct disorder has distinct correlates (e.g., attention deficit and hyperactivity) that are unrelated to delinquency, we are in a better position to argue that conduct disorder and delinquency are different constructs that happen to capture many of the same behaviors. In this situation, the possibility that conduct disorder causes delinquency is left open (Loeber and Baicker-McKee 1989). However, in studying behavior onsets, it can be misleading to speak of the onset of an adolescent delinquent career when identical childhood behaviors are labeled conduct disorders. For example, if we fail to note that a child diagnosed as conduct disordered steals from others, we may erroneously conclude that larcenous behavior observed later in life signals the onset of theft. The problem is that the behavioral elements of a diagnostic scheme can be obscured by classifications of people, which in turn make it easy to overlook the first instance of an act. The proposal to collect data on specific behaviors at all ages helps us to get around this problem since we can study acts apart from the classifications of people that they allow us to impose.

Retrospective Data

Most of the data we suggest collecting can be considered retrospective in the sense that at the time data is collected reports will be solicited on past behaviors. When collecting retrospective data from official records, concerns tend to be limited to degree of access and quality of coverage, items largely outside the control of researchers except to the extent that they are made important considerations in site selection. In contrast, researchers more directly control the quality of interview data. The proposed accelerated longitudinal design has two sets of considerations involving retrospective interview data: (1) information collected on behaviors that occur during the interval between successive interviews, and (2) information on experiences and events outside the standard interview reference period (which we here refer to as retrospective data) that can be used to link cohorts in the analyses.

The interval between data collection efforts relates to decisions that must be made about the frequency of interviews over the follow-up period. For older cohorts, the interview schedule would include a self-reported offending component, and there have been numerous studies on the reliability and validity of self-report data, some of which have focused on how data quality is affected by the length of recall period. In general, these studies show that the accuracy of data falls off substantially as the recall period extends beyond one year (Hindelang, Hirschi, and Weis 1981). Although an interval shorter than one year will yield more accurate data, trade-offs always have to be made with regard to available resources. Undoubtedly, some researchers would consider the gains of semiannual or more frequent interviews as marginal in relation to the increased costs, while others would take the opposite view. Our proposal is to interview subjects at least annually, with more frequent data collection during critical periods of rapid developmental or behavioral change. In our view, this flexible approach to the frequency of data collection allows us to strike a balance between competing demands of data quality and resource constraints.

The other set of considerations, that of linking together cohorts in the data analyses, is specific to the accelerated longitudinal design. One of our reasons for advocating this type of design is that by using multiple, overlapping cohorts we can study long-term developmental processes in less time than would be required to study a single cohort. However, in order to make statements about developmental processes spanning ages covered by different cohorts, we need to be able to link the cohorts together. One approach to linking, which is a variation on case-matching procedures, requires that we identify comparable sets of subjects across cohorts. To the extent that comparability is to be demonstrated in terms of experiences or events at an age or developmental stage not covered by prospective data in the period of overlap between cohorts, retrospective data will be needed for linking older with younger cohorts. For example, in tracing the effects of school failure over time, we can anticipate that some of the younger subjects will show academic problems during the follow-up period. In order to extend the description of the developmental sequences using older cohorts, we would have to know which of the adult subjects had difficulty in school as children. Although we discuss the specifics of linking strategies in Chapter 11 (on data analysis), including strategies that do not involve matching procedures, we offer at this time some general observations.

The viability of a case-matching approach to linking cohorts hinges in part on the accuracy of retrospective accounts. If, as we have just indicated, one year is an outer limit for accurate recall, the natural limitations of memory do not bode well for our plan. Nonetheless, some researchers argue that for many purposes the limitations of retrospective data have been overstated and that evaluations should be made in light of the planned uses of the data (Robins 1988).

In our case, long-term retrospective data are needed to facilitate the study of long-term causal processes. The purpose of our collecting retrospective data is not so that we can duplicate all analyses across all cohorts, although the data will provide for some replication, but to allow for continuity of investigation into extended developmental sequences. The plan to link cohorts therefore does not require that we assemble retrospective information for older subjects on every item collected prospectively for younger subjects. At a minimum, we need retrospective data that allow for the broad classification of subjects along theoretically relevant lines. For example, we will want to identify older subjects as early, typical, or late starters in terms of different types of crimes, and broad categorizations such as these create fewer opportunities for error, especially when focused on salient events that tend to stand out in a person's memory. In addition, to the extent that we can identify reliable intermediate effects in long-term processes, data on the initial events in a sequence are less critical. Finally, if the maximum time between cause and observable effect is of the order of a decade or so, the most useful retrospective data are those needed to link adjacent cohorts, which, taken together, cover a span of 11 years, with five years of overlapping data collection.

On the other hand, situations that require detailed information on past events for linking cohorts may present difficulties. Among the problems we face are instances in which information is not available or is not easily accessed. For example, it will be more difficult to locate parents, caretakers, teachers, and school records for the oldest cohort subjects, especially when family structure changes or a family is mobile. It also may be difficult to collect sufficient detail on past events to allow for the most theoretically relevant classifications. Parents, for example, may not remember how they disciplined or supervised their now-grown children, and changing attributes on which subjects lack knowledge (e.g,. IQ at age 8) cannot be retrieved retrospectively (unless reported in archival records). Finally, on the practical side, the amount of retrospective information to be collected increases with the age of cohort subjects. Since collecting data becomes more unwieldy as the amount of data increases, at some point it may pay to think in terms of separate interviews for collecting retrospective data on older subjects.

In deciding on a specific agenda of retrospective items to be collected, some general principles to follow are listed here:

1. Data should be collected from multiple sources (e.g., self-reports, criminal justice and school records, parents and teacher reports) whenever possible. In particular, archival records are a useful supplement to interview data because they are uncontaminated by memory and recall problems. More generally, a strategy of using multiple sources of data helps avoid the biases that are present in any one source and allows for demonstrations of convergent validity.

2. The amount of data and the level of detail should be keyed to the recency of events, provided that the data allow for classification of subjects in theoretically useful terms. Recent experiences will be most useful in linking adjacent cohorts and, by collecting less data in less detail on distant past events, the plan accommodates the fact that memory decays over time. For example, people will find it easier to recall the general timing or sequence of past events than the exact dates and, for many analyses, a general indication of when events occurred will provide a satisfactory description of developmental progressions.

3. Techniques for enhancing recall, such as using significant life events (e.g., school entry) as reference points, should be used extensively.

4. We should consider using contemporary measures to provide information about past events in situations where this strategy appears viable. Examples of such situations include instances where prior experiences have relatively long-lasting consequences (e.g., if attachment style is an enduring product of early childhood experiences), where individual characteristics are thought to be stable (e.g., if temperament is a constitutionally based feature of psychological orientation) and where developmental trajectories are sufficiently well documented that we can reconstruct a developmental path with confidence (e.g., there is substantial research on individual changes in IQ scores that might prove useful).

11
Statistical Methods and Analysis

The data analysis tasks we face are complex and challenging. Our proposed research has many objectives and, to be most effective, analytic strategies must vary by the nature of the research problem. In some cases, our research questions resemble those that have been asked before, allowing us to use familiar statistical tools with well-developed applications. Other questions we are interested in reflect more innovative approaches to research issues, and thus we have few precedents to build on. In most such instances, the statistical techniques that appear to be most useful and relevant have been developed only recently, and no universally accepted analytic procedure has yet emerged.

Our discussion of data analysis proceeds by laying out a framework for addressing various issues. We have consulted several statisticians who are experts in the analysis of longitudinal data, and our thinking draws heavily on their input. Nonetheless, we recognize that more needs to be done on this topic and recommend continued work on a data analysis plan. We view the development of data analytic strategies as a continuing activity for several reasons. To begin with, the list of statistical techniques that might be used is long, making it difficult to lay out a single, detailed plan for data analysis. In any given situation, the choice of analytic strategies is contingent on many factors, and important considerations include attributes of the data set, only some of which are predictable in advance. In addition, the newer techniques we suggest using represent very recent developments in statistical theory and methods. Although these techniques look promising, we need time to become familiar with their applications. Finally, given that the proposed data collection effort will span nearly a decade, we can anticipate further advances in statistical methods over the course of the project. It is even possible that, when researchers are in a position to carry out the data analysis, they will have the option of using newly invented techniques not now available.

We recognize that the relation between data attributes and statistical analyses can work both ways. That is, just as characteristics of data can dictate types of statistical methods to be used, we need to consider ways in which assumptions different statistical techniques require can inform plans for data collection. For this reason, we have tried to be alert to the implications that various techniques hold for attributes of data to be collected.

Our approach to data analysis incorporates essential strategies for the analysis of any large and complex data set. Although the following principles often are taken for granted, we feel they are worth stating because they place in broader perspective the discussion of specific analytic procedures. As a general rule, we recommend that researchers become very familiar with the data, plotting the distribution of variables and relationships between them in different ways, so that when summary measures, such as means, variances, and correlations are used, we will have a fuller understanding of what these statistics represent. We also suggest that different statistical methods be used to address the same question. When the results of different analytic procedures converge, we can be more confident of the findings' validity, and, when the results differ according to the technique used, it becomes important to determine why this is so. In this manner, we will become aware of situations in which results are artifacts of a particular statistical technique. Finally, we recommend an incremental approach, starting simple and building toward more complex analyses. In part, this strategy means that less concern is given to estimating a total theoretical model at the outset, and instead analysis begins by investigating more delimited issues, the results of which will be used in subsequent analyses.

Descriptive Analyses

A primary interest of ours lies in studying patterns of experience and behavior both within and across time intervals. This mandate requires study of the consistency or variability of an individual's behavior over time and the degree to which differences in behavior patterns vary or remain the same across individuals. As part of the effort to address these issues, we endorse a variety of descriptive analyses, with an emphasis on criminal career parameters and related matters. For example, descriptions might focus on participation rates, offending rates, and lengths of criminal careers in conjunction with the prevalence, incidence, and timing of many different antisocial behaviors. At each step, it is important to look for differences across offender subgroups. Although many of these analyses will be relatively straightforward, they should be very productive and informative.

Data Reduction

The proposed research plan involves a substantial amount of information on subjects, and processing extremely large quantities of data can be exceedingly awkward. One option for making large-scale statistical analyses more manageable is to use data-reduction and scaling techniques. For example, factor analysis can be used to consolidate many variables into a few sets that reflect theoretical dimensions, and some structural equation modeling techniques, such as LISREL, incorporate similar capabilities.

Another appealing data-reduction technique is cluster analysis, which refers to procedures that group subjects with similar characteristics into subsets or types. These pattern analytic techniques are uniquely suited to studying developmental problems, because variables can be coded to reflect the timing of events and thus it is possible to identify progressions and continuities. Another desirable feature of clustering techniques is that they make individuals, not variables, the unit of analysis (Magnusson and Bergman 1988). Finally, these techniques can be used to identify higher-order interactions in which patterns of relations among many variables hold meaning apart from relations between pairs of variables. In using cluster analytic techniques, there often are multiple solutions to a problem, which makes it important to demonstrate the replicability and consistency of any set of results (Breckenridge 1989).

Behavior Progressions

A common method for studying behavior progressions involves a modification of the Guttman scaling technique. The procedure tests for hierarchical models, or sequences in which previous behaviors are required for progression to subsequent behaviors. This method, for example, has been used to study sequences of progressions of drug use (Yamaguchi and Kandel 1984). However, the technique has been criticized for requiring that all individuals have the same progression, an assumption that may be inappropriate if several developmental paths exist.

Alternative strategies include conditional probability analyses based on the likelihood that an event will occur given a particular history. A variation on this approach is stage-state analysis, which also can be described as multistage conditional probability analysis (Runyan 1980). The technique assumes that development can be described as a progression through identifiable stages and that for each stage an individual occupies one of several states. In charting the experiences of a group of individuals, flow tables can be constructed to describe the variety of routes between an early state and a later stage, along with the probability that a given path will be followed (Runyan 1980). A limitation of this method is that, as the number of possible combinations of stages and states increases, larger samples sizes are required to describe fully the developmental paths. In addition, the technique assumes that experience can be characterized in terms of a sequence of stages, and when this assumption is not appropriate, the technique reduces to a state-sequential approach.

Another analytic strategy is to construct transition matrices that display the probability of one behavior being followed by another. When simple correlations are used to study relationships between successive behaviors, the method represents a variation on test-retest reliability procedures (Rogosa 1980). A number of procedures model transition probabilities as functions of covariates, time, stage of process, and prior behaviors. Among the modeling techniques that might be used are random parameter stochastic models (Lehoczky 1986) and Markov models (Wolfgang, Figlio, and Sellin 1972), including mover-stayer models (Goodman 1961).

Age, Period, and Cohort Effects

The proposed sampling strategy represents a variation of a cross-sequential design, and this design will allow us to estimate age, cohort, and period effects, models of long-standing interest in longitudinal research. A problem, however, is that these models typically present serious identification problems. As discussed in Chapter 3, age, period, and cohort effects are often confounded, and it is not always possible to disentangle one from another. However, it is possible to hold one effect constant and investigate the influence of the other two. A major focus of the analysis should be on the relationship between age and crime, and this can be studied with the proposed design.

In the absence of discernible cohort effects, we can consolidate different cohorts into a single group for analysis. A simple procedure for testing for cohort effects is to include a variable on cohort membership in the analysis. If preliminary analyses reveal the cohort membership variable and its interaction terms to be nonsignificant, we can then proceed to amalgamate the cohorts. This strategy will be particularly useful when analysis requires a large number of cases.

Event History Analysis

Event history analysis refers to a set of statistical techniques for studying events that represent discrete changes occurring at specific points in time. An example of an event that is of interest to us is a first-time arrest.

Analysis of event histories typically begins by examining the distribution of survival and hazard rates across different groups. The survival rate refers to the proportion of the total population that has not yet experienced an event in a given time interval. In contrast, the hazard rate refers to the proportion of subjects that experience an event during a time interval among the pool of subjects at risk. As a next step, regression methods can be used to model these rates as a function of explanatory variables. Among the more attractive methods for estimating regression models with continuous time data is the Cox proportional hazards model. The technique estimates the hazard rate, or the instantaneous probability of an event given that it has not happened, as a log-linear function of the independent variables (Allison 1984). The popularity of the Cox proportional hazards model stems in part from the fact that it places few restrictions on the type of data being analyzed.

A useful feature of event history techniques is that they allow us to incorporate the time of an event or between events into the model, and more sophisticated versions of the method can accommodate predictor variables that change in value over time. In order to take full advantage of event history techniques, however, accurate information of the timing of events is needed. Problems of censoring, which stem from the fact that events of interest can occur outside the limited observation period being studied, will also have to be addressed.

Causal Models

Longitudinal designs hold out to researchers an attractive potential for inferring causal relations from nonexperimental data because changes in predictor variables associated with changes in outcome variables can be studied over time. Given this potential, the literature on causal modeling for longitudinal data is growing rapidly.

Many of the research questions of interest to us can be studied with structural equation modeling techniques. Among the more popular computer programs for this types of analysis are LISREL and EQS. These programs generate structural equation models with two components — a measurement component comprising latent factors and manifest variables and a structural component for estimating causal paths. These techniques have several advantages over path analysis, a commonly used approach to causal modeling that is based on standard regression procedures. In particular, the ability to combine multiple observed variables into a single latent construct can be used to simplify the structure of the causal model. Also, the capacity for specifying a measurement model prior to analysis allows us to adapt the statistical assumptions of the model to the characteristics of the data and to theory. Finally, these techniques can be used to investigate recursive models with reciprocal effects between variables over time. For example, we could test a model that hypothesizes that a decrease in school performance leads to an increase in delinquency, which in turn results in a further decrease in school performance. In this type of analysis, we would be interested in both the strength and duration of reciprocal effects.

Although most structural equation modeling techniques use maximum likelihood estimation procedures, EQS also allows for distribution-free estimation. This option might be especially useful in studying highly skewed outcomes. For example, at least one researcher found that it can be difficult to get a LISREL model to converge with delinquency data and that successfully converged models can generate nonsensical findings, problems attributable in part to the skewed distribution of delinquency outcomes (Elliott, Huizinga, and Ageton 1985). These problems might also be addressed by specifying a reasonably accurate theoretical model at the outset of the procedure, a strategy that generally makes for more efficient and productive data analysis.

In the discussion of event history analysis, we noted that the Cox proportional hazards model with time-dependent covariates identifies variables that predict the instantaneous probability of failure at a specific time. Some statisticians, however, have pointed out that, although this technique is an effective method for identifying risk factors, it has limitations when it comes to determining whether predictor variables are causal factors. In particular, it can be misleading to infer causality when the models contain a time-dependent confounder or a variable that changes in value over time and that is correlated with the outcome variable and with other variables in the causal model (Robins and Morgenstern 1987). Recently, a new class of structural equation models, referred to as multivariate structural nested means models, has been developed to address this problem (Robins 1986; Robins 1987). These models are analogous to path analysis for failure time data. Computer algorithms also have been introduced to estimate these models, and further advances in computational techniques are likely to follow. In order to use these methods, however, data on the timing of events are required, including knowledge of when events occurred during the survey reference period. Although we are not fully acquainted with these newly developed statistical methods, we anticipate that they will have useful applications in the proposed research.

Growth Curves

In simple form, growth curves represent a plot of scores or values over time. Growth curves can be generated for individuals and, by charting the mean values of a collection of individual curves, growth curves can be generated for groups. Growth curve analysis ranks among the most useful ways of analyzing changes over time (Rogosa, Brandt, and Zimowski 1982; Rogosa, Floden, and Willett 1984; Rogosa and Willett 1985). As one statistician put it, "research about growth, development, learning and the like center on systematic changes in an attribute over time and the individual growth curves are the natural foundation for modeling longitudinal data" (Rogosa 1988).

A useful technique for describing the consistency of differences across individual growth curves is based on the concept of tracking. More specifically, a tracking index (Foulkes and Davis 1981; McMahan 1981) can be computed to indicate the probability that two growth curves will not intersect over a given time period. From another perspective, the tracking index reflects the degree to which growth curves maintain their rank order. Tracking methods derive from the biometric literature, where they have been applied to continuous variables such as height and blood pressure, and concepts underlying these procedures might be extended to other types of data.

Most structural equation modeling techniques involve a combination of factor analytic models and structural models that are based on an analysis of correlations and variances. Recently, new models have been developed that provide an integrated structure for correlations, variances, and means (McArdle and Epstein 1987). These models, referred to as latent growth curves, are attractive because they allow for tests of patterns of change in coefficients over time by including factor mean changes in the model (McArdle 1988; McArdle and Anderson 1989). Techniques for analyzing latent growth curves can be used to test a variety of models of change and development. For example, in a recent paper, McArdle and Anderson (1989) used the technique to test the fit of a no-growth baseline model, a linear age basis model, a latent age basis model, an occasion basis model, and both an occasion and age basis model to individual changes in IQ scores over time. The data we recommend collecting will meet the primary requirements for latent growth curve analysis, which are repeated observations for the same subjects on the same variables in the same measurement units. We anticipate that these methods will prove useful in addressing many of our research questions.

Linking Cohorts

Our research design follows a cross-sequential sampling plan in which multiple cohorts are selected across different ages in the same year. A rationale for this sampling plan is that, by linking successive cohorts in the statistical analyses, a long-term picture of development can be constructed in less time than would be required by following a single cohort. At this point, we have identified three strategies for linking cohorts: matching, convergence analysis, and multiple imputation.

In discussing plans to collect information on a set of common variables, including retrospective data on early life experiences for older subjects, we mentioned the possibility of using matching procedures to link cohorts. The basic matching strategy involves finding sets of equivalent subjects so that developmental sequences can be laid end to end and traced out across cohorts. Matching is a relatively straightforward procedure, with simple intuitive appeal, and for some research questions it can be a useful analytic strategy. However, matching procedures have a variety of well-known limitations, including the practical difficulties of being able to define equivalence on only a few variables and of having a sufficient number of equivalent subjects for statistical analysis.

Another approach to linking is to view the problem as one in which data are missing at random in large blocks for cohorts and to use techniques for longitudinal estimation with missing data. These procedures do not match individual subjects but rather use statistical quantities such as means, variances, and correlations to link the cohorts. This strategy resembles techniques for estimating models based on incomplete pedigrees, which is an attractive feature, because the emphasis on collecting information at both the community and individual level, which calls for multilevel analyses, is consistent with longitudinal or pedigree models of missing data.

A statistical approach for piecing together separate longitudinal data sets into a single function is convergence analysis (Bell 1953, 1954; McArdle, Anderson, and Aber 1987). In this context, a model is said to converge when the longitudinal and cross-sectional components provide the same information. Recently, it has been demonstrated that concepts of linear structural equation modeling and latent growth curve models can be merged to test convergence hypotheses (McArdle, Anderson, and Aber 1987).

In order to carry out convergence analyses successfully, cohorts should overlap as much as possible to test for convergence of longitudinal and cross-sectional curves; sample sizes should be relatively large so that alternative curve forms can be tested; and the sample should be representative of the population. The proposed design meets these basic requirements. Additionally, lack of convergence of individual and group curves can result from sampling bias. For this reason, we have emphasized in the sampling plan the need for comparability of subjects across cohorts.

Finally, multiple imputation might be used to link the cohorts. This procedure involves defining a set of observations on variables that span the entire age range the cohorts cover and treating this set of observations as the complete data for an individual. The next step is to impute responses for each subject for the periods for which direct observations are not available by randomly drawing values from a specified distribution. The technique requires that we specify in advance the variables that will be used to construct the distributions from which we impute. An advantage of this procedure is that the statistical theory underlying the process is well developed (Rubin 1989).

Postscript

In the process of reviewing statistical procedures, we have tried to pay attention to the data requirements for various techniques. We have identified several such requirements, some of which reflect general concerns that apply to many statistical methods used in large-scale empirical research.

Many commonly used statistical techniques assume interval scaling of the dependent variable. In some situations, the data will not meet this assumption, and we either will have to use a less demanding statistical procedure or document the effects of violating this assumption on the results of the analysis. However, given the focus on studying rates of behavior and on oversampling high-risk subjects, we expect that data analysts will be in a reasonable position to address this issue. Moreover, we note that event history and other related statistical methods require information on the timing of events. As part of this requirement, we need to know at each wave of data collection exactly when events occurred during the reference period.

Along with measurement level, the distribution of variables can pose difficulties for statistical analysis. For example, problems can arise when responses are badly skewed because nearly everyone answers a question in the same way, and such highly skewed distributions may require that we improvise on existing statistical techniques. Some people may never commit a delinquent act, and for some analyses this may present a problem. A simple strategy for dealing with this is to use a two-stage model in which we first model a discrete variable and then model a continuous variable for subjects who show the behavior we are interested in.

Another potential source of problems in statistical analyses is missing data, which occur when subjects cannot be located or are unwilling to cooperate. We have already pointed to the need for assiduous tracking of subjects as they move between residences and communities, and we again emphasize the critical nature of this task. More generally, unfailing concern must be given to data quality issues, including reliability, validity, learning effects, and misclassification errors. For example, because we want to study attributes that change and develop, it may be desirable not to select test instruments with the highest test-retest reliability and instead use tests that combine high internal reliability and low retest stability. In the next phase of activities, we suggest that work concentrate on these issues.

We also suggest that attention be given to analytic difficulties that might arise from the fact that sample size and statistical reliability move in tandem. In Chapter 7 we offer estimates of the number of cases with outcomes of interest and generally conclude that the design will provide sufficient yield for reliable statistical analyses. However, given an interest in using descriptions that stay as close as possible to the behaviors and experiences being studied, we can expect a continuing tension between the level of detail we would like to incorporate into the analyses and the statistical properties of the data. Although it is difficult to present in advance specific ways of resolving this conflict, a simple illustration may help to clarify the types of situations that will be faced. For example, a transition matrix with ten categories of behavior will contain 100 combinations, and if we arbitrarily require 15 cases per cell to ensure reliability, we will need 1,500 cases for analysis. However, if we reduce the number of behavior categories to five, there will be 25 combinations requiring only 375 cases. To a large extent, the option of amalgamating cohorts into a single sample for some analyses will provide flexibility in addressing this type of situation.

Finally, we note that the research plan offers only general hypotheses about growth and development, a situation that partly reflects the lack of attention criminologists have given to these matters. Consequently, the causal models to be investigated may be only weakly specified, and one useful strategy for increasing the chances of success in statistical modeling is to develop more explicit hypotheses. For this reason, we recommend continued review of relevant theory throughout the course of the project.

Cohort Studies

12
Prenatal and Preschool Cohorts

This chapter describes the prenatal cohort and successive cohorts of 3- and 6-year-old children. These three cohorts, in combination, are designed to study constitutional, behavioral, and social risk factors and to test hypotheses about early experience, health, and temperament as causes of conduct disorder and delinquency.

We recommend that the study of risk factors associated with conduct disorder start with the monitoring of fetal development in the prenatal cohort. Pregnant women might be sampled as early in gestation as possible, and their surviving male and female offspring followed to age 8, covering the period during which evidence of disruptive behavior (hyperactivity, oppositional behavior, fighting, cruelty) first appears. Success in studying this cohort over an eight-year period will, we hope, encourage continued follow-up to later ages. A longer study period is desirable because girls have a later age of onset for conduct disorder and delinquency than boys (Offord et al. 1987). Thus, by extending the research on this cohort into adolescence, we can determine the circumstances under which conduct problems arise in girls. Continued study of the prenatal cohort beyond eight years also can profit from the results of studies on the older male cohorts, which will then have been completed.

Similar to most other cohorts in the design, but unlike the prenatal cohort, the age 3 and age 6 cohorts consist only of males. The 3-year-old cohort extends the study into the first few years of primary school (to age 11), thereby permitting continued examination of the emergence of conduct disorder and its links to language development, school performance, and early peer influences. The 6-year-old cohort allows us to examine in detail the social, behavioral, and physiological processes associated with the transition from middle childhood to early adolescence, the period when we are most likely to witness deviant behavior heralding the emergence of serious crime.

The detailed longitudinal study of these three cohorts represents an unparalleled opportunity to examine the independent contributions to the development of conduct disorder of temperament, health, and developmental status; parent-child relationship; family environment; and community structure. Among conduct disordered children the same variables also can be studied for their impact on the persistence of conduct disorder and the onset of delinquency. Because many children in the sample will not be at high risk for conduct disorder, the study should also increase our understanding of why some children who grow up in high-crime urban areas do not become delinquent.

Because study of the prenatal and age 3 cohorts begins well before behavioral manifestations of conduct disorder typically appear, experiments aimed at prevention can add to the knowledge gained in longitudinal studies. For example, interventions designed to offset conduct disorder and delinquency, with similar content but separately packaged for infants, 3-year-olds and 6-year-olds, could investigate the relative advantages of changing health and personality characteristics of children as opposed to changing characteristics of parent-child interaction, family environment, or community structure. The same experiment could also be used to discover if there is a sensitive period in the early development of conduct disorder. The prenatal cohort may be an attractive one for experimentation because it offers the opportunity for introducing an intervention in the first year of life.

The remaining sections of this chapter are devoted to a discussion of the design and methods required to study the three youngest cohorts. We begin with a review of knowledge on risk factors in the first five years of life for conduct disorder.

State of Knowledge

Because few studies of conduct disorder cover the earliest years of life, developmental sequences have to be inferred from knowledge on the nature and correlates of conduct disorder at later ages. Conduct disorder is diagnosed on the basis of acts that could be grounds for identification as a delinquent, whether or not such identification occurs. Children with conduct disorder are believed to lack empathy and to be more impulsive, impatient, hostile, and irritable than others. These traits are presumed to be the psychological underpinnings of theft, vandalism, and violence, which are important components of the diagnosis of conduct disorder (American Psychiatric Association 1987). This project's task is to measure predisposing traits in infants and to find correlates of these traits in the child, family environment, and community structure. Several reviews of literature have compiled the individual characteristics and environmental circumstances that are associated with conduct disorder and delinquency (Rutter and Giller 1983; Wilson and Herrnstein 1985; Kazdin 1987). The risk factors include:

Child characteristics:
1. Males are more often delinquent than females.
2. Delinquents have low verbal intelligence compared to peers.
3. Many delinquent youths are hyperactive and distractable, traits that appear to precede the onset of delinquency.
4. Delinquents are unpopular with nondelinquent peers.

Family environment:
1. A family history of crime and delinquency is common among delinquent youth.
2. Families of delinquents are marked by discordant relationships — marital instability and erratic, harsh disciplinary practices.
3. Delinquents frequently come from families experiencing economic adversity.

Community structures:
1. Higher delinquency rates occur in socially disorganized communities than in other communities.
2. Human services in socially disorganized communities are often inadequate to meet the needs of families and young children.

A full assessment of the state of knowledge requires that we go beyond reviews of existing literature, which are limited to studies completed prior to 1985. Two published studies are of particular importance; an analysis of data from an ongoing study of a birth cohort in Dunedin, New Zealand, is also relevant.

The Newcastle One Thousand Family Survey, begun in 1947 in England, has studied the impact of psychosocial deprivation during the first five years of life on the development of adult patterns of criminal behavior (Kolvin et al. 1988). The research demonstrates that environmental deprivation in the first five years of life can be linked to conduct problems at age 10, to delinquency at age 15, and to criminality at age 33. Children who suffered multiple deprivations (about 7 percent of the sample) were particularly likely to show stable patterns of deviant behavior.

Schonfeld and colleagues (1988) reanalyzed data from the Columbia University site of the Collaborative Perinatal Study to examine separately the effects of IQ and parental management style on conduct disorder. Their findings show that inadequate child management skills produce both low verbal intelligence and aggressive behavior in preschool children. However, once a pattern of aggressive behavior is established, delinquency can be predicted independently of IQ at age 17.

In order to explore the separate and combined contributions to conduct disorder of family environment and individual characteristics, the Program commissioned an analysis of the Dunedin Multidisciplinary Child Development Study data (Moffitt and Silva 1988). This prospective longitudinal study has followed a birth cohort at regular intervals for nearly two decades. The analysis compares 50 children with persistent conduct disorder to children with other psychiatric problems and to nondisordered children. The findings show that family instability, maternal low intelligence, and maternal personality deviance are associated with conduct disorder. Some health, development, and cognitive variables differentiate children with psychiatric problems from the nondisordered group, but these variables fail to distinguish children with conduct disorder from those with other types of problems. Surprisingly, low birth weight and other perinatal measures are not related to conduct disorder.

By far, the variable most strongly related in the analysis to conduct disorder is undercontrolled behavior, which is also associated with hyperactivity and with deficits in children's capacity to sustain attention during cognitive tasks. Laboratory observations, maternal reports, and teacher ratings support the relation, which proves to be stable from age 3 to 13. A combination of maternal descriptors and preschool behavioral variables correctly predicts 41 percent of the boys with conduct disorder, a considerable improvement over the sample base rate of 7 percent. It is worth noting that only 2 percent of nondisordered boys are misclassified as conduct disordered.

In sum, the existing research indicates that family environment makes a significant contribution to conduct disorder and that some children show behavioral precursors of the disorder as early as age 3. However, our capacity to predict which children will develop conduct problems is not well established, and better measures of family environment and of children's characteristics may help to improve predictions.

We have identified three obvious gaps in our knowledge of conduct disorder. The first is in the area of biological measures. Families' criminal histories have not been included in many studies, and thus even this indirect proxy for heritability is unavailable. Some evidence suggests that perinatal factors may not be as important as formerly assumed, but only a limited range of biological measures has been examined during fetal and early postnatal development.

The second shortcoming is in the area of peer influences and delinquency. Most studies rely on contemporaneous measures of peer associations. Yet, there are indications that predelinquents are rejected by nondeviant peers and that exclusion from networks of nondelinquent associates may itself be a catalyst for the onset of delinquent behavior (Tremblay, LeBlanc, and Schwartzman 1988). Recent studies on social competence and friendship-building capacities in young children are helping to increase our understanding of these issues (Rubin and Daniel-Beirness 1983; Howes 1988). We suggest that measures developed in these studies be incorporated into research on the early risks for conduct disorder and delinquency.

The third gap in knowledge concerns the role of community organization in the origins of conduct disorder and delinquency. Socially disorganized communities lack safe play facilities, day-care programs, and health services, and in such contexts familial and constitutional risk factors may have a greater impact on the development of deviancy. In most delinquency research, community organization has been studied in relation to adolescent and adult deviancy. An important area for future work involves the role of community structure in the care and rearing of infants and preschool children.

Key Concepts, Theories, and Hypotheses

As a general principle of development, influences shaping the growth of personality widen as a child matures from infancy to middle childhood to adolescence. The three youngest cohorts should provide a detailed longitudinal picture of intrinsic developmental milestones and life transitions that progressively heighten the risk for conduct disorder and delinquency. The research agenda begins with a concern for possible genetic determinants of behavior and the health of the mother and fetus during pregnancy. Following birth, aspects of the child's physical health and growth are risk factors for conduct disorder, and the key issue is how characteristics of health and behavior influence maladaptation to the family and community.

An unresolved issue in human social development concerns critical periods, or specific time intervals in development, when children are especially sensitive to social deprivation. Research on imprinting in birds and maternal deprivation in mammals represents variations on this theme. Using nonhuman primates, Harlow and colleagues provide experimental evidence that social contact is required for the normal development of social and sexual behavior (Harlow and Harlow 1973). In relation to risks associated with conduct disorder, the research suggests that the timing, as well as the quality, of social experiences are crucial factors. Indeed, critical periods are believed to exist in other areas of development such as language and cognition, that are tied to conduct disorder. Current research in developmental neurobiology may demonstrate how early experiences directly influence brain development (Schanberg and Field 1988; Meany et al. 1988; Carlson, Earls, and Todd 1988), and these findings may suggest measures that should be brought into the design of the proposed study.

A number of expectable life experiences common to most, if not all, children must be monitored between birth and age 14. The experiences include transitions between settings from home to preschool, from preschool to primary school, and from primary school to high school. At each transition point, the child is faced with a number of new tasks. The transition to preschool exposes many infants and young children to their first interactions with unfamiliar adults and peers. Early signs of easy or difficult adjustment can be observed and may serve as important pointers for later behavioral functioning. This transition takes place in both the prenatal and age 3 cohorts.

Between the ages of 5 and 7, children begin primary school and typically confront greater demands for intellectual achievement and self-control than in preschool settings, and their self-esteem is closely associated with success or failure in meeting these demands. This transition can be studied in the age 3 and 6 cohorts.

Between the ages of 9 and 14 most children begin, and many complete, the somatic changes associated with puberty. During this period they make the transition from primary school to high school and establish new personal interests and friendships. This is also the period when males typically progress from disruptive behavior to delinquency. The age 6 cohort, along with the age 9 and 12 cohorts, provides opportunities for studying links between biological changes associated with puberty, transitions in school and community life, and emergence of delinquent behavior.

Theoretical Perspectives

Three major theoretical perspectives on early development, described in Chapter 2, are temperament, attachment, and social learning. Temperament theory proposes that the psychological constructs underlying conduct disorder (impulsivity, impatience, easy boredom, and irritability) are enduring traits that become evident during the first year of life (Garrison and Earls 1987). It is widely held that temperament has a constitutional basis, the origins of which are tied to genetics (Plomin et al. 1988). The temperamental traits linked to conduct disorder also may be responsible for shaping parents' responses to children and for influencing other environmental contingencies (Scarr and McCarthey 1983).

Attachment theory places prime importance on the nature of an infant's relationship to the mother (Bowlby 1969). The period from the end of the first year of life to the beginning of the third year is considered a critical stage during which the quality of the mother-child relationship establishes a foundation for subsequent interpersonal development. Specifically, an avoidant attachment relationship, as identified by situations in which the infant fails to approach the mother following separation, represents a type of insecurity that increases the child's propensity for aggressive behavior (Sroufe 1979). In this scheme, the psychological characteristics of children with conduct disorder can be traced to an insecure attachment to the mother during infancy (Erickson, Sroufe, and Egeland 1985).

Social learning theories of conduct disorder and delinquency have a longer research history than either temperament or attachment theories. Social learning perspectives find support in the results of many studies showing that harsh and inconsistent discipline and exposure to discordant family relationships are closely linked to conduct disorder (Patterson et al. 1975). However, these conditions alone do not explain why children become delinquent. Therefore, although the disciplinary climate in the home may be an important factor in the development of conduct disorder, it is not a complete explanation.

Hypotheses

The foregoing review of concepts and theories serves as a background for articulating a series of hypotheses on risk factors for conduct disorder and delinquency in the first decade of life. In formulating these hypotheses, we assume that behavioral characteristics of infants and preschool children constitute an essential and enduring risk for conduct disorder. We proposed nine central hypotheses:

1. The behavioral characteristics of impulsivity, easy boredom, irritability, low empathy, and impatience increase the risk for conduct disorder.
2. These behavioral characteristics are not all present at birth. However, they are reliably detected by age 3 and remain relatively stable until adulthood.
3. These behavioral characteristics are more frequently identified in males than in females.
4. Low heart rate variability, low circulating levels of cortisol and high levels of androgens represent physiological markers for these behavioral characteristics in males.
5. Criminal parents produce children with these characteristics more often than noncriminal parents.

6. Children with these characteristics are more likely to have suffered insults to the brain during fetal development (e.g., exposure to drugs) than children without these traits.

7. The quality of the early relationship between infant and primary caregiver as well as the type and consistency of discipline parents use are important factors in the development of conduct disorder.

8. In responding to the environmental conditions associated with conduct disorder (i.e., poor health, insecure attachment, harsh and inconsistent discipline, disorganized communities), males are more vulnerable to adversity than females.

9. The probability that high-risk behavioral characteristics result in conduct disorder can be reduced by a combination of good health practices, early language and social skills development, and competent child-rearing practices. However, it is unlikely that any one of these measures will produce a significant effect alone.

Research Design and Measurement

The proposed research design allows for tests of the relative significance of risk factors during the first decade of life (independent variables) in the development of conduct disorder in middle childhood and delinquency in early adolescence (the dependent variables). School achievement and peer relations can also be examined as dependent variables, given temporal proximity with conduct disorder. The prospective longitudinal design should help delineate the mechanisms responsible for the onset of conduct disorder and its relation to delinquency. There are ten essential questions, similar in substance to the hypotheses, that guide the research design.

1. What is the earliest age at which behavior traits of impulsivity, empathy and impatience, easy boredom and irritability can be measured reliably?

2. Are there early physiological markers of these behavioral traits that can be identified before the traits themselves can be measured?

3. Are these behavioral traits sex-linked?

4. How stable are these traits over time?

5. How strongly are these behavioral traits correlated with intelligence?

6. What proportion of children with these traits develop conduct disorder; what proportion go on to become delinquent?

7. To what extent do adverse family experiences, school underachievement and peer rejection represent necessary conditions, either singly or in combination, for development of conduct disorder and delinquency?

8. Is the answer to question 7 the same for males (in the prenatal, age 3 and age 6 cohorts) and females (in the prenatal cohort)?

9. What role does puberty play in the development of conduct disorder and delinquency? Is the role mainly physiological, as represented by differences

in androgen levels or in the timing of hormonal changes; or is it mainly psychological, involving adjustments to changes in social roles and expectations and in personal goals?

10. Can protective factors that insulate children from influences leading to conduct disorder and to delinquency be identified? Are these factors the same for males and females? Can they be addressed in experimental interventions?

Variables and Measures

At this point, we list our recommendations for essential variables by category and indicate how these variables can be measured or assessed. Some of the variables represent key constructs (e.g., impulsivity, parental disciplinary techniques, etc.), while others reflect potentially important characteristics of the sample.

1. We recommend that demographic variables include age, sex, employment status, grade in school, income, and marital status of each member of a household. It is important to distinguish between biological and social fathers and to establish the availability of these men to participate in the research. These variables should be collected for all cohorts.

2. Family histories of delinquency, adult criminality, antisocial personality, and substance abuse should be covered. Retrospective data on parents can be obtained to allow for comparisons with subjects in the young adult cohort. Most important in this connection is the history of behavior problems, delinquency, and school achievement.

3. Physical dimensions of growth are crucial variables during the first seven years of life, because they can be used as indicators of health, nutritional status, and extreme social deprivation. We suggest that prenatal variables include measures of the mother's health and of fetal development. Aspects of the mother's health should include prior gestational experiences, general health, and specific measures of health during pregnancy; fetal development might be assessed directly by means of a physician's examination. The possibility of using ultrasound for fetal assessment should be explored. Indirect assessments of the fetus can be based on reports from the mother (for example, her substance abuse).

   Birth weight and gestational age for newborns can be collected from medical records. However, it will be important to repeat these measurements and to include head circumference, height (or length in infants), and body mass index. We recommend that semiannual measures of height, weight, head circumference, and body mass index be routinely collected to age 7. Thereafter, measurements can be made annually. Reliable measures of height require careful training and monitoring. Resting pulse rate and blood pressure can be measured starting at 12 months. Blood samples from the umbilical cord should be collected and tested for the presence and concentration of heavy metals and drugs.

Major and minor physical anomalies need to be evaluated. Major congenital defects having serious developmental consequences are usually noted in medical records. In contrast, minor physical anomalies, often referred to as stigmata, may go unrecorded. They do not, in themselves, impair development; instead they represent possible abnormalities in prenatal development that may have resulted in insults to internal organs (such as the brain), leaving the stigmata as a benign clue.

Hormonal assays of cortisol and testosterone should be periodically determined. Cortisol can be used to monitor levels of psychosocial stress; testosterone can serve as a marker for the rate of physical maturation and for levels of aggressive behavior. These hormones can be measured from blood plasma and saliva.

4. We suggest that both minor and major illnesses be evaluated semiannually. The number of sick days can be recorded for each child; a similar measure might be taken for other family members, especially mothers. In addition, numbers of health visits, emergency room visits, and hospital days are additional useful measures of health. Specific medical conditions that may have behavioral consequences, such as head injury, meningitis, and seizures, should be recorded.

5. Developmental quotients and IQs are needed as measures of cognitive development. The conventional testing approach for infants involves scales that measure neuromotor performance and mental development according to age-expected norms. These measures provide a developmental quotient, an index that is correlated with later measures of intelligence but is sufficiently unlike these measures to warrant a different label. At age 3 standardized measures of intelligence with verbal and performance scores can be used. These measures are identical or similar to measures of intelligence designed for school-age children and adults. It is important to choose a measure of IQ that accommodates sensitive age periods in development and overlap in ages between cohorts.

Currently, research on infant perception is attempting to develop measures that predict verbal ability at later ages (Bornstein and Sigman 1986). The methods devised so far can only be applied during a restricted age period (3 to 8 months), and there are no reports showing a relation between these measures and later attention-deficit or conduct disorder. The measures also require a laboratory setting that may make impractical their use in a large study. Thus, while these measures represent promising developments in infancy research, we advise that they be used in the prenatal cohort carefully and with caution.

Apart from measures of verbal and performance intelligence, specific measures of receptive (i.e., the capacity to decode spoken messages) and expressive language development are needed. Once schooling has begun, measures of school achievement (reading, spelling, and math skills) should be collected.

6. Temperament is a critically important variable in theories and hypotheses for the prenatal and preschool cohorts. However, our capacity to measure temperament accurately is less well developed than that for other constructs, such as intelligence.

   A number of temperament measures based on parental reports are available for infants and preschool children; some of these provide fairly consistent definitions of temperamental traits over several years of development. Observational measures should be used to provide comparisons with parent reports. As a corollary, operational definitions of impulsivity at any one age should be based on more than one source of data, even though it may be difficult to apply the same criteria from infancy to school age. Finally, pulse rate, blood pressure, and levels of cortisol and testosterone should be examined in relation to temperament.

7. Family interactions, especially those between parent and child, are of great theoretical importance for the prenatal and preschool cohorts. Relevant measures may be designed to tap global aspects of interactions or specific features. In selecting measures and methods, attention should be given to the degree of coverage of the domain of interest, relative advantages of interview and observational approaches, and a subject's age.

   Measures of bonding should be used during the neonatal period, while measures of attachment can be used starting from between ages 8 and 12 months until age 24 months. Measures of warmth and criticism in the parent-child relationship generally may be applied from late infancy to adulthood. These measures typically characterize global aspects of relationships.

   From age 12 months, measures of parental discipline become important. Both interview and observational methods are available. Because observational methods can be expensive and laborious, their use might be limited to a subsample of particular interest. Observational methods are also useful in confirming results from interviews.

   Measures of marital interaction should include ratings of general satisfaction and a description of tactics used to handle conflict. In addition, background information on each parent's previous marriages, separations, and divorces should be obtained. Extended family relationships, including those with grandparents, other relatives, and nonrelated individuals who have functioned as parental surrogates, should be assessed with appropriate consideration given to cultural factors.

8. Measures of physical and social characteristics of the home environment are also needed. Housing quality should be rated, as should the availability of play materials, space for play, and the order and organization of the physical environment.

   Religious beliefs and practices, moral values, and moral behavior is an underresearched area with poorly developed methods of assessment. However, developmental psychologists are giving increasing attention to how such values and behavior are acquired in early development (Damon 1988).

Finally, the social networks of family members should be evaluated. Degree of psychological support and concrete acts of help are essential aspects of networks to be rated separately.

9. Important events in the life of a child, such as the birth of a sibling, hospitalization, beginning day care or school, and prolonged separation, should be assessed.

10. Descriptions of neighborhood and community characteristics should include evaluations of the quality of schools, playgrounds, day-care, and healthcare facilities.

11. Measures of conduct disorder and school achievement are the primary dependent variables for the youngest cohorts. We recommend that measures of conduct disorder be based on parent, teacher, and child assessments. Both interviews and checklists might be used, although a consideration in selecting direct assessment methods is that children under age 9 or 10 may not be reliable reporters. Measures of school achievement can be based on standardized tests of reading, math, and spelling skills and on grades in school. In contrast, measures of peer relationships in preschool will have to depend on teacher reports and observational methods.

Since the success of the proposed study depends on the strengths of the outcome measures, measures should be chosen on the basis of reliability, validity and relevance to children between the ages of 6 and 14. Outcome measures for the prenatal cohort might be used as explanatory variables for the age 6 cohort in studying progressions from conduct disorder to delinquency.

A number of technical and logistic data collection issues are of special importance for the three youngest cohorts. First among these is the need for careful training and supervision of interviewers and examiners. As already mentioned, the reliability of temperament measures may be poor. Since temperament is a crucial variable, it may be necessary to use multiple measures, including parent and teacher reports, observational methods, and physiological tests. It is also important to consider informants other than mothers for measures of behavior problems, family history, child-rearing practices, and family functioning. It would be highly desirable to include interviews with fathers for many variables. Once measures of the same variable are successfully obtained from several informants, consideration will have to be given to ways of resolving discrepancies.

Sampling Issues

The most challenging sampling issue is that of locating 2,000 women in the second trimester of pregnancy. Actually, the sample will have to be slightly larger to obtain 1,000 male and 1,000 female infants. Pregnant women must be sampled in a way that ensures comparability to a known population and to other cohorts. It may not be possible in a given site to obtain a sample of women of this size within five to six months of gestation. Thus, the sample may have to include children in the first few postnatal months. Samples of 500 3- and 6-year-old children for the preschool cohorts should be representative of the same population as infants in the prenatal cohort.

Sampling procedures should begin by selecting a diverse set of communities within a geographical area, such as a city or SMSA. Household probability samples will then be drawn from each of the selected communities. We anticipate that this procedure can be used effectively to sample for pregnant women as well as for preschool children. As part of the sampling strategy, families at high risk of having children with conduct disorder and delinquency will be oversampled.

Experimental Interventions

A compelling argument exists for trying out experiments that have proven successful in education of children at risk for conduct disorder (Berrueta-Clement et al. 1987). Indeed, a national mandate exists to implement such programs (Both and Garduque 1989). The three youngest cohorts provide a unique opportunity to examine the effectiveness of differential exposure to specific components of a prevention curriculum. Exposure can be varied by starting interventions at different ages (e.g., at birth, age 3, and age 6), and specific components of a program can be evaluated by randomly assigning subjects to different combinations of treatments and to different levels of intervention. In this way, an experiment can be used to test particular theories, identify sensitive periods in development, and compare the relative importance of parent-focused and child-focused intervention programs.

To date, many of the preschool programs demonstrating long-term improvements in adaptive behavior and school achievement have been global interventions. These programs typically combine multiple components into a package such that all children are invariably exposed to all program components. The inflexibility of this approach minimizes consideration of the individual needs of children and families, thus overlooking the fact that a given program may benefit some children and not others despite similarities in risk for conduct disorder.

An experimental approach we recommend is a hierarchical design in which successive curricula are given separately and in combination, such as in an A, B, C, $A + B$, $A + B + C$ pattern. Program components most relevant to the prevention of conduct disorder should center on good healthcare and nutrition; child-rearing practices, particularly in terms of appropriate use of rewards and punishments; cognitive stimulation to develop language and prereading skills; and social skills training, especially with regard to peer relations. To what extent temperament is modifiable is an open question. Innovative programs for teaching impulsive and overactive children to be patient and considerate of the rights and welfare of others should also be explored.

Interventions with the age 6 cohort might incorporate features of several ongoing studies aimed at preventing the onset of conduct disorder or treating boys who already show the disorder. For example, experiments by Kolvin et al. (1981) in

Newcastle and Patterson's (1975) extensive work on parent training could serve as the basis for intervention programs.

Experiments should be designed along the lines of a formal preventive trial with random assignment, blinded assessment, and subsamples of sufficient size for appropriate statistical testing. High-risk features of the sample should be documented in early infancy, including the history of criminality and antisocial behavior in the biological parents and siblings, prenatal health status of the mother and fetus, perinatal events, and health status of the infant in the neonatal period. Intervention programs should build up enrollments slowly, unless ongoing efforts in the research site can be incorporated into the design. A sufficient number of high-risk families should remain outside the experimental protocol as a control group and as a part of the core longitudinal project.

The choice of sites and of experiments should take into consideration the implementation of PL 99-457, which mandates states to provide health, educational, and social services for high-risk children from age 3 to 5, with a strong recommendation for downward extension of the age of eligibility. It may be possible to include aspects of services initiated in response to PL 99-457 in the experimental protocol. Alternatively, it may be possible to carry out a quasi-experimental design in relation to programs under this law.

A final consideration involves the measurement outcomes. Although the cross-sequential cohort design involves an eight-year period, measurement of conduct disorder and delinquency in the prenatal cohort can benefit from a longer follow-up interval, perhaps to age 10 or 12. Because this cohort includes girls and because girls have a later age of onset of conduct disorder and delinquency than boys, the possibility of eventually studying the prenatal cohort for 15 years should be seriously considered. Nonetheless, behavioral antecedents of conduct disorder will occur by age 5, and a proportion of high-risk children will show fully developed conduct disorder before age 10. Thus, it will be possible to study outcomes of interest within the eight-year span of the cohort design.

Existing Data Sets, Ongoing Studies, and Pilot Research

No existing study of criminal careers begins with a sample selected during pregnancy, and secondary analyses of such data that do not include important explanatory and outcome variables can only be of limited value. Despite this reservation, two data sets could profitably be reanalyzed. They are:

1. The National Child Development Study. This project is a longitudinal study of all children born in Great Britain between March 3 and 9, 1958. The subjects have been studied on four occasions since 1958: in 1965 (at age 7), in 1969 (at age 11), in 1974 (at age 16), and in 1981 (at age 23). Of the 17,000 infants enrolled in the study, 76 percent were included in the data collection at each wave. A great deal of work relevant to conduct disorder has already been carried out with this data set and, before initiating a reanalysis, this work should

be reviewed. The data set is available through the Murray Center at Radcliffe College. It should be extended by the inclusion of criminal records.

2. The National Longitudinal Survey of Labor Market Experience of Youth (NLSY). This project involves 12,686 males and females who were first interviewed in 1979, when they were between the ages of 14 and 21. The sample has since been interviewed annually, and at the time of the eighth survey in 1986, a child supplement was added to collect information regularly on employment, education, and family life. The supplement provides information on the health, schooling, and behavior of all children born to members of the 1979 cohort. Data tapes are currently available through the Center for Human Resource Research at Ohio State University. The tapes contain data on maternal and child health, child cognitive development, home environment, and longitudinal patterns of relationships within families for nearly 3,000 mothers and their 5,000 children. A behavioral problems checklist was included as part of the data collection, making it possible to estimate the number of children with conduct disorder. Thus, it should be possible to investigate longitudinal patterns of parent and home environment characteristics occurring before the onset of conduct disorder. Although a substantial investment of time would be needed, consideration might be given to secondary analysis of these data.

Ongoing Studies

Six ongoing studies are recommended for close monitoring and possible collaboration. They are:

1. Dunedin Multidisciplinary Health and Development Study; Deputy Director Terrie Moffitt. This project is one of the best-maintained longitudinal studies involving an unselected birth cohort. At this time, the sample of 1,000 children, born in 1972 and 1973, is entering the age when persisting and desisting patterns of criminal behavior could be discerned. Relatively low sample attrition and extensive data on subjects make possible continued analysis that may shed light on early developmental antecedents of serious criminal behavior.

2. Infant Health and Development Program; principal investigators, Jeanne Brooks-Gunn and Cecelia McCarton. This project, originally supported by the Robert Wood Johnson Foundation, is investigating the health, behavioral, and cognitive development of over 900 low-birth-weight infants. The first phase of research has concluded, and the second phase is beginning. The first consisted of an experiment designed to improve the health and social competence of infants with a birth weight of below 2,500 grams. The intervention contained components that might conceivably decrease the risk of conduct disorder. Initial results should soon be published, and a dialogue has been established with the investigators.

3. Risk and Prevention Intervention Group, MacArthur Network II Collaborative Study; principal investigators, Kathryn Barnard, Joy Osofsky, Arthur

Parmelee, and Leila Beckwith. In this project a consortium of three research teams combined the resources of separate studies, each on a high-risk infant sample, to complete a school-age follow-up. The group has been particularly interested in methods for improving the mother-child relationship and has fashioned a number of experiments along these lines. Thus far, work has concentrated on links between improving the mother-child relationship and language development. As children approach school age, the researchers are turning their interest to problems of school achievement and conduct disorder.

4. The Minnesota Mother-Child Project; principal investigators, Alan Sroufe, Byron Egeland, and Martha Erickson. About 200 children from low-income, predominantly single parent families have been followed from birth to middle adolescence in this project. Particular interest has been given to attachment theory and to the nature of the mother-child relationship. Findings show that an insecure attachment bond predicts aggressive behavior in middle childhood with moderate success. The investigators are now anxious to study conduct disorder and delinquency as the subjects approach adolescence.

5. A Prospective Longitudinal Study on Substance Use During Pregnancy; principal investigator, Nancy Day. This project is studying the effects of maternal alcohol, marijuana, and cocaine use on child physical and cognitive development. Detailed measures of substance use during and after pregnancy provide important opportunities to investigate specific contributions to conduct disorder of alcohol, marijuana, and cocaine exposure during the prenatal period. Some subjects have already reached school age, and others will enter school in the next few years. Sample attrition has not been high.

6. The Montreal Longitudinal Study of Disruptive Boys; principal investigator, Richard Tremblay. This project is a longitudinal-experimental study in which boys with propensities for fighting, inattentiveness, and oppositional behavior are being followed from age 5 to adolescence. A sample of over 1,000 boys were initially screened from kindergarten classes serving low-socioeconomic families in Montreal. Boys with high scores on a teacher-rated disruptive behavior scale were then randomly assigned to one of three groups. An experimental group received parent training for two years when the boys were between the ages of 7 and 9. Parents were trained to monitor their children's behavior, provide positive reinforcement for desirable behavior, use punishment effectively, and manage family crises more efficiently. The experimental group is being compared to two control groups. One group had frequent observational sessions, similar to the experimental group, but received no parent training. The other group received no training and no observation. Normal boys without disruptive behavior are also being followed, allowing yet another contrast with the experimental group. Initial results from the experiment are encouraging. The findings show a decrease in disruptive behavior scores and greater rates of retention in regular classes for the experimental group (Tremblay et al. 1989). In addition to features of the experiment, many of the behavioral, physiological, and family measures used in the longitudinal phase of this project are relevant to the research we propose for preschool cohorts.

Pilot Research

Four pilot projects are recommended. First, a variety of physiological measures of temperament need to be tried on high-risk samples to see if impulsive and disinhibited infants and preschool children can be identified. These physiological measures should then be compared to parent and teacher reports and observational measures of temperament. It would be particularly interesting to learn if temperament characteristics associated with risks for conduct disorder occur with greater frequency in children whose parents are criminal and antisocial.

Second, an effort should be made to locate and interview biological fathers of a high-risk sample. Some data on difficulties in locating fathers and on successful strategies for engaging them in a research project would be helpful.

Third, androgen and cortisol levels can be measured from saliva samples. A small pilot study is necessary to determine how easy it is to obtain samples of saliva from infants and how closely salivary levels of these hormones correlate with blood samples. Laboratory methods to measures steroids in saliva also need to be reviewed and feasibility and costs determined.

Finally, measures of prosocial behavior and empathic expressions of emotion have not had a wide application in developmental psychology. Because these types of variables might identify children at high risk for persistent antisocial behavior, the development of appropriate measures is not only an important area for pilot study but may become an essential ongoing research activity of the project.

13
Young Adolescent Cohorts

This section discusses the study of two cohorts of males, the first from age 9 to age 17 and the second from age 12 to age 20. In order to avoid repetition, theories and measures for the two cohorts are described together. Essentially, we are describing a study of development between ages 9 and 20, although, where possible, the applicability of measures at specific ages is noted (e.g., up to age 15). Additional cohorts of siblings and females at age 12 are discussed in Chapter 15.

Current State of Knowledge

Predictors and Correlates of Teenage Offending

A great deal is known about the predictors and correlates of teenage offending that official records and self-reports measure, and there are numerous exhaustive reviews of this topic (e.g., Rutter and Giller 1983; Wilson and Herrnstein 1985). Hence, it is neither necessary nor desirable to go over this well-worn ground in detail. Rather, we summarize a few key results to set the context for the proposed research.

Teenage offending has been linked to hyperactivity, impulsivity, and attention deficit (e.g., Farrington, Loeber, and Van Kammen 1990). It has also been associated with low intelligence, low educational achievement, and truancy (e.g., Loeber and Dishion 1983). Teenage offenders tend to have antisocial, alcoholic, or criminal parents (e.g., Robins 1979). Also, poor parental supervision or monitoring, erratic or harsh parental discipline, marital disharmony, parental rejection of the child, and low parental involvement with the child are all important predictors of teenage offending (Loeber and Stouthamer-Loeber 1986).

The relation between socioeconomic deprivation and offending is uncertain (e.g., Thornberry and Farnworth 1982). Research findings seem to depend on the definition of socioeconomic deprivation (e.g., low occupational prestige vs. poverty), on the method of measuring offending (official records vs. self-reports), and on the level of measurement of socioeconomic deprivation (individual or area). More consistently, teenage offenders tend to come from large families and to have been separated from their parents for reasons other than death or hospitalization (e.g., West and Farrington 1973). They also tend to have delinquent friends (e.g., Elliott, Huizinga, and Ageton 1985) and to live in inner-city areas characterized by physical deterioration and social disorganization (e.g., Shaw and McKay 1969).

Numerous other predictors and correlates of teenage offending could be mentioned here, and numerous studies could be reviewed. However, there is good agreement about the facts of teenage offending, as Farrington, Ohlin, and Wilson (1986, p. 2) note:

We know a great deal about who commits crimes. We know that the typical high-rate offender is a young male who begins his aggressive or larcenous activities at an early age, well before the typical boy gets into serious trouble. We know that he comes from a troubled, discordant, low-income family in which one or both parents are likely to have criminal records themselves. We know that the boy has had trouble in school—he created problems for his teachers and does not do well in his studies. On leaving school, often by dropping out, he works at regular jobs only intermittently. Most employers regard him as a poor risk. He experiments with a variety of drugs—alcohol, marijuana, speed, heroin—and becomes a frequent user of whatever drug is most readily available, often switching back and forth among different ones. By the time he is in his late teens, he has had many contacts with the police, but these contacts usually follow no distinctive pattern because the boy has not specialized in any particular kind of crime. He steals cars and purses, burgles homes and robs stores, fights easily when provoked, and may attack viciously even when not provoked. While young, he commits many of his crimes in the company of other young men.

Problems of Interpretation

Unfortunately, as Farrington, Ohlin, and Wilson (1986) also pointed out, current knowledge about the predictors and correlates of teenage offending leaves unanswered many crucial questions about causal influences. For example, we know that offenders tend to have delinquent friends, but we do not know whether this is because birds of a feather flock together or because delinquent friends facilitate offending. We know that offending is linked to school failure, but we do not know whether crime causes school failure or school failure causes crime. It is also possible that offending and school failure are coexisting characteristics of antisocial people that are not causally linked. Similarly, we know that offending is linked to drug use, but we do not know if drug use causes offending, if offending causes drug use, or if both reflect antisocial personalities. As a final example, we know that offenders disproportionately live in inner-city areas, but we do not know if this is because antisocial people migrate to such areas (e.g., because of low rents) or if the neighborhoods themselves in some way facilitate offending.

These problems of interpretation largely follow from the fact that most studies essentially compare offending *between individuals*—that is, most research shows that offenders (however defined) differ from nonoffenders in intelligence, peer delinquency, parental child-rearing techniques, school failure, or whatever.

Between-individual comparisons do not allow unambiguous conclusions about causal influences with high internal validity, especially when predictor variables are highly interrelated. More convincing conclusions about causality can be drawn from *within-individual* comparisons, such as by showing that an individual's offending decreased after his or her school performance improved (Farrington 1988b). Also, successful prevention or treatment of offending requires changes within individuals. One of the major contributions of the proposed project is to study within-individual changes, which can only be done with longitudinal data.

Development of Criminal Careers

Another problem with existing studies is that they lack a developmental perspective. Most criminological research is on teenage offending in full flow. However, an important conceptual development in recent years has been the focus on criminal careers (Blumstein et al. 1986). This approach emphasizes the need to explain why offending begins, why it continues after onset, why it ends, and why some people commit offenses more frequently and more seriously than others.

The criminal career approach also highlights the possibility that known predictors and correlates of offending are differently related to onset, continuation, and desistance (Blumstein, Cohen, and Farrington 1988). For example, harsh or erratic parenting may only influence the onset of delinquency; delinquent friends may only be a factor in continuation; and leaving school and getting a job may only be related to desistance. Thus, another important contribution of the proposed project would be to identify factors uniquely influencing onset, continuation, and desistance.

Given subjects between the ages of 9 and 20 years, the proposed project could throw light especially on the onset of different types of offending and antisocial behavior (see Farrington et al. 1990). Offenders who begin their careers at an early age tend to commit many offenses over long periods at high rates (Blumstein, Farrington, and Moitra 1985). Early onset also predicts a high frequency and a long duration of drug use (Kandel and Raveis 1987). More information is needed about links between age and other features of onset—such as whether it occurs alone or with others—and features of criminal careers, such as frequency of offending and career length. Criminological research has rarely taken a developmental focus and has often overlooked continuities between offending and other types of problem behavior, such as child conduct problems or adult alcohol abuse.

The onset of officially recorded offending is also important because it represents the first opportunity for intervention by social welfare or criminal justice systems to prevent the continuation or escalation of future offending. Thus, advancing knowledge about onset may help in devising prevention and rehabilitation programs.

It is especially important to study sequences of onsets of different types of offenses. Conceptually, there are three main reasons why one act follows another in some kind of predictable sequence. First, different acts may be different manifestations of the same underlying construct, with no facilitating effect of an earlier act on a later one (e.g., where an antisocial tendency manifests itself first in shoplifting, later in burglary, and later still in family violence and child abuse). Second, different acts may be different behavioral manifestations of the same underlying construct and also part of a developmental sequence, as when one act facilitates another (e.g., smoking cigarettes leading to marijuana use). Third, different acts may be indicators of different constructs and may be part of a causal sequence, such that changes in the indicator of one construct cause changes in the indicator of a different one (e.g., school failure leading to truancy).

The first of these ideas can be distinguished empirically from the second and third. If all acts in a sequence are different behavioral manifestations of the same construct (like symptoms of an illness), then preventing or changing an early act in the sequence will not necessarily affect the probability of later acts, unless there is some change in the underlying construct. However, for developmental and causal sequences, changing an early act in the sequence will affect the probability of later acts. It is harder to distinguish the second and third ideas empirically, since the key distinction between them is conceptual.

Information is needed especially on the ages of onset of different acts; the influence of explanatory factors at these ages; the interrelations between onsets of different acts; the predictive implications of age of onset for later stages of the criminal career; and strategies to prevent or delay onset and continuation after onset. These questions should be addressed in the proposed longitudinal project.

Key Theories, Hypotheses, and Concepts

Life Transitions

Many offenses are committed for the first time between ages 9 and 17, and the prevalence of offending peaks in the teenage years, declining by age 20 (Farrington 1986). Between ages 9 and 20, parental influence probably declines, peer influence is probably greatest, and the influence of girls (or even wives and cohabitees in some cases) probably increases. For example, West (1982) found that getting married led to a decrease in offending, but only for male offenders who married unconvicted women.

Puberty occurs at about age 14 for males, and roughly between ages 15 and 18 boys graduate from school or drop out and afterwards may start full-time jobs, go to college, and leave home. The effects of these key life transitions should be investigated. For example, Elliott and Voss (1974) showed that the rate of official offending by boys decreased after they had dropped out of school. Similarly, the effects of other key life events should be studied, such as getting arrested or convicted, moving, and parents splitting up. Farrington (1977) discovered that a boy's (self-reported) offending increased after a first conviction, while Osborn

(1980) found that official and self-reported offending decreased after families moved out of an inner city. Some of these events (e.g., puberty, leaving school) will happen to all boys in the young adolescent cohorts, while other events (e.g., being arrested, parents separating) will be less than universal.

Theories

Existing criminological theories have limited relevance to our proposed research because they were devised to explain cross-sectional relations in the teenage years rather than development from childhood to adulthood. Also, theoretical propositions are not sufficiently specified to make unambiguous quantitative predictions. Hence, it would be a mistake to focus our research on testing any one particular theory, although it would be quite reasonable to measure and evaluate some of the key constructs in existing theories. Some of these key constructs are as follows:

1. the gap between a person's aspirations and what can be achieved by legitimate means (Cloward and Ohlin 1960);
2. status frustration experienced especially by lower-class boys who fail in school (Cohen 1955);
3. differential exposure to delinquent or law-abiding attitudes in the immediate social environment (Sutherland and Cressey 1974);
4. strength of the bond to society (Hirschi 1969);
5. strength of conscience and patterns of reinforcements for antisocial behavior (Trasler 1962);
6. immediate situational opportunities, and the probabilities, costs, and benefits of outcomes for alternative courses of action (Clarke and Cornish 1985);
7. impulsiveness, or the extent to which choices are influenced by future outcomes as opposed to more immediate ones (Wilson and Herrnstein 1985);
8. the degree of negative labeling by parents, teachers, or the justice system (Lemert 1972).

Recent theoretical formulations in criminology (e.g., Elliott, Huizinga, and Ageton 1985; Hawkins and Weis 1985) have attempted to integrate several of the classic theories into a more comprehensive theory.

What is lacking in most theoretical approaches is the attempt to integrate individual and situational approaches. Generally speaking, criminal behavior results from the interaction between a person (with a certain degree of criminal potential or antisocial tendency) and the environment (which provides criminal opportunities). Given the same situation, some people will be more likely to commit offenses than others, and, conversely, the same person will be more likely to commit offenses in some situations than in others.

Our proposed project focuses more on individual development than on immediate situational influences on offending, although we do focus on community and neighborhood contexts. Nevertheless, for a more complete explanation of both the development of offenders and the occurrence of criminal events, situations that provide opportunities for crime at different ages should be measured.

Hypotheses

Between ages 9 and 20, the research should focus on the onset of offending and, once initiated, on the continuation and intensification (increasing frequency and seriousness) of offending careers. As already mentioned, existing theories typically do not specify whether predictions apply to onset, continuation, or desistance, and in most cases, explanatory factors are linked to prevalence (differences between offenders and nonoffenders). However, some hypotheses about onset, continuation, and intensification can be derived. We can predict that a younger age of onset and a higher probability of continuation and intensification will be linked to:

1. low intelligence
2. high impulsiveness
3. child abuse
4. harsh and erratic parental discipline
5. cold and rejecting parents
6. poor parental supervision
7. parental disharmony, separation, and divorce
8. one-parent female-headed households
9. convicted parents or siblings
10. alcoholic or drug using parents or siblings
11. nonwhite race
12. low occupational prestige of parents
13. low educational level of parents
14. low family income
15. large family size
16. poor housing
17. low educational attainment of the child
18. attendance at a high delinquency school
19. delinquent friends
20. high crime area of residence

Factors that are especially important in development before the teenage years (e.g., parental child-rearing methods) are likely to be related to onset, while later factors (e.g., delinquent friends) may be more related to continuation or intensification. It is important to investigate how factors are independently related to offending and how factors interact with each other. It is also important to investigate factors that can change within individuals (e.g., educational attainment), especially in response to some kind of experimental intervention, compared to constants such as race or nonmanipulable factors such as age.

Research Questions

Answers to some basic questions on the natural history of offending and antisocial behavior are needed before we can formulate adequate developmental theories. In particular, we need to determine the prevalence and frequency of offending between ages 9 and 20 and the ages of onset of different types of acts. It should then be possible to specify the ages of maximum deceleration and acceleration in offending (see Farrington 1986).

It is also important to link up within individuals the frequency of offending at one age with the frequency of offending at another, in order to establish continuity (relative or absolute) between different ages and the extent to which one act predicts another. By studying relations between onsets of types of acts, it should be possible to specify developmental sequences. For example, we might suspect a developmental sequence exists involving hyperactivity between ages 2 and 5, conduct disorder between ages 8 and 10, shoplifting between ages 13 and 15, robbery between ages 19 and 21, and family violence and alcohol abuse between ages 20 and 25. The proposed project could track this kind of sequence in far more detail than ever before. It could also help in timing intervention strategies to increase effectiveness. For example, a key intervention point might occur just before the typical transition from less to more serious behavior, or at the time when the correlation between predictor and outcome variables is relatively low, suggesting that the person is still relatively changeable. Other key features of criminal careers, such as specialization, crime-switching, and escalation, should also be established from within-individual sequences of acts.

More is known about developmental sequences involving substance abuse than about other kinds of sequences. For example, Yamaguchi and Kandel (1984) showed that involvement with drugs typically begins with alcohol and cigarettes, progresses to marijuana, and then to other illegal drugs. Elliott, Huizinga, and Menard (1989) studied sequences of delinquency, drug use, mental health problems, and sexual activity. They found that minor delinquency usually occurs first, followed by alcohol use and then marijuana use. Serious offending, use of other illicit drugs, and mental health problems typically follow marijuana use. Of course, people drop out at all stages of developmental progressions, and only a small minority of those who begin a sequence reach a later stage. The proposed project should help to investigate this dropout process in more detail, thereby yielding clues about how such developmental sequences might be interrupted.

Given subjects between the ages of 9 and 20, it is unlikely that complete desistance from offending can be studied satisfactorily, in view of the need to wait several years to establish desistance. However, within this age range, it should be possible to investigate factors influencing early desistance after onset as well as intermittency or gaps in criminal careers.

The proposed project should make it possible to identify protective factors that explain, for example, why some conduct-disordered boys do not continue into juvenile delinquency. Farrington and colleagues (1988) discussed the various interpretations of protective factors and the extent to which they might be the opposite of risk factors. They also studied unconvicted boys from criminogenic backgrounds and found that the most protective factors were being shy or withdrawn and having few or no friends. Given that juvenile delinquency tends to be a group activity, it is perhaps not surprising that more solitary boys are less at risk of becoming delinquent.

It is also important to investigate the degree to which chronic, serious, frequent, or high-rate offending behavior can be predicted at an early age. For example, Farrington (1985) developed a prediction scale based on early antisocial behavior, convicted parents, socioeconomic deprivation, low intelligence, and poor parental child-rearing. The 55 boys with the highest prediction scores included the majority of chronic offenders having six or more convictions up to age 25 (15 out of 23), 22 of the other 109 official offenders having between one and five convictions, and 18 of the 265 unconvicted youths (Blumstein, Farrington, and Moitra 1985).

It is also important to investigate the effect of explanatory factors (biological, individual, family, peer, school, community, etc.) and key life transitions on the development of offending and features of criminal careers, and to address the problems of interpretation discussed previously. These issues include relations between drugs and crime, between offending and school failure, and reasons why offenders tend to have delinquent friends and to live in inner-city areas. Another crucial issue is the effect of juvenile justice system processing (arrests or convictions) on offending. Numerous other questions could also be illuminated in a longitudinal survey such as that proposed here. For example, victims tend also to be offenders (e.g., Singer 1986), and a longitudinal survey could assess whether there is a causal link between victimization and offending, or whether antisocial people or those living in poor areas simply happen to be both victims and offenders.

Research Design and Measurement

Practical Considerations

In any study, there is a problem of fitting all the desirable measures into the inevitably limited time available. Practical and funding constraints will limit the length and frequency of interviews with the males who are the primary focus of this study. As a starting point, we assume that subjects will undergo yearly face-to-face interviews, lasting about one hour, in which they will be asked about experiences in the previous year.

The frequency of interviews depends to some extent on the rate of change in the phenomena of interest, and the choice of the reference period depends on how far back in time valid information can be obtained—in view of memory limitations, for example. The major choice in practice is between annual and semiannual interviews, and it seems unlikely that the benefits gained in a twice-yearly schedule would outweigh the costs or would be preferable to other ways of allocating resources (e.g., having another type of respondent). More frequent interviews might be planned around key transition points (e.g., puberty) when rapid changes in development are anticipated.

It would be best to have each interview at about the same age (e.g., within a month after a boy's birthday) rather than at the same time of year (e.g., during the month of January). Interviews could then be spread throughout the year; it is easier to maintain a smaller interviewing staff throughout the year than to recruit a larger interviewing staff anew for a short period each year. Also, if interviews are always in progress, tracking can be always in progress, thereby minimizing attrition. It is inevitable, however, that some people in some years will take a long time to trace. We are more likely to be interested in behavior at an age (e.g., age 8) than in behavior during a calendar year. Hence, the first interview for the 9-year-old subjects might be conducted just after their 9th birthdays, leading to a distinction between the age of interest or reference age (i.e., age 8) and the age at interviewing (i.e., age 9).

In addition to the cohort subjects, mothers (or primary caretakers) should be interviewed once a year until the last age at which the vast majority of the males are still living in their parental homes. Also, teachers should fill out questionnaires once a year until the last age at which the vast majority of cohort subjects are still in school. In addition, official police and court records should be collected. Information from multiple sources is desirable, in order to counteract the errors and situational specificity present in any one source (see e.g., Achenbach, McConaughty, and Howell 1987).

Essential Measures

It is essential to measure different types of offending and antisocial behavior between ages 9 and 20, including stealing, burglary, robbery, violence (including threats and use of weapons), damaging property, sexual behavior, drinking alcohol, smoking cigarettes, using drugs such as marijuana and cocaine, glue sniffing, cheating, lying, truancy, disobedience, bullying, running away, and behavior leading to arrests or school suspensions. Except for age-inappropriate behaviors, information should be collected annually about each of these behaviors.

Types of behavior can be subdivided or specified more exactly—for example, stealing from home, from a shop, from school, or from a vehicle. It would be desirable to have information on each act—for example, how many times in the last year, with whom, why, where, when. However, it is unclear how far subjects will tolerate such detailed questioning and how far it might suppress admissions. Methodological research on strategies for detailed questioning about crime and antisocial behavior is thus desirable. Also, in order to draw conclusions about developmental sequences, information on the exact timing of events is needed. Methodological research on how best to obtain such information and how far it could be collected retrospectively is also desirable.

Information should be obtained from the cohort male, from his caretaker, and from his teacher (up to about age 15). The National Youth Survey Self-report Questionnaire (Elliott, Huizinga, and Ageton 1985) and the Achenbach Child

Behavior Checklist (Achenbach and Edelbrock 1983a) would be useful starting points in the development of instruments, since both are widely used measures of antisocial behavior.

It is also essential to measure two clusters of individual difference factors:

1. impulsiveness, hyperactivity, attention deficit, ability to delay gratification, daring, risk-taking (using caretaker, teacher, and self-reports, and possibly also psychomotor tests); and
2. intelligence, cognitive ability, ability to manipulate abstract concepts, academic attainment (using neuropsychological tests, teacher reports, and school records).

Evidence about the importance of these factors can be found in Wilson and Herrnstein (1985) and in Farrington, Loeber, and Van Kammen (1990). Impulsiveness and cognitive abilities should be measured annually.

It is also essential to measure several aspects of parent-child interactions by questioning both caretakers and boys. Key constructs to be measured are supervision or monitoring of boys' activities, methods of discipline, parental reinforcement for desirable behavior, parent-child relationships, separations of boys from parents, parent-child communication, involvement of fathers with boys, parental harmony, warmth or coldness of emotional relationships, and mutual or shared activities of family members (see Loeber and Stouthamer-Loeber 1986). These variables should also be measured annually.

For younger adolescent cohorts, it is essential to collect information annually on boys' friends, such as on antisocial or prosocial activities of peers, time spent with peers, popularity among or rejection by peers, peer influences, and peer leaders.

It is also essential to collect information from records on boys' schools and communities and to solicit relevant perceptions from caretakers and teachers. Data should be obtained on delinquent influences of other boys, quality of housing in the neighborhood, demographic characteristics of schools and communities, residential mobility, truancy rates, recreational resources, school and neighborhood safety, and so on. This information need not necessarily be collected annually, depending on the extent to which measures change over time.

It is also essential to measure certain characteristics of the parents, notably antisocial behavior, drug and alcohol use, physical health, ethnic backgrounds, age (including age at the time of the first child; see Morash and Rucker 1989), education, perceived stresses, attitudes (e.g., to antisocial behavior), and concerns about boys' deviant behavior and school problems. In addition, basic information should be collected on family structure (e.g., people in the household and their dates of birth), housing, employment, and income. This information should certainly be obtained in the first interview and subsequently if there are changes.

In the first interview, retrospective data should be collected that will permit linkage with earlier cohorts. Retrospective data covering the previous three years (that is, the three years before the reference year) would be particularly important, as those data would permit linkage with the immediately preceding cohort. The accuracy of such retrospective data might be tested in methodological research.

Retrospective data should be obtained in the first interview, especially on commission of types of offending and antisocial behavior in the previous three years, on whether boys had ever done each act, and on the age of first commission of each type of behavior. The data should permit assessment of conduct disorder in order to link these cohorts with younger ones. Retrospective information should also be obtained from boys and their caretakers on contact with or separation from biological or operative parents since birth. Retrospective information might also be obtained from school records (e.g., scholastic achievement or truancy) or hospital records (e.g., birth weight or obstetric problems).

Desirable and Supplementary Measures

It is desirable to measure self-esteem or self-concept; morality, guilt, strength of conscience or religiosity; altruistic or prosocial behavior; and attitudes (e.g., law-abiding or antipolice). It is desirable also to measure variables relevant to rational decision making, such as perceived probability of being caught and perceived costs and benefits of committing different types of offenses. Rutter and Giller (1983) and Wilson and Herrnstein (1985) review the relevance of these kinds of factors to offending.

Biological and health measures should be taken where feasible. Height, weight, and pulse rate should be assessed repeatedly over this age range. In general, violent offenders tend to have low pulse rates (e.g., Farrington 1987). A questionnaire such as the DISC might be used to measure mental health classifications (including attention deficit-hyperactivity, conduct disorder, oppositional defiant disorder, anxiety, depression, eating disorder, somatic complaints, obsessive-compulsive and schizoid-psychotic conditions). The DISC takes so long to administer that it could not be given annually; however, it could be given at less frequent intervals.

Supplementary studies could be carried out to investigate biological correlates of the onset, continuation, and intensification of offending, using blood or saliva samples to measure hormone levels, for example. In addition, it would be useful to supplement interview measures of family interaction by intensive systematic observations, following Patterson (1982). Also, it would be useful to supplement the subject's reports on peers by interviewing friends to build up a picture of peer networks at each age in terms of recruitment, stability, main activities, and roles of actors in the network (see Reiss 1988). These three supplementary studies could be done with small subsamples (e.g., 50 boys) from each cohort.

Another supplementary study could be carried out with a separate sample of arrestees in the city, selected at first arrest, in which criminal careers are followed. One of the most important aims of this study would be to investigate the impact of juvenile and adult criminal justice experiences both quasi-experimentally and in randomized experiments. It is easier to conduct such experiments among arrestees than in the general population.

Another supplementary study could be carried out to interview fathers (biological and nonbiological but operative). It is questionable whether accurate information about fathers can be obtained from mothers, and it is important to investigate the role of fathers in boys' upbringing. Also, it would be desirable to relate boys' own fathering in due course to the fathering they were exposed to in childhood and adolescence. Another supplementary study might interview boys' girlfriends to obtain information about their relationships.

Experimental Interventions

Given the great influence of peers during the teenage years, it would be highly desirable to investigate the effectiveness of interventions to train teenagers to resist deviant peer influences. Several studies show that school students can be taught to resist peer influences encouraging smoking, drinking, and marijuana use. For example, Telch et al. (1982) had older high school students teach younger ones to develop counterarguing skills to resist peer pressures to smoke, using modeling and guided practice. Similarly, Botvin and Eng (1982) successfully used same-age peer leaders, and Evans et al. (1981) used films. It would be worth mounting experiments on teaching teenagers to resist peer influences to commit delinquent acts.

Other possible experimental interventions for this age group include parent management training (e.g., Patterson 1982), promoting social competence through skills training (e.g., Ladd and Asher 1985), and promoting academic competence through special tutoring (e.g,. Coie and Krehbiel 1984). However, bearing in mind the lack of convincing evidence for competence-based approaches and the fact that parent management training is likely to be more effective for children at younger ages, interventions targeted on peers would be most useful with these cohorts.

Existing Data Sets, Ongoing Studies, and Pilot Research

It is important that any new large-scale longitudinal projects be complemented by analyses of existing literature, reanalyses of existing data sets, augmentation of existing projects where appropriate and feasible, small-scale supplementary research, and pilot studies, especially on methodological issues pertinent to the main project.

Several previous longitudinal projects have collected data that might be reanalyzed to throw light on some of the questions we are interested in. Farrington (1988a) has reviewed many of these projects and three detailed tables in that paper specify some of the major possibilities for reanalysis. Some data sets (e.g., collected by Delbert Elliott, Lyle Shannon, Kenneth Polk) are available in the Criminal Justice Archive in Michigan; others (e.g., collected by Joan McCord, Donna Hamparian, Sheppard Kellam) would have to be obtained from researchers.

The three longitudinal studies funded by the Office of Juvenile Justice and Delinquency Prevention (directed by David Huizinga, Rolf Loeber, and Terence

Thornberry) are prime candidates for augmentation, together with the project funded by the National Institute of Mental Health and directed by Gerald Patterson. These projects might be augmented by additional data collection for existing cohorts, experimental interventions, or additional (younger) cohorts. Another possibility is to collect offending data in projects in which it has not so far been collected, as in some projects of the Consortium for Longitudinal Studies (1983).

Methodological research is needed especially on the feasibility of interviewing biological and nonbiological but operative fathers, who are excluded from most research projects on teenage offending. Research is also needed to investigate how much detailed questioning on self-reported offending is feasible, and how the validity of responses by different groups (e.g., blacks vs. whites; see Hindelang, Hirschi, and Weis 1981) can be maximized. Research is also needed on maximizing the validity of retrospective questions covering several years. Another topic that might be investigated in pilot work is the feasibility of interviewing a boy's friends and the friends of his friends (etc.), to build up a detailed picture of peer networks in relation to offending. Pilot work is also needed on the feasibility of collecting biological (e.g., hormonal) data in a community survey.

14
Young Adult Cohorts

The life-span segments covered by the 15- and 18-year-old cohorts encompass many important developmental transitions, particularly in social and criminal justice arenas. Cohort members, for the most part, will be high school students, and we can anticipate that over the course of the study many will graduate or drop out, creating a transition from school to work. At the beginning of the research, the majority of subjects probably will be living with parents; later on some will move out on their own. Many also will be involved in serious, romantic relationships, some of which will lead to marriage. In the criminal justice sphere, some subjects will have accumulated substantial juvenile records, including institutionalization in juvenile detention centers or in other facilities, such as psychiatric hospitals. Finally, at a point about midway in the follow-up for the 15-year-old cohort, most cohort members will shift from juvenile to adult court jurisdiction, qualifying them for long-term prison incarceration.

The stages of development of criminal careers are not subject to clearly defined demarcations. They fuse into one another and may occur at different age levels. To expedite work in planning, three career stages were identified: pathways to delinquency, onset of delinquent activity, and desistance from or persistence in delinquent and criminal careers. These three stages predominate at different ages. Thus, pathways issues are primarily concerned with the determinants of conduct disorders during the prenatal, neonatal, and childhood periods of child development. Onset questions focus on early and middle adolescent years, when delinquency is most likely to begin. Similarly, desistance and persistence issues are more relevant to periods of late adolescence and adulthood.

It is clear, however, that the correspondence between chronological age and career stage is only approximate. For example, behavior disorders in late adolescence and adulthood, such as alcoholism and drug addiction, may lead to a late onset of criminal behavior. Similarly, early experimentation with delinquency may quickly come to an end as a result of the countervailing influences of official sanctions and parental or peer pressures. Criminal careers and antecedent pathways may be long or short and may occur at different ages, making it necessary to explore most career stages across most age-graded cohorts. At each stage of the criminal career, explanatory factors change in saliency and in theoretical and policy relevance. The influences that account best for the emergence of conduct disorders may differ significantly from the causal factors most relevant to the onset of delinquency or to desistance or persistence issues. Similarly, relevant explanatory factors may also differ considerably in early and late stages of the criminal career.

Our primary research mission for young adult cohorts is to describe and explain the development of criminal careers, with an emphasis on persistence and desistance issues. The main focus of attention therefore should be on the career paths of known offenders. Blumstein et al. (1986) have reviewed the current state of knowledge, and we need fuller information on many critical questions. We need better data on offense career patterns and on offenders. For example, we need to know more about how frequency of offending varies by type of offense. To what extent is there a tendency toward offense specialization or toward progressions in seriousness as careers develop? How much variation is there in the duration of offense careers or in the periodicity of offending as reflected in bursts and lulls of activity? To what extent is there versatility in offending or mixing of different crimes in a career? In addition to better descriptions of criminal-career patterns, we need to know more about chronic offenders, not only with regard to demographic characteristics, such as sex, race, and age, but also in terms of other familial, social, and individual characteristics that may provide a better basis for prediction and intervention (Blumstein et al. 1986, chap. 2).

In the final analysis, we would like to know more about why individual offenders persist in or desist from criminal activity. To what extent can we sort out the influences of biological factors and the early developmental experiences of family, school, and peers, of different life events, and of situational and contextual factors that create opportunities and inducements for crime? To what extent can we determine causal connections and sequential or reciprocal effects of different career paths with sufficient plausibility to justify experimental interventions?

Longitudinal studies and experiments responsive to these issues raise a number of critical methodological questions. What are the best methods for reliable and valid estimation of rates of individual offending? What are the most appropriate sampling units and populations for study of desistance and persistence issues? What are the likely sources of sample attrition in studying known offenders, and what are the best methods for minimizing the adverse effects of such attrition? How can we best study desistance and persistence processes, given that many active offenders escape detection? Which sampling strategies permit study of the careers of undetected offenders or careers in which offending begins in adulthood? These design and methodological issues reflect some of the critical decisions that will bear on the validity and usefulness of the final research products. A number of these issues may require preliminary study or continuing investigation as the research proceeds.

In the simplest terms, desistance implies a transition to a crime-free life-style, and persistence the obverse. But characterizing an offender as a desister or persister is obviously conditional on the period of observation. The termination of

TABLE 14.1. Glossary of basic symbols and relationships describing criminal careers.

Measure	Symbol and definition	
Measure based on crimes and arrests	*Crime process*	*Arrest process*
Aggregate crime rate per capita per year	C Crimes per capita per year	A Arrests per capita per year
Individual frequency per active offender	λ Crimes per year per active offender	μ Arrests per year per active offender
Current participation rate	d Percent of a population committing a crime within a year ("*doing*")	b Percent of a population arrested for crimes within a year ("*busted*")
Cumulative participation rate	D Percent of a population *ever* committing a crime	B Percent of a population *ever* arrested
Aggregate crime rate per capita: frequency per active offender times participation rate	$C = \lambda d$	$A = \mu b$
Other measures		
Arrest probability	q = Probability of arrest following a crime ($q = \mu/\lambda$)	
Career length	T = Total criminal career length	
Residual career length	T_R = Average time remaining in a criminal career	
Career dropout rate	δ = Fraction of a criminal population whose careers terminate during an observation period	

Source: Alfred Blumstein, Jacqueline Cohen, Jeffrey A. Roth, and Christy A. Visher. 1986. *Criminal Careers and "Career Criminals,"* vol. 1. Washington, D.C.: National Academy Press. Reprinted with permission.

all criminal activity can only be determined with certainty by the offender's death, and whether an offender is categorized as a persister or desister may depend on how long we follow that person's career. Criminal justice workers interested in policy matters are inclined to adopt a more relativistic position. Intervention programs or official sanctions may be deemed successful if offenders are diverted from more serious crimes to relatively minor law violations, if individual rates of offending are significantly reduced, or if periods between offenses are significantly lengthened. Issues of persistence or desistance are thus qualified by considerations of seriousness, frequency of offending, and duration of crime-free periods.

The NAS Panel on Research on Criminal Careers (Blumstein et al. 1986) found it useful to create a glossary of basic symbols and relations in order to distinguish more precisely dimensions of individual criminal careers and aggregate crime rates. This glossary is reproduced in Table 14.1. These symbols can be used to capture the essential concepts of the criminal career in quantifiable terms as illustrated in Figure 14.1, which is also adopted from the panel's report. The panel noted that this simplified representation of an individual criminal career can be extended to reflect more complex aspects of the career, as follows:

Possibilities include a "start-up" time during which an offender's frequency increases, a decrease in frequency toward the end of a career, and sporadic spurts or intermittent

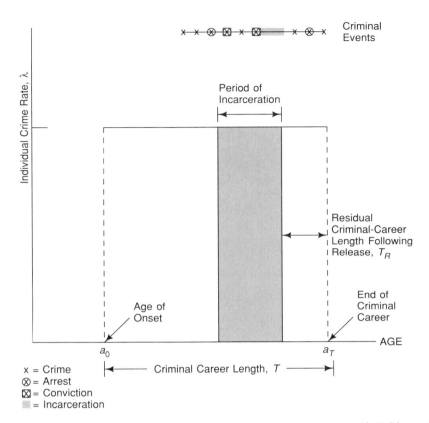

Figure 14.1. Illustration of an individual criminal career. (From Alfred Blumstein, Jacqueline Cohen, Jeffrey A. Roth, and Christy A. Visher. 1986. *Criminal Careers and "Career Criminals,"* vol. 1. Washington, D.C.: National Academy Press.) Reprinted with permission.

recesses from criminal activity. If the intervals between spurts are much shorter than a typical sentence, the intermittent pattern may be ignored and the average lambda used as a consideration in setting sentencing policy. But if the intervals of inactivity are long, then separate estimates are needed for high- and low-rate periods and for the duration of these periods, to adequately estimate average lambda. In addition, spurts in activity make it difficult to obtain information from offenders for use in estimating average annual rates. Distinctions among different offense types can also be made, permitting attention to single offenses (e.g., "robbery careers") or to patterns of switching among offense types during a career. In this context, it is important to know whether offenders are more likely to be "specialists" (who engage in only one or a small group of offenses) or "generalists" (who switch more widely among a range of offenses). Last, extensions of the basic model can address whether offending patterns typically "escalate" in the seriousness of successive events so that crimes later in the career are more serious, or whether they peak in seriousness in mid-career and then begin to decline in seriousness as a career nears its end. (Blumstein et al., p. 22)

Research on criminal careers has become increasingly sensitive to the need to identify and account for periodicity in offending (lulls and bursts, or intermittency), tendencies for specialization or crime mixing, and trends of escalation or deescalation in seriousness of offending. The tasks are not easy, because estimates of the actual rate and types of individual offending are invariably subject to biases and limitations implicit in self-report and arrest data. Researchers in recent years have given serious attention to problems in establishing valid accounts of criminal activity; the NAS Panel report discussed such problems at length, most notably in the papers by Jacqueline Cohen (1986) and Joseph Weis (1986).

Desistance, and probably persistence, can profitably be viewed and analyzed as a stochastic process using Markov, semi-Markov and survivor statistical models. These analytic strategies allow offenders to move along multiple parallel paths, each possibly having different determinants and hazards, with transitions in, out, and across paths. Desistance from crime is unlikely to be the product of one decision made at a single point in time. Instead, the transition from a criminal to a more conventional way of life involves at least three stages: motivation to change, learning new behaviors, and practicing new behaviors. Research based on conventional arrest information overlooks the complexity of the process just described, with its implicit assumptions of occasional relapses and opportunities to learn and practice new behaviors with appropriate reinforcers. Willpower alone is rarely a sufficient condition for behavioral change. Research on desistance and persistence needs to be sensitive to the transition process by considering the barriers offenders face in trying to develop prosocial life-styles.

Theoretical Considerations

We have identified three theoretical perspectives that seem most relevant to the oldest cohorts: lifetime social control, peer networks and co-offending, and community social disorganization and person-environment interactions. Each of these perspectives includes many subsidiary issues and hypotheses, and we cannot hope to do justice to them in a short discussion. Moreover, the theories provide explanations that are to some extent interrelated and that ultimately might be integrated. There is an increasing tendency to see different theoretical perspectives as complementary and occasionally overlapping rather than competitive, which has led to the creation of models of developmental processes in criminal behavior. For the most part, these models focus on factors leading to the onset of criminal behavior (Empey 1978; Glaser 1979; Elliott, Huizinga, and Ageton 1985; Thornberry 1987). The theory Thornberry developed holds special significance for persistence and desistance in stressing the reciprocity of relations among variables. In this scheme, delinquent acts can have feedback effects on explanatory variables, which in turn affect further delinquent behavior. The desirability and usefulness of integrative theories, however, are still matters of considerable debate among criminologists (Messner, Krohn, and Liska 1989), and therefore we found it useful to think in terms of three broad theoretical perspectives in tracing out hypotheses and design strategies.

Social Control

An important theoretical perspective on juvenile delinquency is social control theory, which can be traced back to Emile Durkheim (1897) and has been most fully articulated by Travis Hirschi (1969). The theory assumes that tendencies toward delinquency represent the natural state of affairs; hence the theory focuses on patterns of control that bond individuals to society (conformity). Hirschi's version of the theory focuses on attachment to parents and significant others (e.g., friends, teachers), commitment to the conventional social order (e.g., education, occupation), a belief in shared (common) values, and involvement in law-abiding activities. The overarching hypothesis is that delinquent acts result when an individual's bond to society is weak or broken. For example, as attachment to others (in terms of respect, affection, supervision, monitoring, etc.) decreases, the likelihood of delinquency increases. Empirical support for control theories has been strong in past cross-sectional studies of delinquency.

As we see it, the concept of social control is embedded in a more general theory that can be applied to human development in adolescence and early adulthood. Indeed, the key concepts of bond and society are complex and hold rich potential for the study of crime and delinquency. With regard to the oldest cohorts, it is important to focus on varying sources of social control in the transition from adolescence to adulthood. For the younger ages (e.g., 15 to 17 years), sources of control include bonds to parents, peers, teachers, and school. In young adulthood (e.g., 18 to 25 years), sources of control include marriage, work, and parenthood. Moreover, official sanctions operate as formal controls, which also vary over time (e.g., juvenile courts emphasize treatment, whereas adult courts emphasize punishment). Consequently, social control influences, both formal and informal, change throughout life (Glaser 1979).

Cross-sectional designs have studied between-individual differences in social bonding. However, a dynamic conceptualization of the social bond requires temporal study of the changing sources of social control. For example, what is the effect on subsequent delinquency of losing a job, becoming divorced, or being arrested? If we cannot specify the causal order of events, dimensions of control may be confounded with crime itself. In short, a longitudinal design allows us to examine how changes in age-graded sources of social control affect trajectories of criminal careers.

Social control theory can be applied not just to serious criminal behavior but also to drug abuse, alcoholism, and other forms of antisocial behavior, and nothing inherent in the concept of social control limits its application to older cohorts. This broad focus provides a natural linkage with the younger cohorts.

Peer Networks and Co-Offending

We know that much delinquency is committed in groups and that most delinquents have delinquent friends. In fact, one of the strongest predictors of delinquency is the delinquency of friends. However, while the empirical association is well-known, the causal status of peers and peer networks has yet to be established, and there is widespread disagreement over the meaning of the statistical relation. More generally, we have little information on the ways that peer social networks might be a factor in recruiting people into criminal careers and in continuation and desistance processes (Reiss 1988).

We recommend explicit study of issues of co-offending and social networks. Rather than focusing on one overall hypothesis, we stress several critical questions that can be examined by means of network analyses. The social network approach emphasizes linkages among and between sets of social relationships. Two characteristics of networks, multiplexity and density, seem especially relevant to offenders. Multiplexity refers to the number of activities or exchanges (foci) in which the same people interact jointly. Multiplexity is high when overlapping ties exist across several different foci (e.g., school, work, church, neighborhood). Individuals involved in multiplex relationships are less able to withdraw from a network, because withdrawal may jeopardize participation in more than one context. For this reason, multiplexity in social relationships is likely to constrain behavior.

Network density is the extent to which all actors in a social network are connected by direct relations, commonly measured by the ratio of observed ties in a network to the maximum number of possible ties. More dense networks place greater constraints on behavior within the purview of a social network. To the extent that network associations and foci are prosocial, multiplexity and density are predicted to inhibit crime.

Network analyses of criminal careers can benefit from longitudinal data on entry into and exit from cliques and peer groups. For example, researchers can test competing hypotheses on entry into co-offending careers: do birds of a feather flock together, as the Gluecks (1950) hypothesized (a variation on self-selection bias)? Or, do peers have a causal effect by recruiting actors into co-offending networks, as Shaw and McKay (1931, 1942) argued? If Shaw and McKay are correct, are co-offenders recruited through strong or weak ties? Does participation in multiplex networks insulate an individual against the effects of delinquency recruitment? Are there group processes that interact with dense peer networks to increase persistence in offending? Are subcultures (e.g., drug subcultures) maintained via strong or weak network ties (Granovetter 1973)?

Clearly, the temporal ordering of network ties needs to be established with respect to acts of crime and delinquency. For example, evidence suggests that most delinquent pairings are of short duration—less than six months (Klein and Crawford 1967; Sarnecki 1982). An important implication of this finding is that, unlike stable aspects of human development, shifts among cliques of peers and co-offenders are common. This lack of stability in delinquent associations highlights the need for a study of peer networks over time in order to understand how crime is related to the strength of ties and to the density and multiplexity of networks.

Longitudinal studies are also needed to follow changes in co-offender influences on criminal careers during the critical transition from juvenile to adult. As Reiss (1988) notes, no study has examined patterns of co-offending into the adult years.

More generally, Suttles (1968) observed that changes in salient life events are associated with transitions to new networks and social roles. Thus, a key issue to be studied is whether network transitions are the source of desistance or whether desistance itself leads to new friendships. Again, in order to address this issue we need to study changes in affiliations over time. Moreover, we need to examine whether early desistance of offenders who seemingly prefer to commit crimes in groups accounts for the greater concentration of solo offending among persisters (Knight and West 1975).

An advantage of a network approach is that it can integrate several theoretical perspectives on crime. Elements of social control theory (Hirschi 1969), learning theory (Akers et al. 1985), differential association theory (Sutherland 1939), and subcultural theory (Cloward and Ohlin 1960) can be incorporated into it. Such an approach also provides insight into the effects of sanctions. In particular, network theory suggests that crime may be reduced if sanctions are targeted at breaking up or disrupting co-offending networks, especially those with weak ties (Reiss 1988; Ekland-Olson 1984).

Community Disorganization and Person-Environment Interactions

Crime appears to have a history in particular locales, possibly regardless of the composition of the population inhabiting those locales (Shaw et al. 1929; Shaw and McKay 1942; 1969). Relatedly, community effects on crime (i.e., contextual effects) apparently remain even when individual-level characteristics are controlled. Therefore, community structure must be considered in the study of persistence and desistance patterns.

The concept of social disorganization does much to bring the variety of theories on community structure together. In general terms, social disorganization refers to the inability of a community to maintain effective social controls. Community attributes are important not only because they relate to social control but also because they relate to subcultural formation and opportunities for crime (Cloward and Ohlin 1960). Hence, both the rate and form of crime vary systematically by dimensions of the community (Reiss 1986; Bursik 1988; Stark 1987; Byrne and Sampson 1986).

Moreover, there is evidence that community structure directly affects criminal behavior in ways that cannot be attributed to individual characteristics and that it interacts with individual characteristics to explain crime (Simcha-Fagan and Schwartz 1986). This area of research is generally known as contextual analysis. For example, Gottfredson and Taylor 1986) have shown that parolees with an extensive history of criminal involvement fail more often and more quickly when released to socially disorganized communities, a finding directly relevant to the desistance of criminal careers. Consequently, they argue that recidivism among high-rate offenders is best understood by a person-environment model in which individuals, environments, and behaviors mutually influence one another.

In brief, we think that the social disorganization perspective goes a long way toward bridging community social control, opportunity structures and notions of rational choice (Clark and Cornish 1985), subcultural development (Schwendinger and Schwendinger 1985; Anglin 1986), and behavioral strategies (Cohen and Machalek 1988).

Hypotheses

Most community research has been cross-sectional, and we expect to study between-community variations. Nevertheless, communities change as do individuals, and people may selectively migrate to communities with certain attributes. Therefore, longitudinal designs that track the structure, composition, and organization of communities and that track the movements of community residents are needed to ascribe variation in crime to individual and to community factors (Reiss 1986). Overall, our major point is that by combining information on both individuals and communities in a longitudinal study, which has never been done, we will be able to assess more accurately the causes of criminal careers.

Our knowledge of factors related to criminal behavior derives largely from correlations on cross-sectional samples of offenders and nonoffenders. By drawing on these research findings, a number of empirical conclusions can be stated about the experiences, characteristics, and behavior of offenders. What we do not know, however, is whether the insights, understandings, and expectations generated by this work will survive the more rigorous tests provided by longitudinal research designs. In the following sections we have extracted from the literature some findings on crime that relate to the development of criminal careers, the effects of social control and social disorganization, the role of school and developmental experiences, the influence of peers in social networks, the effect of criminal justice sanctions, the relation of drug use and crime, and the impact of community contexts. These findings can be used to generate hypotheses framed in terms of changes in the level of criminal activity, including the possibility of desistance. Many of the hypotheses document commonsense or intuitive expectations that may hold up in a longitudinal perspective. Also, each of the propositions can be stated in the converse to emphasize the possibility of counterintuitive findings that challenge conventional wisdom on these matters.

Criminal Careers

In studying the older cohorts, one of our primary objectives is to chart the unfolding of offending careers. Although the criminal career paradigm emphasizes description over explanation and, in this sense, is atheoretical, it identifies a number of research issues that can be framed as empirical expectations. Among a representative group of active offenders, we will observe a variety of career patterns that might be characterized as chronic, intermittent, and occasional. For example, chronic offenders constitute a distinct group that can be distinguished from other offenders in terms of personal characteristics, both in kind and in degree. They are disproportinately early starters who show signs of behavior problems (e.g., conduct disorder) at a young age. In addition, chronic offenders demonstrate, both historically and contemporaneously, a greater degree of social and psychological pathology (e.g., drug and alcohol abuse, mental illness, and chronic unemployment).

Among some offenders, different sequences of onsets are related to different patterns of subsequent behaviors. For example, drug abuse followed by crime is related to a different career path than the reverse sequence of onsets. Also, many offenders show versatility in offense behavior; however, a distinct subset of offenders show offense specialization or an escalating pattern of seriousness. Among chronic offenders, abrupt desistance is an infrequent event that tends to be involuntary (e.g., resulting from death, disease, or disability).

Social Control and Disorganization Effects

Social control and disorganization theories emphasize constraints on behavior that derive from interpersonal and institutional attachments and commitments. Some of these constraints are social or psychological in the sense that they can be traced to attitudes and beliefs. Other constraints are structural in that they derive from patterns of behavior that direct people away from criminal opportunities and influences. The two types of constraints (reciprocal causations) probably interact over extended periods of time, such that changes in psychological orientations precipitate changes in behavior, while outward changes in behavior facilitate shifts in personal orientations. For example, marriage demonstrates commitment and attachment to another person; dispositions that lead a person to get married may also lead to reform from criminal activity. On the other hand, marriage will tend to restrict the time a person spends with friends and associates, which may reduce opportunities for crime, and although a couple may not be greatly attached at the outset of a marriage, strong bonds may develop as they spend time together.

Social control and disorganization theories, and to some extent social learning theory, emphasize the importance of role transitions that involve attachments, commitments, and increased levels of responsibility. For the older cohorts, important life events include marriage and employment, and we expect that they will be related to rates of offending. Marriage (and possibly cohabitation) can lead to a reduction in crime, and the effect should be greater if marriage involves a noncriminal spouse, a strong, positive interpersonal attachment, and a change in life-style. Employment can lead to a reduction in criminal activity, providing it satisfies a person's interests, abilities, and economic goals and expectations. These effects may be contingent on considerations unrelated to a job, such as changing life circumstances and life-style (e.g., having to support a family or becoming a drug addict with an expensive habit).

School Experiences

School experiences play a prominent role in the lives of children and adolescents, and many propositions can be generated regarding the effects of school achievement and classmate associations on delinquency. Although we expect that school-related variables will largely be covered in the younger cohorts, the 15-year-old cohort will be in high school while the 18-year-old cohort will be approaching high school graduation. Thus, subjects in the older cohorts will be finishing school or making the transition to spheres of adult life.

Although we assume that for the older cohorts the most important research questions will revolve round transitions to other social roles, we may possibly find that this is not the case. For example, in Ann Brunswick's Harlem Youth Study (1985) subjects between ages 12 and 15 showed serious problems of school achievement and performance. Two-thirds of them were in elementary school; one-half attended at least four different schools; one-quarter had a notation in their school file regarding a "special disability"; and the mean number of days students were absent during the preceding school year was 21.

Developmental Changes and Related Psychological Factors

Many developmental changes involving shifts in perspectives and world views accompany aging, and a variety of explanations might account for these changes. The explanations most often advanced focus on learning, which may include elements of rational choice, although we cannot rule out the possibility that biological processes of aging are involved at some level. While some developmental changes may be universal (or virtually so) in that they occur for most people, the timing of changes may differ critically among individuals. For this reason, by studying the timing of known developmental changes in relation to levels of criminal behavior, we will be in a position to elaborate on the age-crime relation. Goals, expectations, and self-concepts regarding success, achievement, and accomplishment develop over time, and changes that improve the fit with one's life situation should reduce criminal activity. For example, goals may be shifted downward, as in a process of accommodation, or life situations may improve.

Reductions in criminal activity are most likely to result from a shift in time perspective from short-range to long-range views; a shift in orientation to a more risk-aversive stance; an upward shift in moral development (e.g., from an egocentric to other-centered world view); an increased ability to tolerate frustration and to delay gratification; and changes in attitudes and beliefs, both prosocial and antisocial. Chronic offenders are more likely to have emotional disorders, especially disorders involving impulsiveness, impatience, and impaired cognitive abilities. Thus, it may be that psychological deficits and emotional disorders among chronic offenders inhibit the developmental changes that typically lead to a reduction in criminal behavior. However, some evidence suggests that anxiety disorders may be related to a lower level of criminal activity.

Network and Peer Relations

Differential association theory emphasizes that criminal behavior, including related techniques, skills, attitudes, and motivations, is learned from people favorably disposed to violate the law. In addition, the theory states that prosocial behavior, which is learned from conventional people, acts as a buffer and that the balance between competing prosocial and antisocial influences determines whether a person engages in crime. Differential association and other learning theories highlight the importance of criminal and noncriminal associations, providing a link to our concern with peer networks and co-offending. Network analyses with concepts of dense, bridging, and multiplex ties promise to be useful for studying interpersonal influences; however, because learning theories of crime are built around the transmission of skills and values, we will have to go beyond simply charting the structural aspects of networks (i.e., who interacts with whom) and describe the criminal orientations of actors. The descriptions might involve a simple determination of the extent of criminal activity, or preferably a more detailed inquiry about criminal orientations.

Life events (such as marriage, employment, residential mobility) frequently lead to the breakup of criminogenic peer networks. For some offenders, a change in attitude and outlook will precipitate a change in networks and in criminal activity (self-selection) while, for other offenders, such changes follow a change in networks, particularly if replacement networks hold a different set of values.

Observed differences in co-offending might be attributed to the fact that offenders who commit crimes in groups tend to desist earlier than other offenders. Alternatively, it is possible that persistent offenders shift to committing crimes by themselves.

Punishment and Incarceration Effects

Both deterrence theory and labeling theory predict that criminal justice sanctions influence criminal propensity, albeit in opposite directions. Labeling theory argues that punishment leads to internalization and solidification of a criminal self-concept, particularly in the early stages of a criminal career, resulting in increased criminal behavior. In contrast, deterrence theory argues that punishment teaches offenders that crime has negative consequences, a lesson that can alter cost-benefit assessments such that individuals refrain from crime.

Theories on prison socialization and postprison adjustment also address the effects of criminal justice sanctions. In general, we would expect that prison inmates who resist the potentially crimonogenic influences of the inmate culture, accept the legitimacy of their confinement, and after release adopt law-abiding life-styles are most likely to refrain from criminal activity.

Other factors influence criminal behavior as well. The transition from juvenile to adult court jurisdiction is probably a key juncture in desistance from crime. An offender's experiences with the criminal justice system in terms of the severity and celerity of punishment will affect perceptions of the risks of crime. However, the relation between punishment and subsequent criminal activity may be contingent on the stage of the criminal career. Official reactions that occur very early in the career might reduce criminal activity, rather than amplify deviance, depending on the offender's evaluation of the negative consequences of punishment. Finally, prison can either increase or decrease levels of subsequent criminal behavior, depending on the transferability of learned skills to the outside world, the effect of relationships in prison on the formation of prosocial and antisocial values and attitudes, and whether parolees are released into strong, positive community support networks.

Drug Use and Crime

Many studies document the fact that criminal activity and drug use are intimately connected. In general, we find higher levels of criminal activity during periods of drug use, especially acquisitive or property crimes that can finance drug addiction, although some offenses are direct products of addiction itself (i.e., drug possession and use offenses).

Drug use also can alter the cost-benefit assessment of engaging in crime. Some offenders will generally accept greater risks, leading them to engage in crimes that have a greater chance of official detection and apprehension, and other offenders will commit crimes while under the influence of drugs, thus risking a greater probability of arrest.

Community or Geographic Factors

We have emphasized that community attributes are important factors in understanding criminality, because they represent the contextual frameworks within which individuals respond differently (person-environment interactions) and because they may have direct effects on behavior (environmental effects independent of the person). While this general framework is applicable across all cohorts, among older subjects we can anticipate greater residential mobility, which means that environmental contexts will be changing more frequently over the course of the study. We have already discussed how geographical movement can relate to changes in the peer networks that affect the level of criminal activity. Moving to areas with more social disorganization and criminal opportunities, including the availability of drugs, guns, and gang activity, can be expected to increase the level of criminal behavior. In some cases, greater social isolation will be conducive to more law-abiding activities.

Variables and Measures

Measurement of the primary dependent variable, criminal behavior, will be a substantial undertaking, because prospective and retrospective data on the incidence, timing, seriousness, and circumstances of detected and undetected offenses will have to be collected. Extremely active offenders will present special problems in collecting data by virtue of the amount of data to be collected. Interviews for this group should enhance cooperation and recall. We also recommend collecting data on a variety of other antisocial or deviant behaviors that might be viewed as correlates of causes of crime or that might be analyzed separately as dependent variables. The list includes alcohol and drug use, family violence, emotional disorder, chronic unemployment, transience, and institutional disciplinary infractions. Drug and alcohol abuse are important variables that may require fairly detailed data collection.

Although a variety of self-report instruments have been developed, none appears to meet the needs of the proposed research, primarily because they fail to inquire about specific details of offense behavior. An attractive option is to modify one or several existing instruments (e.g., National Youth Survey), because this would allow researchers to capitalize on work that already has gone into developing these instruments. Nonetheless, it will be very important to allocate sufficient time and resources to developing instruments, given that off-the-shelf instruments fall short of our requirements.

An interest in studying the effect of experiences with the criminal justice system makes it important to document the chronology and nature of a variety of official actions involving arrest, prosecution, sentencing, community supervision, and incarceration. Data collection instruments will have to be modified for incarcerated people because many items on community experiences will not be applicable. Jail experiences differ from prison experiences, and these differences also need to be accommodated in data collection. As cohort members are followed over the course of incarceration, we should at least continue to collect self-report data on criminal behavior (i.e., crime behind the walls), supplemented by institutional records on disciplinary infractions.

Much information on criminal justice experiences should be contained in official agency records. It therefore becomes important to scrutinize the record-keeping systems of potential sites for comprehensiveness and ease of access. In addition, it will be critical to maintain good relations with official agencies throughout the study, such as by avoiding negative publicity and by minimizing the administrative burden of data collection.

Similarly, relevant information on school experiences should be available from official records. As subjects leave school during the follow-up period, collecting data from teachers becomes unnecessary. However, for subjects who are not in school at the start of the study, we suggest contacting teachers for retrospective evaluations. Although it may be desirable to collect information from employers, it will probably be difficult to get them to cooperate. Data will have to be collected from family members (especially parents and spouse), either because they are the best sources of information (e.g., parents are best able to report on many of the early childhood experiences of subjects and on their own criminal behavior) or because they can corroborate reports from subjects (e.g., by asking a wife about a husband's behavior at home). Prison and jail staffs will be in a good position to report on incarcerated subjects, and it should not be difficult to enlist assistance.

Our theoretical approach to studying the older cohorts emphasizes the concept of social control stemming from multiple sources. The relevance of various sources of social control will vary with individuals' life situations, which are more closely tied to age ranges than to specific ages. Older cohorts present a particular problem because they span a number of important life transitions. For this reason, it is difficult to rule out in advance the relevance of many social control elements, which means that a wide-ranging inventory of life circumstances will have to be developed.

Critical life events for subjects in the older cohorts include leaving school, getting married, starting families, holding jobs, and being incarcerated or institutionalized. We suggest documenting occurrences and assessing the nature of each of these events. Detailed assessments of attitudes, perceptions, and behaviors for each change in status (or repeated assessments to detect changes that occur in a continuing status) are unrealistic given the level of resources that would be necessary and problems of testing effects. We therefore suggest that several global items from existing instruments be identified, such as those on job and marital satisfaction, that reliably and validly tap into the constructs of interest. Since this strategy would preclude dimension-specific or item-specific analyses, another possibility is to combine more frequent global assessments with occasional detailed assessments, reserving in-depth data collection for specific times or for critical junctures.

Another aspect of social control we recommend collecting data on is that of social activities, such as time spent with friends, at home with family, at work, in school, involvements in organizations, and other conventional activities. To the extent feasible, the nature of the activities (e.g., hanging out with friends on the street corner, fighting with wife and children, not showing up for work, being truant from school) should be described. This aspect of data collection also requires development of instruments covering a broad range of behaviors. For significant interpersonal relationships, we suggest measuring the nature and strength of attachments, including assessment of prosocial and antisocial orientations, and instruments that have already been developed on this topic might prove useful.

An issue that will need to be resolved in developing instruments to gauge the influences of social controls is the extent to which emphasis is placed on the specific mechanisms through which controls operate. Some control mechanisms stand outside the person (e.g, constraints due to surveillance, or time allocations of daily activities that impinge on crime opportunities), while other mechanisms are socio-psychological (development of attitudes, beliefs, values, morals). Questions that might be investigated include the following: How do these two classes of mechanisms (internal and external) relate to different sources of control (parents, teachers, spouse)? What are the interrelationships between different control mechanisms? Do external controls lead to internal controls or vice versa? To what extent will investigation of specific control mechanisms facilitate theory testing or lead to theoretical integrations?

From the point of view of external controls, we need to study structural constraints on behavior imposed by key life events or transitions. From a more psychological point of view, we can ask how significant life experiences affect the development of critical attitudes and beliefs. Both sets of influences constitute intervening variables that we presume operate but that we rarely study directly. To the extent that intervening processes are studied, we will be able to clarify associations discovered among variables. However, the level of resources involved in collecting these data can be substantial, which raises the issue of how much effort to devote to this line of inquiry.

We have also highlighted the desirability of collecting data on a variety of attitudes and beliefs regarding values, criminal justice experiences, interpersonal relationships, self-concept, and personal goals and expectations, and of documenting changes in these variables over time. The task is a substantial one, requiring an extensive review of the literature for instruments that might be used. In addition, repeated data collection raises the possibility of testing effects, although the rate of change in many variables of interest is probably not great, thereby allowing measurements to be spaced out over time.

Another important group of variables involves psychological attributes including temperament, attachment, personality traits, and emotional disorders. The pool of psychometric tests to draw from is large, and if more than one test is used it is important to minimize overlap in the type of information collected. We suggest that a standardized psychiatric diagnostic test (e.g., DIS) and an intelligence test (e.g., WAIS) be administered to subjects, since they broaden the appeal of the research by including mental health issues. Although these tests will require a substantial investment of resources, they will not have to be administered often. We hesitate to recommend the MMPI, because this test has been used frequently with criminal populations (e.g., *Criminal Justice and Behavior*, the official journal of the American Association of Correctional Psychologists, has issued a moratorium on articles reporting MMPI results) and because the test tends to generate seemingly tautological or circular relations (e.g., criminals are more likely to have high psychopathic deviate scores). Similarly, esoteric or exotic instruments that might raise questions about the reliability and validity of findings are also unattractive.

Finally, at the community level, we suggest looking at such factors as availability of day care, healthcare, playgrounds, and so on. Aside from using this information to document aspects of neighborhoods, connections to individual level behavior can also be pursued. That is, implied causal processes can be traced and links made to individual behavior by asking subjects about their use of day care, healthcare, and so on. Again, it is important to decide how much effort will be put into clarifying causal links and processes of factors expected to be important.

Variables Providing Links to Younger Cohorts

Several major hypotheses for the birth and childhood cohorts relate to the crucial role that infant-parent relationships play in the subsequent psychological development of children. These experiences may be too far back in time to be captured retrospectively for the older cohorts, which means that some propositions concerning the pivotal role of early childhood events may not be testable for older subjects. However, given that the outcomes of early childhood experiences are assumed to be stable over life (e.g., attachment styles are relatively enduring features of how a person approaches interpersonal relationships), it seems important to measure these outcomes among older cohorts in order to facilitate cross-cohort analyses. This can be done without necessarily detailing the events and processes that led to the outcomes.

Research on the youngest cohorts also highlights several hypotheses regarding environment-trait interactions. Although contemporary trait descriptions for older cohort subjects can be substituted for retrospective data because traits are presumed to be stable over time, it will be difficult to collect detailed retrospective information on early environments to provide links with developmental sequences studied in the younger cohorts.

Hypotheses generated for the younger cohorts also suggest that low IQ is related to antisocial behavior through a mechanism that differs from that of crime-prone traits. In particular, low IQ delays the acquisition of social skills, which in turn encourages aggression as a means of influencing others. If the hypothesized mechanism operates, then low IQ becomes for older cohorts a marker for a variety of social deficits of a late-onset variety, and it will be difficult to reconstruct retrospectively the time when social skills are acquired. If, however, low IQ prevents the acquisition of social skills, this outcome will be measurable among older cohorts. Low IQ may operate more directly by impairing cognitive and reasoning abilities, leading to skewed assessments in the cost/benefit crime calculus. This hypothesis seems especially appropriate for older cohorts and can be tested directly.

Many of the behavior onsets of interest would have already taken place among older cohorts. We can expect that there will be some late onsets, and it will be important to capture these events. For some types of crime (probably the most serious offenses, such as armed robbery, but not the deviant behaviors young adolescents typically engage in, such as shoplifting, drinking, and smoking), the older cohorts may capture the majority of onsets.

In collecting retrospective onset data, it will be difficult to detail the timing of events in the distant past. One strategy for improving data collection among older cohorts might be to use common experiences as a reference point, such as by asking, "What grade were you in when you first did x?"—and then to determine how old the subject was at that time. Retrospective information collected on onsets for the older cohorts should allow for classifying subjects as early, typical, or late starters with regard to particular behaviors and for identification of sequences of behaviors (e.g., cigarettes to marijuana to cocaine). It is important to make these assessments given hypotheses on relations between early onset and subsequent chronicity and on developmental behavior progressions.

The quality of family relationships—in particular, interactions between child and primary caretaker during sensitive developmental periods and parental discipline styles—are critical variables that may be difficult to capture retrospectively but that should have measurable ramifications throughout a person's life. We suggest, if possible, tapping the outcomes of these critical developmental experiences for older cohorts so that they can be used to link cohorts together in the analyses.

Peer acceptance and rejection are also identified as possibly critical factors in the onset of conduct disorder and delinquency. Among older cohort subjects, many peer socialization issues will have been resolved by finding peer niches, and many onsets will have taken place. However, significant interpersonal experiences occur throughout life, and the emphasis on network theories for older cohorts addresses this issue. Social learning theory suggests that delinquency is learned partly through attachments to deviant others, while in contrast, control theory argues that the orientation (prosocial or antisocial) of significant others is irrelevant because delinquents are incapable of forming strong attachments to anyone, thus placing the strength of attachments at issue. It seems important to collect data that will allow for a test of these competing hypotheses. Although network theory (with weak, strong, bridging, dense, and multiplex ties) may capture some important theoretical elements, techniques may have to be adapted so as to reflect better the psychological or emotional processes that undergird interpersonal attachments.

We suggested physiological measures for early cohorts, of sustained attention and reaction time, autonomic functions (heart rate and blood pressure), and neuroendocrine functions (sex hormones and cortisol). All these items are good candidates for inclusion in research on older cohorts, and each measure should be evaluated in terms of types of analyses that will be possible both within and across cohorts.

Interventions and Experiments

We have identified two general types of interventions for older cohort subjects. The first, developed by Peter Greenwood, can be described as a relapse prevention program. The basic strategy involves continuous case management by a single individual or agency using a single, conceptual approach; intensive community supervision (two or more contacts a day) and assistance by well-trained, well-supervised, youthful, enthusiastic trackers; and a heavy emphasis on resolving family problems. The second strategy, developed by Douglas Anglin, can be characterized as a dynamic system of social intervention for drug use. The strategy involves early detection of drug abuse, assessments at the individual level for developing an integrated intervention system, and voluntary or mandated participation in the program with monitoring for compliance.

On the criminal justice side, interventions might involve court diversion into treatment; or treatment as a condition of probation, early release from prison, or parole. On the community side, interventions can range from education programs, to outpatient counseling, to methadone maintenance, to residential treatment. A comprehensive program of case management is required to monitor intensity of treatment and levels of social control. The model is similar to that of the mental health system in managing chronically ill patients.

We recommend that interventions target active offenders because many older subjects should be well into their criminal careers and because prevention efforts directed at nonoffenders have relatively less payoff at later ages. The proposed programs combine a variety of treatment strategies intended to demonstrate the efficacy of intervention efforts, rather than to test theoretical propositions. They build on decades of research on criminal recidivism by acknowledging that the motivations of adult criminals are complex, influenced cumulatively by personal experiences and life events, and that the specific life circumstances that need to be dealt with are extremely varied. Thus, recommendations for interventions were shaped not so much by advocacy of a particular intervention strategy or program as by recognition of the facts that in order for treatments to be successful we have to attack the problem of criminality on a number of fronts and that treatment programs need to be carefully tailored to individuals.

Arguments in favor of embedding experiments in a longitudinal study of offenders have been reviewed in Farrington, Ohlin, and Wilson (1986). For the older cohorts, experiences with evaluating offender rehabilitation programs, many of which have been disappointing, are especially relevant. We now realize that we need background information to determine which intervention strategies are most likely to work and, because treatment outcomes are not always captured by simple criteria of success or failure, we also need detailed follow-up information describing the timing and nature of subsequent offenses over an extended period. These requirements suggest that treatment programs are best evaluated longitudinally, indicating a convenient fit between descriptive developmental research and research intended to demonstrate program effectiveness. Reservations we have stem from an assessment of the probable costs and benefits. The recommended interventions are unlikely to have very substantial effects on recidivism in general but may show a marked effect on rates of offending for different types of offenses. Even these effects, however, may be very difficult to replicate given the highly individualized treatment strategies involved.

At this time, the major question that needs to be addressed is whether possible experiments for the older cohorts should drive design and site selection issues. Given issues of treatment effectiveness and transferability of intervention technology and the fact that any intervention attached to a longitudinal study may threaten the integrity of the core study, the answer to this question, at least for the older cohorts, is probably not. However, this conclusion does not mean that we have abandoned the possibility of experiments and interventions with adult offenders, and we suggest that the option of incorporating such programs into the project as the research proceeds be left open.

Special Sampling Issues

As currently planned, the 15-year-old cohort consist of 500 males, and the 18-year-old cohort of 1,000 males. The increased sample size for the oldest cohort is intended to provide a sufficient number of subjects at the upper end of the age spectrum, since the 15-year-old cohort does not overlap with the 18-year-old cohort for the 24 to 26 age range. There are other special sampling concerns for the older cohorts.

The research strategy calls for oversampling high-risk subjects to increase the yield of outcomes of interest; for older cohorts we are especially interested in identifying active offenders. Older subjects are distinct in that at the time of screening we are in a position to identify some of the behaviors we are interested in studying, something that cannot be done for all cohorts. The most efficient procedure to increase the yield of active offenders is to screen potential subjects for the onset of a criminal career. Thus, one option we considered is to include an official arrest record as one of the criteria for identifying a high-risk sample among older subjects. However, because comparability across cohorts is needed to facilitate analytic linkages, we hesitate to recommend targeting arrestees for inclusion in the core sample. More generally, we have had difficulty identifying common individual-level risk criteria that can be used for all cohorts to increase sampling yield. The difficulties relate to the fact the optimal predictors differ across cohorts, because the type of behavior subjects are at risk for varies with age, as does the availability and relevance of specific predictor variables.

For household sampling, we recommend including single-person households because potential subjects in the older cohorts may not be living with their families, although we set the age of the oldest cohort at 18 to minimize this possibility. Screening single-person households may require repeated visits, especially during the evening. Another potential problem is that subjects in the older cohorts may be semitransient, rotating living arrangements among friends, lovers, and so on. If potential subjects have stable, albeit temporary, residences, they can be identified fairly easily from appropriate inquiries. However, to the extent that they are nomadic and do not have a primary residence, screening and data collection will be difficult. Finally, while we leave open the possibility of excluding otherwise eligible subjects residing temporarily at distant institutions (prisons, schools, etc.), we recommend including people in local jails. Our rationale is that jails contain active offenders who may live in single-person households or who may be nomadic; that the length of stay in jails is relatively short; and that inmates are usually discharged back to the communities the jails are located in. Eligible subjects in jails, and possibly in other local institutions, can be identified either by canvassing local facilities or by asking questions in household screenings on the whereabouts of family members not present.

Another problem of special importance with older cohorts relates to the need to elicit retrospective information in order to assess comparability with younger cohorts. The overlap in age groups built into the multiple-cohort strategy makes cohorts comparable, but retrospective data can further assist this. The critical question is how much effort and interviewing time can profitably be spent in collecting retrospective data. Some information can be gathered from school, social service agency, and police and juvenile justice agency records. Nonrecorded information on early family composition and relationships, early conduct disorders, peer group or gang involvement, however, may need to be obtained from subjects and possibly from interviews with parents, siblings, teachers, or other authorities. Significant events such as family deaths, family disruption by separation or divorce, early processing by juvenile justice agencies, school dropout, and similar occurrences need to be recorded.

Older cohorts are likely to cause problems of attrition. Some subjects may be dealing in drugs and thus may be difficult to locate. A few subjects may enter the military, and a more substantial proportion will be floating about the community, staying with friends intermittently. Some, wanted by the police, will be in hiding, making it difficult to obtain reliable information on their whereabouts from family members or friends. Still other subjects will be in jail or prison or under probation or parole supervision and therefore easier to trace and contact. However, once a cohort is formed and an initial contact has been made, it may be possible to mitigate many of these problems. In the Harlem Youth Study (Brunswick, Merzel, and Messori 1985), which involves a 12-to-17-year-old cohort ($n=688$) of black males, 80 percent of the original sample was available for a second wave of data collection after seven years, approximately our proposed follow-up period, and 64 percent for a third wave after 15 years. This latter figure is relevant to any plans for continuing the study beyond the originally proposed follow-up. Most of the attrition in the Harlem Youth Study resulted from the inability to locate subjects or from their deaths. In our case, if attrition is concentrated among the most active offenders, we may have problems in analyzing data.

A problem we face is that we do not know the rate of change for many variables of interest. Although we recommend assessments at one-year intervals, the rapidity of change in life circumstances and the occurrence of critical events in reshaping relationships among the older cohorts makes some twice-yearly contacts attractive, at least for the transition years from 18 to 22. More frequent interviews might also be desirable to help active offenders or drug users recall the number and types of crimes they have committed. One option is to use a supplemental interview schedule for very active offenders. While the core content of the interviews may need to be repeated for certain items, interviews can vary in content, scope, and depth to avoid fatigue and to maintain interest in the research. We also recommend use of a bounding interview, which might be the screening effort.

Another argument in support of frequent assessments is that we want to collect information before and after significant events within a reasonable time. It would be helpful if key events could be used as triggers for assessment, but this strategy is probably unrealistic, because the timing of events such as marriage and employment is unpredictable, which means that a notification process would have to be set up or that researchers would have to be in continual contact with subjects. Experiences that involve the criminal justice system (or other centralized agencies) might provide opportunities for notification of certain events. In any case, we suggest that consideration be given to in-depth interviews around important life experiences in order to develop a better understanding of the subjects' perspective.

Given that for the older cohorts we may not need repeated interviews with teachers and parents, it might be possible to redeploy the resources allocated to these interviews. Among the options that might be considered are interviewing peers, interviewing spouses, and more frequent interviews with high-rate offenders. These options might be used for part of the sample over a delimited portion of the follow-up period on a semiannual or more frequent schedule.

Supplementary Studies

Network Study

We have placed considerable emphasis on the influence of peer networks and on the associated phenomenon of co-offending. For the oldest cohort, the proposed research may intersect the sample at a point that is too late to resolve causal order issues regarding group delinquency, at least in terms of onset. Nonetheless, we should be able to assess how changes in group affiliation relate to rates of offending. It also would be interesting to document how changes in peer networks affect a person's routine activities as well as attitudes and beliefs. In order to study socialization processes and subcultural issues, it would be advantageous to include direct assessments of attitudes over time. Assessments would have to include both subject and network affiliates to demonstrate assimilation; this will be problematic if networks and cliques change rapidly. The study of co-offending issues requires information on the details of criminal events. This will not be difficult for casual offenders but will be problematic for high-rate offenders. One option is to use a different interview schedule or a supplemental interview format for high-rate offenders. Another is to collect detailed information only on selected offenses, such as the most recent.

Given the types of data that need to be collected as well as the methodological and resource problems we are likely to face, we recommend that network and co-offending issues should be generally investigated across an entire cohort and more aggressively pursued in a substudy. Thus, we suggest that a network study be conducted on a subsample of subjects in the older cohorts (e.g., 50 or 75 subjects). In this supplemental project, the network will be the unit of analysis followed over time. Given that the methodology of network research is relatively new, it may be that techniques are not developed sufficiently for this purpose and thus pilot research may be necessary.

Prison Study

We have recommended that sampling include eligible subjects in local institutions, and we have also noted that it may not be possible to collect data on many items in the core design during periods of institutionalization. Incarceration is clearly a significant event in offenders' careers, and we want to ensure that these experiences can be studied in sufficient detail. Although it will be possible to chart the institutional experiences of subjects in the core sample who are eventually sent to prison, the yield of our sampling procedures in terms of active offenders will determine the number of incarcerated subjects and ultimately the level of analyses that can be carried out. If the yield is too low, the incarcerated group may be so small that it cannot be analyzed separately. On the other hand, if the yield is too high, there may be other problems, since incarcerated offenders, while institutionalized, may have to be excluded from analyses of the core sample. Incarceration can encompass a substantial portion of the proposed follow-up period, given that the average prison term runs over two years.

An alternative is to launch a separate study that focuses on institutional experiences. The study could identify a group of prison inmates at intake, if possible from a prison offenders in the communities we study are likely to be sentenced to, and undertake periodic assessments of this group, incorporating variables relevant to issues of prison adaptation. Alternatively, one could screen the prison population to create a sample of those who resided in the communities being studied at the time of their arrest for their current convictions. It may be possible to collect some data from prison staff (e.g., counselors).

We recommend measuring self-reported prison rule violations. In order to minimize perceived risks of repercussions, questions on offenses within prison might best be asked when inmates are preparing to return to the community. Self-reports could be incorporated into a more general review of the prison experience, asking inmates about the high and low points of their institutional career. The retrospective review could be organized around inmates' stays at different facilities, which constitute significant and memorable experiences. For example, an interview might start by reminding an inmate that on April 1 he was transferred to Attica and ask about experiences during the first few weeks, proceeding to collect additional chronological material.

It might also be possible to extend an interest in networks to prisons. Network analyses of prison populations would allow for the study of a number of important theoretical questions that relate to the social organization of prisons, prisons as schools of crime, and the importance of ties to family members and significant others for successful reentry to the community. However, we recognize that participation in a network study may place subjects at risk for retaliation by fellow inmates, which may create serious problems in cooperation.

High-Rate Offender Study

Among the older cohorts we are especially interested in criminal career development, including desistance. In order to study these issues, we need a substantial group of active offenders. Although the research design calls for oversampling on the basis of high-risk criteria, it is difficult to know at this point whether the strategy will identify enough active offenders for studying persistence and desistance. Elsewhere, we recommended carrying out analyses of existing data to study possible use of various sampling criteria. This pilot work will be useful in resolving tensions between comparable and efficient risk criteria across cohorts. To the extent that sampling criteria are unlikely to produce an adequate number of high-rate criminals, a supplemental study targeting this group for analysis should be considered. That study would allow for detailed investigation of issues of desistance and continuation among a group of offenders in which chronicity is high.

15
Sibling Study

This chapter introduces behavioral genetic research methods, and then discusses how they can be used to advantage in the proposed multiple-cohort design. Design choices are presented with an emphasis on why one research design is to be preferred over another and on how a behavioral genetic strategy can help to identify the causes of crime and delinquency. The last section of this chapter describes the sibling-cohort design and addresses a series of questions concerning design choices.

To preview, we recommend that a cohort of siblings who are between 9 and 15 years old at the first wave of data collection be included in the core longitudinal study. A sibling study is particularly valuable for its ability to distinguish *between* family from *within* family causal influences. The proposed design would be unique in the study of crime and delinquency; no previous study in criminology has incorporated longitudinal data on siblings.

Behavioral Genetic Methods

Behavioral genetic methods are useful for understanding the origins, or distal determinants, of behavioral variation (Plomin, DeFries, and McClearn 1990). Behavioral genetics does not deal with traits shown by all members of a population, for example, with cross-cultural universals such as the high rate of aggression among adult males. Instead, the goal is to articulate the origins of variation among individuals in terms of behavioral traits.

Before discussing specific behavioral genetic designs, it is important to correct two common misunderstandings. The first is that heredity and environmental influences are so intertwined in development as to be inseparable. The second is that behavioral geneticists concern themselves only with heredity and not with environment.

The first misconception arises because the goal of behavioral genetics, articulating origins of individual differences, is confused with the developmental history of a single organism. The mix of heredity and environment producing a single organism's development is unknown, and certainly both factors are necessary for physical and psychological growth. The question a behavior geneticist asks, however,

TABLE 15.1. Primary and secondary designations of environmental variables as representing between-family and within-family influences.

Variable	Between-family	Within-family
Social class	P	
Parental religion	P	
Parental values	P	
Child rearing styles	P	S
Father absence	P	
Maternal employment	P	
Neighborhood	P	
Family size	P	
Birth order		P
Perinatal trauma		P
Peer groups		P
Teachers	S	P

Note: P = Primary designation; S = Secondary designation.
Adapted from Rowe (1987).

is, to what extent are *deviations* from the population average genetically or environmentally determined, or both? The question requires a separation of influences because different traits may be determined to different degrees by environmental and genetic factors (e.g., Southern speech accents versus IQ).

Behavioral genetic research designs attempt to disentangle environmental and genetic influences. But, how, one might ask, can family environmental influences be correctly assessed if they are confounded with genetic influences? The study of family environments among biologically related family members can reflect this problem because parents contribute both to family environment and to children's heredity. Only with proper quasi-experimental controls (for example, adoptions) can we know exactly how strongly environmental exposures influence the development of particular traits. Recent research indicates that heredity can affect measures of environment as well (Plomin et al. 1988; Rowe 1981, 1983). Once we recognize that most measures of environment are actually assessments of individual behavior (for instance, parents must decide to purchase books if books are to be in the home), genetic influence on environmental measures follows logically from genetic influence on a diverse range of intellectual and personality traits (Plomin 1986).

Behavioral genetic techniques can be used to ascribe behavioral variation to theoretical (in the sense of mathematically defined) components (Rose and Plomin 1981). Environmental differences among families are a possible source of behavioral variation. The between-family effects, representing the environmental component of variation that is shared in a given family, operate to make family members alike but different from members of other families. The behavioral genetic strategy is to estimate how much behavioral variation results from all types of environmental influences between families, which is a composite of any number of specific environmental influences. As shown in Table 15.1, the effects of many environmental influences mentioned as possible determinants of crime and delinquency should be predominantly between-family effects. For example, families differ in social class, structure (e.g., single versus two parent), religion, parental alcohol use, and so on, and the impact of such influences is usually similar across siblings.

Other influences affect individuals uniquely. The within-family effects, representing the environmental component of variation that is nonshared in a given family, refer to all influences uniquely affecting each person. The within-family effects account for dissimilarities among family members precisely because they are nonshared. Since measurement error also reduces correlations among relatives, true within-family influences should be separated from measurement error, and the separation is made possible by information on trait reliability. Rowe and Plomin (1981) identified several broad categories of nonshared environmental effects: (1) perinatal trauma; (2) family structure, such as birth order; (3) parents' differential treatment of siblings; and (4) extrafamilial influences, such as peer groups.

Genetic variation refers to genes that vary in a population (e.g., genes such as the *A-B-O* blood groups). Heritability (h^2) refers to the extent that genetic variation affects variation in a trait in a particular population. The formula for h^2 is V_g/V_p, where V_g is genetic variation and V_p is phenotypic (e.g., observed trait) variation. We can estimate V_g indirectly, from correlation on phenotypes (e.g., traits) between pairs of relatives, where the pairs differ in degree of genetic or environmental relatedness. Further divisions of genetic effects, such as genetic dominance and genetic interactions, are discussed in behavioral genetic textbooks (Hay 1985; Plomin, DeFries, and McClearn 1990).

Figure 15.1 displays the full partitioning of variation for siblings. Siblings are made similar by between-family influences, shared heredity, and family environment, whereas they are made different by within-family influences. The latter set of influences consists of nonshared environmental and genetic differences among siblings (e.g., siblings may inherit different genes for a particular trait). The remainder of the trait variation can be attributed to between-family (shared) and within-family (nonshared) environmental components.

Choice of Research Design

Various behavioral genetic research designs can apportion behavioral variation between different sources (e.g., heredity, shared environment). Selecting the best combination of research designs depends on the research questions of utmost concern, as well as on the practicality and expense of various options. Possible design choices include: (1) a twin study; (2) a sibling study; (3) a sibling study supplemented with half-siblings and step-siblings; and (4) a sibling study supplemented with an adoption study.

Our recommendation is for a sibling study to be incorporated into the basic longitudinal cohort design, with a supplemental study of adoptees. The rationale

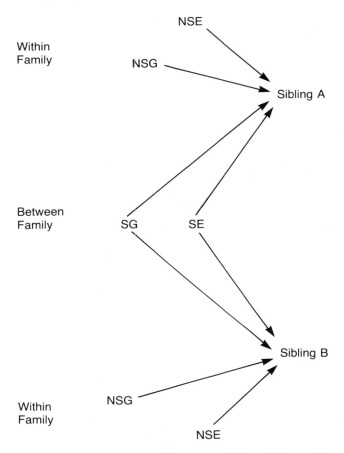

FIGURE 15.1. Environmental and genetic influences on siblings (NSE=nonshared environment; SE=shared environment; NSG=nonshared heredity; SG=shared heredity).

for this recommendation is that comparisons of siblings are theoretically interesting for what they can reveal about total family effects. Consider two extreme, but improbable, outcomes. On one hand, if siblings are no more alike in delinquency than children in different families, then between-family influences would be unimportant. On the other hand, suppose we have a perfect sibling correlation (i.e., 1.0). In this case, variation in causal influences between families would completely determine delinquency, and no relevant causes would exist within families. Real-world situations fall between these two extreme cases, but exactly where can be determined only by empirical study. The sibling study method also permits exploration of sibling effects, such as when one sibling imitates the delinquency of the other. In the absence of between-family environmental influences, the sibling design can be used to estimate trait heritabilities directly as well as to explore alternative models of developmental process. The main disadvantage of a sibling study, however, is that it cannot separate environmental from genetic influences. Hence, we recommend augmenting the sibling study with additional subjects that can help answer the question, how much of family influence is genetic or environmental?

One choice might be to combine siblings, half-siblings, and step-siblings into a single design. A problem of the full-to-half-sibling comparison is that it lacks statistical power, because the difference of genetic correlations is only 0.25 (0.50 for full siblings less 0.25 for half-siblings). Large samples would be required to show that the greater genetic resemblance of full siblings accounts for similarities in behavior. However, a third group, step-siblings, could be used to increase statistical power, because they lack genetic relatedness. Together, these three informative pedigrees would provide sufficient information to identify genetic models, given large sample sizes.

In high-risk areas, it may be possible to find sufficient numbers of step- and half-siblings to solve the problem of statistical power. Depending on the population, the proportion of individuals who are half- or step-siblings can range from 5 percent to over 20 percent. The major difficulty with this pedigree design is that it may not provide satisfactory information about environmental etiology. Half-siblings are often widely separated in age, and step-siblings spend varying periods in their reconstituted families. Hence, the degree of environmental correlation within each sibling type would be uncertain. Given unanswered questions about environmental similarity, this design is not our first choice as a means of separating environmental and genetic effects. Nonetheless, we recommend pilot work on the feasibility of this type of add-on study.

A twin study involves the comparison of monozygotic (MZ) and dizygotic (DZ) twins having a degree of genetic difference of 0.5 (1.0 for the MZ twins less 0.5 for the DZ twins). Clearly, this method provides more statistical power than the previous pedigree design. On the other hand, assessment of family environmental effects is indirect, being much stronger for horizontal environmental influences shared by siblings than for vertical parent-child ones. Environmental influences can be inferred when the MZ twin correlation is greater than the degree of trait heritability. For example, if the MZ twins correlated 0.50 and the DZ twins 0.50, then the estimate of trait heritability would be zero, indicating that greater genetic similarity fails to make MZ twins more alike and leaving family environmental effects prominent. Nonetheless, a confounding persists in twin studies if the interest is in measures of family environment based on parental behaviors. Both types of twins possess an equal genetic relatedness to their parents, so relationships between family environment and twin behavior are confounded. In addition, twins are the same age and have a unique social status. Between-family environmental influences of various types may be greater for twins than for nontwins, leading to overestimation of their importance. Sibling effects, too, may be more important for twins. For these reasons, we will probably have more generalizable results if we use nontwin family relationships.

Another disadvantage of a twin design is the number of households that must be sampled to obtain a sufficient number of twin pairs for study. About 1.25 percent of all births are twin births, and slightly under one-sixth of these will be identical males, and one-sixth will be same-sex fraternal males. This low prevalence presents a formidable challenge to a household sampling strategy. The proposed household sampling procedure would yield about 6 twin pairs per cohort. To acquire a large twin sample, other sampling procedures (e.g., schools, birth records) and an expanded catchment area are probably required.

Our recommendation for a combination of sibling and adoption cohorts avoids these problems and has many advantages. For many personality traits, most family resemblance appears to be predominantly genetic in origin (Loehlin, Willerman, and Horn 1988; Rowe and Plomin 1981). This conclusion rests on a variety of evidence, such as the similarity of twins reared apart or, conversely, the lack of resemblance of adopted siblings raised in a family from infancy. Trait correlations among adopted family members are typically less than 0.05, indicating that, despite rearing together, they are no more alike than individuals raised in different families. As Loehlin, Willerman, and Horn (1988) comment, these circumstances can make a sibling design a full behavioral genetic study:

If it is indeed the case that the influences of shared [between-family] family environment are negligible for most personality traits, then ordinary families should be as informative for behavior genetic work as more exotic groups like twins and adoptees. (p. 110)

That is, the sibling correlation would then estimate genetic influences directly, and all environmental effects would then be within-family ones. More information on behavioral genetic studies of environmental influences between and within families can be found in Plomin and Daniel's (1987) article in *Behavioral and Brain Sciences* and in the commentaries that follow.

For the traits we propose to study, however, some between-family environmental influences may exist. If so, we should be able to demonstrate these influences convincingly in a study of adoptees. Adoptees (adopted in infancy) lack any genetic correlation with adoptive parents; hence, correlations within adoptive families can estimate vertical family environmental effects directly, without the need for statistical manipulations. Adoption studies, of course, can be complicated by selective placement, whereby adoption agencies place children with adoptive parents who are similar in some traits to the children's biological parents. Empirically, such nonrandom placement sometimes causes a weak bias in correlations of IQ scores, but it is rarely, if ever, a problem for nonintellectual traits, because adoption agencies tend to place children selectively for religion, race, and physical characteristics. A selective placements effect so large as to induce a substantial correlation for antisocial behavior implies that subsequent antisocial behavior in infants can be predicted by the characteristics of biological parents. Because the literature shows only weak predictive ability for antisocial behavior regardless of the information used, we must resort to our full design. In any case, various statistical methods can be used to estimate and remove any biasing effects of selective placement.

The supplementary adoption study should be cross-sectional or short-term longitudinal. It might involve an adoption group comparable in age to the sibling cohort. Assuming that genes and environment contribute equally to a parental risk factor and that the risk factor correlates 0.30 with outcome, 100 adoptees give a statistical power of about 33 percent for detecting the environmental component, 300 adoptees give about 75 percent power, and 500 or more adoptees give about 90 percent power. On the other hand, if genes play a trivial role in parental risk factors, then 100 adoptees give almost 90 percent power. Thus, adoptees provide a strong statistical test for one of the important objectives of this supplemental sample, which is to verify that associations found in the nonadoptive sibling longitudinal cohort are environmentally mediated. By combining adoption and nonadoption data, a full behavioral genetic design is achieved that can be used to estimate the size of heritabilities and between-family environmental effects. If, however, few between-family environmental effects are found for delinquency and crime, a result in line with many behavioral genetic studies referenced previously, then the sibling design becomes itself a full behavioral genetic design. Although matching adoptive families to the highest-risk families in the longitudinal cohort study may be difficult, adoptive families comprise a wider range of social class levels than is commonly supposed, because a major impetus to adoption—infertility—ignores social class boundaries. Thus, it may be possible to find matches for a broad range of families in the cohort samples. Lack of adoptions of minority youth may limit the external validity of the design, and the extent of this problem, and possible ways of handling it, should be explored in pilot work. The importance of the adoption comparison will be elaborated in a later section.

Because the adoption study is included to test assumed mechanisms of family influence, it need not be exactly equivalent in composition to the sibling and cohort studies, nor need it be restricted to the same site, since mechanisms of interest should be general across locations and samples. Relatively inexpensive adoption samples can be obtained by culling lists of marketing research firms for adoptees in a given age range, which would provide a nationally representative sample. Alternatively, it might be possible to join Dr. Richard Udry's national study, which includes 100,000 school children, and draw various specialized samples. About 1,000 to 2,000 of these families should be adoptive ones. Another possibility is to draw a new adoption sample in the site selected. Various procedures are possible, but the most practical approach is to survey schoolchildren about their adoption status, because about 98 percent of adopted children today know they are adopted. We can expect that the yield of nonrelative adoptees will be about 1 percent of children surveyed.

Our joint sibling and adoption design can address a number of etiological issues: (1) What is the degree of family influence on crime, delinquency, and related traits, and how do sex differences moderate these effects? (2) What is the degree of sibling effects in which one sibling imitates the other's delinquency? (3) What is the explanation for differences in behaviors between siblings who are exposed to many of the same risk factors for crime and delinquency? (4) What accounts for developmental continuity or change in crime and delinquency? (5) How much of family influence on antisocial behavior is genetic?

Family Influence

A sibling design can be used to investigate causal influences tied to the family unit. The sibling correlation for delinquency (or crime) indicates the total effect of all familial influences, both measured and unmeasured, and thus represents an upper limit on between-family influences. Statistical controls for various between-family covariates (such as social class, family size, IQ) may identify factors that explain some of the between-family variation in delinquency.

Another advantage of a sibling design is that it can be used to decompose correlations among traits into component determinants. Suppose, for example, that in one cohort the correlation between delinquency and positive attitudes toward deviance is 0.52. Only with a sibling design can this correlation be further separated statistically into a family background component and a component representing nonshared influences on each child. A method for this separation is to compute the sibling correlation on double-entry data. In this procedure, values on trait X of one sibling are entered with values on trait Y of the other, and then vice versa, so that the number of paired values is twice the number of siblings. The individual correlation on X and Y minus the sibling (double-entry) correlation on X and Y yields the within-family correlation. The latter would be mathematically equivalent to the correlation of sibling difference scores or to one sibling's trait X minus the other's trait X correlated with sibling differences on trait Y, with the siblings' order of entry preserved and appropriately standardized (see Rowe and Osgood 1984 for details). The apportionment of the correlation is exhaustive, since the total correlation in individuals is exactly equal to the sum of the between- and within-family components.

Consider two possible, albeit unlikely, outcomes for the correlation of delinquency and attitudinal deviance. First, the double-entry sibling correlation (0.52) might equal the correlation in individuals (0.52). In this case, the between-family component would be 0.52 and the within-family component would be zero, indicating that explanations are to be found in variables tied to the family unit. Parental rejection, for example, might lead to both outcomes. On the other hand, if the opposite result was obtained, a between-family component of zero and a within-family component of 0.52, then perhaps tolerance of deviance develops in the peer group sometime after initiation of delinquency. Because siblings may belong to different peer groups, the association of behavioral and attitudinal delinquency would then lack any family background component. The example just given was chosen for didactic purposes. Most likely, some part of the total variation can be apportioned between families and some part within families.

Sex Differences

The analysis of sibling correlations is especially interesting for siblings of different sexes. Although brothers and sisters share many environmental influences, they differ considerably in their propensity for delinquency and crime, as reflected in the well-known sex difference in crime (Wilson and Herrnstein 1985). A cohort study can reveal the correlates of crime and delinquency within each sex, assuming that there are both males and females in the cohort. It cannot, however, indicate which correlations reflect family-transmissible factors and which of these factors are common to males and females.

In the delinquency literature, variables associated with male and female delinquency tend to be similar. In contrast, little evidence is available on whether the family-transmissible influences are the same for males and females; the sibling design is uniquely positioned to address this issue. The hypothesis that between-family causal influences are identical for the two sexes implies that same-sex (i.e., brother-brother, sister-sister) and opposite-sex (i.e., brother-sister) sibling correlations are equal. A much lower opposite-sex than same-sex sibling correlation implies, on the contrary, that between-family influences are different for males and females. One might anticipate a lower opposite-sex correlation, given that delinquency is a sex-linked variable. On the other hand, this result would be quite surprising in light of the failure to identify unique sets of causal variables for males and females. For instance, social control theory variables seem to predict equally well for males and females.

This kind of analysis can be expanded into a multivariate framework. Trait X in the brother can be correlated with Trait Y, which may be the same or a different trait, in the sister. Thus, one can search for nonobvious cross-sex correlates of a behavior. For instance, delinquency in a girl may be better predicted by her brother's level of academic achievement than by his degree of delinquency. These analyses of sex-moderating effects have been rarely conducted and represent a new territory for scientific exploration.

Sibling Effects

Another feature of a longitudinal sibling design is that it can be used to investigate the possibility of a sibling effect in which the delinquency of one sibling is imitated by the other. Although sibling effects may be investigated in the main cohort study—for example, by asking one sibling about the influence of the other—this design is not optimal. Including the other sibling in the study avoids attributional biases that may appear in a single respondent's report (e.g., falsely blaming a sibling for antisocial behavior). Furthermore, if sibling effects are present, they should have pervasive consequences for sibling resemblance, trait variances, and so on. These outcomes can be fully assessed only in the sibling design.

Figure 15.2 displays a statistical model for evaluating sibling mutual influence effects. The latent variables, P, represent the delinquency of the older sibling (A) and younger sibling (B). The siblings were measured on three occasions, as indicated by numbers 1 to 3. Sibling effects are shown by arrows from younger to older sibling, and vice versa, and are labeled with path coefficients, s. The model also allows for a general delinquency proneness trait that is correlated across siblings (G_{cA} with G_{cB}). When analyzed backwards, using known parameter values to estimate a correlation matrix, the model demonstrates that sibling effects will lead to increasing sibling correlations over occasions and to greater test-retest correlations, thus predicting a fairly unusual set of correlations. In a

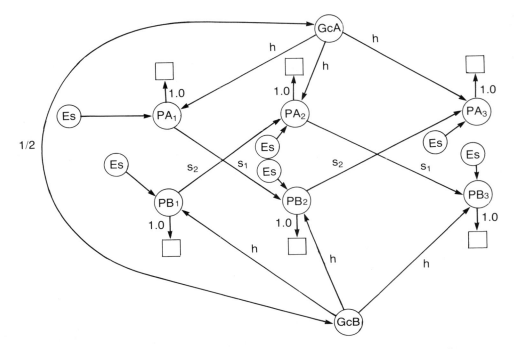

FIGURE 15.2. Developmental model of sibling influence effects and general trait effects over three occasions.

normal analysis, one would enter the correlation matrix as data and then determine whether the sibling effects parameters were statistically significant. In summary, by organizing the data into older and younger sibling pairs, we can test for sibling effects using the statistical model in Figure 15.2. To do this with any degree of statistical power, at least three measurements are required. Hence, the longitudinal design greatly enhances the power of the sibling study.

What Is the Explanation of Sibling Differences?

One of the most striking findings of behavioral genetic studies is that siblings differ in many dimensions of behavior. For example, sibling correlations for personality traits (e.g., sociability) typically are about 0.20 and for IQ and specific intellectual traits about 0.40 (Plomin 1989, p. 109), indicating that siblings are often very different. In the National Youth Survey (Rowe and Britt 1989), same-sex sibling correlations for self-reported delinquency averaged about 0.40 for adolescents between 11 and 20 years of age. In the National Longitudinal Survey of Youth, the correlations averaged about 0.29 (unpublished data). Hence, some family background influence existed that was similar for siblings since children in the same family tended to be more alike in their delinquency than those children reared in different families. Yet, despite this family background effect, enormous differences remained between siblings.

Given the size of sibling differences, it is crucial to explore their basis. What traits or environmental factors make one sibling, but not the other, relatively immune to criminogenic influences? To solve the puzzle of why children in the same family are so different in antisocial behavior, correlation matrices based entirely on within-family difference scores need to be explored. Because siblings differ in both heredity and within-family environment, these difference score correlations reflect both components of variation. Identifying within-family sources of variation will not solve the nature versus nurture problem. Nonetheless, it is a first, important step, one heretofore largely neglected.

What Accounts for Developmental Continuity and Change?

Behavioral geneticists at Virginia Commonwealth University have developed new models for analysis of longitudinal sibling data (Hewitt et al. 1988). These models possess the interesting feature of allowing for comparisons of hypotheses about developmental processes. Rather than presenting all the details of the approach, we will highlight a few relevant ideas. The developmental model can investigate such possibilities as environmental effects at one age that are directly transmitted to the next, nonshared environmental effects on behavior that enter at each age, genetic effects that build on previous ones, and genetic effects that are common to all ages. A pure sibling design cannot label an effect genetic without imposing the assumption of a lack of family environmental influences. Nonetheless, developmental genetic models can be applied to siblings and tested under various sets of assumptions for goodness of fit and for conceptual plausibility.

Figure 15.3 shows a developmental model that can be applied to sibling data. As before, the letter P stands for phenotype, meaning the observed delinquency score; the numerical subscript represents the occasion of observation; and the letters A and B refer to the younger and older sibling, respectively.

The model postulates a latent trait affecting delinquent behavior at each time period (G_{cA} and G_{cB}). Note that in the figure the subscripts of the siblings were omitted for convenience. The latent trait correlates at the genetic expectation of 0.5 across sibling pairs, so that the delinquent behavior of one sibling may become correlated with that of the other. At each time period, a specific genetic variable enters that also correlates 0.5 across sibling pairs (G_s). In genetic terms, this variable represents genes that may be developmentally active, such as those activating pubertal maturation. In environmental terms, the variable may represent period-specific environmental influences shared by siblings, the 0.5 coefficient lacking particular relevance. Both types of genetic influences give rise to a time-dependent genotype (G'_t; here t is the occasion). The regression of this latent trait genotype on the phenotype—that is, the observed delinquency score—is h.

The environmental influences represented in the model are unique to each person and do not correlate across siblings. At each time period, random environ-

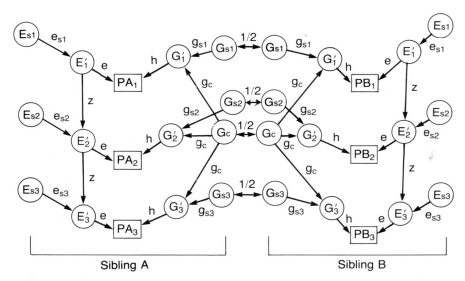

FIGURE 15.3. Developmental model of genetic and environmental effects over three occasions.

mental influences that affect delinquent behavior (E_s) enter the model. These influences create an environmental latent trait that directly affects the phenotype (path e). However, it is possible for environmental influences to transmit forward in time, as represented by the z path coefficients.

In this model, two processes affect developmental status. One is the strength with which the latent trait (G_c) connects with behavior at each time period. The greater the influence of this trait on behavior, the more likely an individual will have the same level of delinquency on all three occasions of observation. As the latent trait is a common factor, it tends to produce consistency across occasions. The other developmental force tending to produce continuity is environmental transmission. Individuals who are high in delinquency at one time due to environmental reasons, such as exposure to particular peer groups, tend to have a high rate on a later occasion, and vice versa. This transmission process suggests that interventions designed to prevent exposure to the environmental influence may reduce both concurrent and future delinquency rates.

A combination of environmental transmission and new environmental influences at each age may have complex effects on correlations from occasion to occasion and on sibling correlations. For example, under some assumptions, sibling correlations would actually decrease with age, as new exposures to non-shared environmental influences make siblings more dissimilar.

The foregoing example makes an important point. Developmental models imply a set of features in the data. If those features are absent (for instance, if sibling correlations increase rather than decrease), one developmental model may be rejected in favor of another. Another point about this kind of developmental model is that its statistical power depends critically on the number of occasions of measurement. Multiple occasions of measurement (four or five rather than the usual two) are more important for distinguishing among theories of developmental processes than a large sample size. Once again, the multiple waves of data collection in a longitudinal study would enhance a sibling study of developmental processes.

How Much of Family Influence Is Genetic?

Jencks (1980) noted that the most policy-relevant conclusions of behavioral genetic studies pertain to the degree of shared (family) environmental influence, rather than to heritability. Although Jencks's comments were directed at IQ, they apply to any family environmental change that is in the direction of families with the best outcomes:

$e^2{}_c$ [shared environment] tells us nothing about the effects of new environments . . . But many policy proposals consist, in essence, of providing all families with advantages currently enjoyed by the privileged. If $e^2{}_c$ is initially large for a given phenotype, successful efforts along this line can be expected to substantially reduce the total variance of the relevant phenotype and greatly improve the relative position of the disadvantaged. (p. 734)

For instance, if the regression coefficient for family environment and child behavior is 0.4, then a one standard deviation change in home environment for the disadvantaged should improve their behavioral outcome by four-tenths of a standard deviation, but only if the regression statistic is not the result of confounding genetic influences.

Behavioral genetic research directed at environmental measures rather than traits has demonstrated the ambiguity of most environmental assessments. Rowe (1983) found that twins' perceptions of parental acceptance-rejection, but not of control, were influenced by genetic variation. This result was later replicated in a Swedish study of MZ and DZ twins raised apart and together (Plomin et al. 1988). If an environmental assessment can contain significant genetic variation, then its association with developmental outcomes may be contaminated as well.

This principle extends to delinquency and children's behavioral problems. An adoption study can check the ostensible family environmental processes discovered in the main longitudinal study. Measures that tap aspects of family environment and that predict children's delinquency, or precursor behaviors, should produce the same kinds of outcomes in adoptive and nonadoptive families. If not, then we might infer that the presumed environmental effects in the main study are mediated genetically, therefore offering less potential for social interventions.

The Sibling Component of the Core Longitudinal Cohort Design

In this section, we review the sibling design component of the core longitudinal study. After describing the core study, we address a number of question pertaining to different design decisions.

The proposed sibling cohort will overlap the 12-year-old cohort. The design will yield 250 sibling pairs of each type (brothers, sisters, and mixed sex), and a total of 1,050 boys and 1,000 girls. The siblings will range in age from 9 to 15 years. We anticipate that, based on the 500 boys in the 12-year-old cohort, we will be able to include 100 brothers and 100 sisters as part of the sibling design. In order to identify additional sibling pairs needed to complete the design, we will conduct a special screening. We anticipate that the screening will produce 150 pairs of brothers (for a total of 250), 150 mixed-sex pairs (for a total of 250), 250 girls of cohort age (12 years), and 250 pairs of sisters.

The females in the sibling design will add to our coverage of etiological processes in female crime and delinquency.

Choices made in this sibling design are considered next:

1. *Why take only two siblings per family?* There are several justifications for this procedure. One is the practical difficulty of interviewing more than two children per family. If two children are the focus of study, a parent will be asked many questions twice. Asking about three or more siblings would place an excessive burden on parents. Another rationale is that it is more convenient statistically to work with a single pedigree type. Finally, if more than two siblings are included in the full longitudinal phase of the study, the cost and difficulty of tracking family groups would be greatly increased.

   We recommend collecting data on two siblings per family with regard to the set of standard measures in the core longitudinal study. Pilot work should explore the feasibility of collecting additional information on other siblings given that targeted data collection on full sibships may be useful for testing specific hypotheses. For example, sibling effects (i.e., imitation or contrast) might be hypothesized to be stronger in siblings who spend more time together or who are at similar ages of development. In this situation, sibling similarity will be moderated by age, and it will be preferable to include all siblings to have sufficient power to test this hypothesis.

2. *Why restrict siblings to within three years of the cohort age?* This decision was somewhat arbitrary. The typical spacing for siblings is about two years, so a three-year range usually catches another sibling in a family, if one exists. The main reason for restricting the age of siblings is that behaviors may change rapidly in early adolescence. With siblings close in age, adjustment of variables for age-related differences is less problematic.

3. *Why use the 12-year-old cohort?* The choice of this cohort was dictated by a desire to capture the period in which the prevalence of active offenders

increases most rapidly. The 12-year-old cohort also captures, for most individuals, the period of pubertal development. Finally, there is merit in studying development from late childhood through late adolescence, because most studies focus on either children or adolescents, but not on the transition between these developmental periods.

4. *Why not sample just older siblings, if younger ones are the target of sibling effects?* The design calls for sampling both older and younger siblings. We cannot assume, at the outset, that sibling effects work only in one direction. Regardless of how siblings are sampled, they can be placed into an older-younger relationship, and both directions of sibling effects can be evaluated using the statistical model presented earlier.

5. *Why study females as a part of the sibling design?* Omission of female siblings reduces the opportunity to discover familial effects specific to females. On the other hand, the addition of sisters to the sibling design adds to its power because sibling correlations could be examined for brothers, sisters, and mixed-sex pairs. The design calls for 250 females of cohort age and a total of 1,000 females in the 9- to 15-year-old range.

6. *How do sibling pairs relate to cohort members?* The design includes the standard cohort of 500 12-year-old males, and an additional cohort of 250 12-year-old females. For many analyses, there is no need to separate the cohort sample from the sibling sample due to concern for possible overrepresentation of large families. Sampling bias in genetic research has been well understood since the beginning of this century, and appropriate techniques for correcting bias are available. A strategy of combining both samples together and correcting for sampling bias increases statistical power for testing hypotheses. In fact, similar bias affects household sampling of individuals, since all things equal, households with large sibships are more likely to contain an individual in the targeted age range than households with smaller sibships.

7. *How will the design deal with changing ages over the follow-up period?* Unlike twins, siblings are different in age, and natural developmental curves for a behavior typically reduce sibling correlations. One way of dealing with the problem is to correct the behavior scores for age with statistical regression techniques which can be used to remove any quadratic trend. In the social sciences, few developmental curves are specified beyond linear and quadratic components.

Another feature, unique to longitudinal data, is that sibling correlations can be produced for siblings measured at the same age, although in different years. This latter comparison is a way of confirming that the statistical corrections of ordinary regression were appropriate.

8. *What if the siblings sampled were twins?* Twins would not count as siblings, and hence would be dropped from the design.

9. *What if adoptees are only children?* In the adoption study, the focus is on *vertical* (e.g., parent-child) environmental effects, so that families with a

single adopted child are eligible for inclusion in this study. These adoptees may be compared to any child in the cohort design, whether the child is ascertained through the sampling of siblings or through the ordinary cohort sampling. In actuality, most adoptive families have more than one child. A horizontal design could include adoptees that have an unrelated sibling in the family. In the experience of the Colorado Adoption Project, over half of adoptees have an unrelated sibling in the household, but, because parents often prefer children of both genders, they are often mixed-sex siblings. Pilot work should determine the feasibility of sampling multiple siblings from adoptive families.

10. *Does the sibling design reflect excessive concern for genetic influences?* The sibling design estimates total familial effects and gives a window on within-family differences. The interpretation of these findings may refer either to family environmental or genetic effects. The sibling design alone does not provide for identification of genetic effects, and therefore we recommend that the longitudinal sibling design be supplemented with an adoption study. The adoption study would help to choose between environmental and genetic interpretations of related sibling results.

Appendix I: Preparatory Field Work and Supplemental Studies

Over the course of many sessions, members of our planning team discussed and critically evaluated numerous proposals for research. Most of these were adjudged meritorious, and the best of these formed the basis for the core plan we present in this book. However, after sorting, evaluating, and synthesizing research ideas, there remained a handful of projects that, although deemed highly important initiatives, were not made part of the core research plan. These fall into two categories: preparatory field research and supplementary research. These studies have been mentioned and discussed throughout the report. In this Appendix, we summarize our recommendations for projects to be carried out in conjunction with the core longitudinal study.

Preparatory Field Research

Producing quality research requires a substantial amount of advance preparation. Just as, for example, the production of a new automobile goes through stages, from concept to drawing to prototype to trial assembly to full-scale manufacture, research also has a production sequence for obtaining quality results. Although we have enjoyed the luxury of being able to invest considerable energy in thinking about research problems, armchair discussion goes only so far before it becomes clear that more action-oriented strategies are needed. This seems especially true when research discussions center on the state of the art and are intended to foster major conceptual and methodological advances. Thus, as part of the research plan, we recommend that several preparatory studies be undertaken before the core longitudinal study is launched.

In social science research, it is not common to earmark substantial resources for in-the-field preparatory work. In our case, given the considerable resources needed for the core longitudinal study, prudence dictates that some advance field research is undertaken in order to reap the maximum yield from the project. We are not alone in the view that preparatory field work is desirable if we are to get the most benefit from a major research initiative. Our conversations with the principal investigators of the Office of Juvenile Justice and Delinquency Prevention Program on the Causes and Correlates of Delinquency revealed a common theme; all of them concluded that too little effort had gone into advance field work because resources were not available. They also concluded that the scientific value of the projects would have been increased had things been otherwise. In particular, they said that they would have liked to have had more opportunities to pretest and refine their instruments and procedures.

The need for preparatory work on instrumentation is especially important in longitudinal research. Although such projects continue for several years, instruments must be finalized at the outset because changes introduced over the course of the study may compromise the symmetry of repeated measurement and possibly threaten the integrity of the design. When researchers plan to coordinate use of instruments across multiple sites or investigators, it is all the more critical for them to develop instruments carefully. This is especially true for the proposed research, because the use of common measures in many sites is a relatively new practice in criminology and no standardized approach has emerged yet from the research community.

Site and Sample Selection

We have identified a number of desirable characteristics for the type of city the research plan should be carried out in. These characteristics, discussed in Chapter 8, represent criteria potential sites can be judged by. As a next step, we suggest a small project that narrows down the list of possible research sites and identifies the most desirable locations. Much of this work can be done using census data and other publicly available statistics, and we estimate that the task will take several months to complete. However, before a particular site can be selected, it is critical that an assurance is given that the research can be carried out in that location.

The selection of research sites is especially critical to the success of the proposed project because work will progress for a decade or more in the same location. We therefore recommend visits to potential research sites to assess firsthand their qualifications and desirability. Because the research depends heavily on the cooperation of local leaders, we also suggest that meetings be arranged with local government and school officials and with community representatives to explain the project, gauge those people's interest, and determine the prospects for long-term cooperation. It would also be useful to inspect school and criminal justice agency records for completeness and ease of access, since these documents will be a major source of information on research subjects.

After selecting a location for the research, the next step would be to work on sample selection issues. For example, our estimate in Chapter 6 of the number of households that will have to be screened to generate the sample is only a rough guess and, in order to develop a more accurate estimate, more needs to be known about the research site. Likewise, the plans in Chapter 5 for community-level sampling are presented in general terms and, once a specific site was selected, it would become possible to be more explicit on the number and types of communities, on sampling ratios, and on the potential advantages of using an individual-level screening procedure. Finally, later in this chapter we will propose a project on tracking fathers that, as a byproduct, will document the family structures of high-risk families, including relationships between primary caretakers and children. This information can be used in defining households and respondents as targets of the research and in refining strategies for sampling siblings and older cohort subjects.

Self-Report Methodology

Self-reported delinquency measures, or information obtained by asking people to provide details on their criminal behavior, is today a nearly universal feature of delinquency research. When first introduced, self-report techniques constituted a major advance because previously researchers had only records from criminal justice agencies for studying illegal behavior. Over the years, substantial work has gone into the refinement of self-report instruments. However, several issues have not been addressed adequately, issues that hold implications for the quality of data to be collected. Furthermore, some methodological questions raised by unique features of the proposed research design have yet to be investigated, and it is desirable to have at least partial answers to these questions in order to carry out the plan. For these reasons, we recommend that several projects be undertaken to refine self-reporting further.

Many objectives can be accomplished by linking up with ongoing studies by researchers who share an interest in studying self-report methods. This strategy will allow results to be achieved more quickly and economically. We have already identified several principal investigators who have expressed an interest in collaborating on methodological projects—namely, David Huizinga (University of Colorado), Terence Thornberry (State University of New York at Albany), Rolf Loeber (Western Psychiatric Institute), and Margaret Ensminger (Johns Hopkins University).

Data accuracy is a long-standing concern with self-report techniques, and we know that a variety of factors can influence subjects' responses to questions on offending behavior. Among these are the range and types of behaviors asked about, the amount of detail requested, the order of questions (trivial to serious, vice versa or mixed), the choice of answers (open-ended or categorical), and the length of reference period (six months or a year). Also important are the method of administration, such as whether answers are solicited by questionnaire or by interview, the use of bounding or focusing aids (e.g., calendar techniques), and the manner in which assurances of confidentiality are presented. We especially are concerned with how these factors relate to differences in reporting levels and validity and to response biases across groups of subjects. We are also concerned with the ability of respondents to report precisely on the timing and details of events and to recall accurately early life experiences.

For example, two large-scale self-report studies have found that black males tend to underreport their criminal involvements (Hindelang, Hirschi, and Weis 1981; Huizinga and Elliott 1986). We do not know the sources of this bias and whether propensities to overreport or underreport can be minimized by changing the way questions are asked. Because we are interested in studying ethnic differences in antisocial behavior, we need to be sure that the data are comparably valid across ethnic groups.

Collecting retrospective information on the early life experiences of subjects in the older cohorts is a central feature of the design. This will be used to link younger and older cohorts, which in turn will facilitate the study of long-term causal processes. The evidence on the accuracy of long-term retrospective reports is conflicting. Research shows that mothers can recall details of the birth of their children many years ago (Hewson and Bennett 1987), but also that people can forget that they were hospitalized within the last year (Cohen, Erickson, and Powell 1984). We need to determine the types of information that can be recalled accurately over an extended time period. One strategy is to cross-check contemporary responses with historical records, and we suggest a collaboration with a long-term longitudinal study in which subjects are reinterviewed about experiences data had been collected on contemporaneously at an earlier time.

Another topic for study is that of the best way to solicit information from high-rate offenders. Extremely active criminals present several problems for researchers, because they can have trouble recalling the details of criminal events, can get tired in interviews, and can be uncooperative. Because frequency and seriousness of offending overlap heavily, any measurement error for chronic offenders also limits our ability to study the most serious offenders.

One of the research objectives of the project is to chart developmental sequences, and this goal requires information on the timing of events. Accurate dating of events is especially critical for some of the statistical techniques we recommend be used (e.g., event history analysis). A variety of methods, such as using calendars or other memory aids, has been developed to assist respondents in locating events in time. Presumably, the use of these methods yields more accurate data. However, we do not know which strategies or methods work best, and we suggest that the relative advantages of various techniques be assessed in a small-scale study.

Tracking Subjects and Family Members and Securing Cooperation

Attrition is a problem that must be given serious attention in longitudinal research. This is particularly so in a study of criminal behavior, because the most interesting subjects can be difficult to track and may be reluctant to cooperate. Some longitudinal studies have very low attrition rates, and this experience can be used to identify techniques that facilitate tracking subjects. However, there will always be difficult cases, and there are substantial benefits in finding ways to improve tracking and increase cooperation. The types of strategies we suggest exploring are those that enlist the help of peers, neighborhood organizations, and friends or acquaintances at school, home, and work. In the interest of efficiency, we recommend linking up with an ongoing study in which a group of difficult-to-find subjects has already been identified.

Past research on child misbehavior shows a strong preference for enlisting mothers, to the exclusion of other family members, as sources of information or as research subjects. In our view, this practice represents a narrow approach to the investigation of family influences on delinquency, leading us to develop a strong interest in including fathers in our research. There are several advantages to involving both parents in delinquency research. To begin with, a mother's report of her child's behavior and of the father's behavior may be biased, so it is useful to have the father as a source of information. More generally, however, we do not know much about the nature and quality of father-son relationships, including the father's role in child-rearing practices when fathers are not full-time residents of households. Also, knowing about the criminal involvements of biological and nonbiological fathers (as well as of mothers) allows us to document continuities in antisocial behavior across generations.

Fathers are often excluded from delinquency research, not only because of a lack of theoretical focus, but also because of the presumed difficulty of locating nonresident fathers and securing their cooperation. We are unsure of the feasibility of studying fathers among high-risk populations, which tend to have unstable family structures. Thus, we recommend undertaking a field study that interviews biological and operative fathers, traces the whereabouts of nonresident fathers, and gauges their willingness to cooperate.

Measurement Development

The ability to measure precisely key constructs and variables stands as a cornerstone of scientific research. Having already discussed aspects of self-report delinquency instruments that warrant further methodological work, we now identify some areas where promising new measures have appeared or where there is a need for new measures.

Temperament, or the constellation of features used to describe individual dispositions, is a key theoretical construct in this research, and a number of measures have been developed, because of the considerable research interest in the temperament of infants and young children. Many of these are pencil-and-paper questionnaires, some involve observations in structured settings and, most recently, biomedical measures have appeared.

For the proposed project, it is important to identify valid and reliable measures of temperament that can be used throughout life. In our view, biomedical measures are especially attractive because they hold opportunities for gauging temperament in a way that is relatively uncontaminated by life experience and associated personality development. Furthermore, by linking physiology to temperamental types, we stand to make easier our task of integrating biological, psychological, and sociological perspectives on development. Jerome Kagan's work (1982), for example, has shown that heart rate variability is a reliable discriminator of inhibited dispositions, and we recommend that this and similar measures be studied to see if they identify children who might be characterized as under-controlled or uninhibited.

As part of the core longitudinal project, we recommend the study of changes in hormone levels of research subjects in relation to antisocial and violent behavior (see Chapter 9 and Appendix II). Recent technological advances that allow saliva samples to be assayed for hormone levels make our proposal feasible. However, since this technology is relatively new, a small-scale trial is needed to gauge the viability of large-scale testing and to gain experience with the technique.

Empathy is defined as "identification with and understanding of another's situation, feelings, and motives." From this definition, obvious hypotheses follow regarding the relation of empathy to criminality. We can expect that people who readily empathize with others, or who routinely put themselves in another's place, are unlikely to engage in harmful antisocial behavior because they will vicariously experience the pain and suffering of victims. Conversely, people who lack empathy should feel less constrained in their relations with others. Psychiatrists have developed the theoretical link between empathy and criminality, often emphasizing in clinical portraits of hardened or psychopathic criminals the fact that some offenders are emotionally insensitive to the situations of other people. Notwithstanding the central position of empathy in some psychiatric theories of criminality, few reliable measures of the concept have been developed. We therefore suggest a modest study to explore measurements of empathy.

Today, in what many observers view as an era dominated by secular influences, it may appear somewhat anachronistic to argue that religion might play a major role in shaping prosocial values and behavior; but for many people, religion remains an important aspect of personal development. As a relevant example, it is not difficult to locate testimonials by ex-offenders attributing a total change in life-style to religious conversion. Furthermore, in many high-risk neighborhoods, religious organizations are an important factor in social, political, and personal spheres. Some research on crime has studied denominational affiliation or has included simple measures of religious commitment, such as church attendance, but few studies have gone beyond this surface level to tap deeper levels of religious commitment and to study the role of religion in fostering values. In the expectation that religiosity may prove to be an important correlate of criminality, we suggest some measurement work in this area.

Supplementary Research

The core longitudinal study, although a highly ambitious research plan, cannot hope to provide answers to all the questions that interest criminologists. In this section, we outline a set of supplementary studies to broaden the scope of the research plan. We designate these as supplementary studies because they are intended to address delimited research questions. We also expect that these studies will draw on separate funding sources and may be carried out by researchers who are not part of the core research team. In keeping with our emphasis on coordination and integration of research efforts, we recommend that the supplementary studies use instruments and measures from the core study for key variables and constructs.

There are several reasons why we suggest these investigations be carried out as supplementary projects. Research strategies must be tailored to the questions being investigated, and optimal designs for different research problems can conflict or can be wholly incompatible in terms of key features such as sampling. By designating some topics for separate efforts that are linked to the core research plan, we can reconcile conflicting design criteria without compromising the project's scientific integrity. Other reasons have to do with practical limitations on the ability to collect data. Funding constraints, for example, make it impractical to use expensive biomedical tests or sophisticated in-home observations on a large number of subjects, and we therefore suggest reserving such measures for specialized investigations on subsamples of the main cohorts.

Studies of Known Offenders

We recommend that two groups of known offenders—arrestees and prison inmates—be selected for supplementary research projects. If possible, the offenders should come from the same city as the core sample, making it more convenient to follow subjects as they move between the criminal justice system and the community. Further details on these proposals can be found in Chapters 13 and 14.

Although the experiences of subjects in core samples will be studied as they come in contact with criminal justice agencies and institutions, there are several reasons for recommending additional studies to complement these investigations. We know that the criminal justice system tends to identify the most active and serious offenders, so that projects starting with known offenders offer greater opportunities for studying the small group of individuals who disproportionately commit crimes. We are also interested in documenting the effects of experiences with the criminal justice system on offenders, and some events, such as prison incarceration, may not occur frequently enough in the core sample to allow for detailed and reliable study. Although we anticipate that many subjects in the core sample will be arrested, a project starting with a sample of arrestees offers more possibilities for experimentation or intervention. Finally, these supplementary studies will provide for quicker research results, since it is not necessary to wait for subjects to become offenders.

Network Study

We have a strong interest in studying how networks of interpersonal associations relate to criminal behavior in terms of onset, continuation, and desistance. In Chapter 14 we discuss network theory and its implications for criminological theory. In general, existing studies of criminal networks have been limited to reports by subjects on their preference for committing offenses in the company of others, or on the delinquency of friends and associates. The core longitudinal study will solicit comparable information, but these data fall short of addressing the full set of network issues we have identified. If the role of networks is to be fully understood, networks themselves should be made the object of investigation, which requires a very different research strategy than past approaches, in which individuals are followed across changing friendship ties. For this reason, we recommend a study to sample and follow networks over time. Because there have yet to be any full-scale network studies in criminology, preparatory work will be necessary in order to gain experience and knowledge on the best way to follow changing affiliations among groups that include active offenders.

Observational Studies

Very often, observational studies, carried out in naturalistic or structured settings, provide important information that cannot be obtained otherwise. In addition to the unique contributions that observational methods can make to understanding a research problem, observational data allows for the demonstration of convergent validity when results obtained by different methods are compared. Many observational techniques, however, are difficult to use on a large scale because they are expensive and require skilled staff to carry out properly.

We have identified several areas where observational data can serve as important complements to survey data and recommend that these projects be carried out on subsets of subjects in the core longitudinal study. Some of the projects we recommend involve observations of parent-child interactions, which might be especially informative in studying siblings and may help to explain why children in the same family turn out differently. Observational studies of family interactions can help to understand how family processes relate to delinquency, while observations of small-group interactions, perhaps carried out in schools, might tell us how peer acceptance or rejection is related to delinquency. Finally, an ethnographic study at the community level can add substance to the demographic and community survey data we propose.

Adoption Study

In Chapter 15, we describe our plan to include pairs of siblings in the core longitudinal study. By contrasting subjects from the same family with those from different families, we will be able to determine the degree to which shared family influences are factors in antisocial behavior. However, family members share both genes and environments, and within the context of a sibling study it is not possible to separate the two sets of influences. Because we are also interested in isolating the contribution of heredity to delinquency, we recommend an adoption study to supplement the sibling analyses. The rationale behind this proposal is given more fully in Chapter 15. At this point, we note briefly that, because adopted children do not share genes with other family members, the confounding effects of heredity are removed from sibling comparisons, helping to isolate effects attributable to environment. Once the environmental effects are estimated, this estimate can be used to adjust the findings from other sibling comparisons, in which the effects of environment and heredity are combined.

As with several other projects we have proposed, a delinquency study with adopted children might be carried out efficiently by augmenting an ongoing project, and a promising possibility for augmentation is the Colorado Adoption Project. By incorporating a self-reported delinquency measure in this project, researchers could capitalize on work that already has gone into sample selection and data collection. In particular, delinquency information on subjects in the Colorado project would make investigating family influences (e.g., poor parenting) on delinquency, inherited predispositions to delinquency and crime, and the relative role of IQ versus nonintellectual personality traits on delinquency possible.

Intergenerational Transmission

The cohort of young girls between the ages of 9 and 15 presents a unique opportunity for studying intergenerational patterns of behavior. We can anticipate that within a relatively short time many of these girls will become parents and that some of their children will show behavior problems. Given that considerable information will be assembled on these female subjects, including details of their antisocial behavior and of their relationships to their parents, continuities in child-rearing experiences across generations can be studied by following those subjects who have children.

We could start by asking the mothers of the young girls in the sample to describe retrospectively the social, economic, and medical circumstances surrounding the birth and early upbringing of their daughters. We could also ask them to describe their child-rearing practices and their illegal activities, including taking drugs. Subsequently, from the point that the females in the cohort become mothers, similar information can be collected prospectively from them. Comparisons can then be made between mothers and daughters regarding maternal roles and behaviors spanning a generation. An intergenerational study of this nature might help clarify different explanations put forward to explain research findings showing that crime tends to run in families.

Expensive, Highly Technical or Specialized Biomedical Measures

Our approach to crime is interdisciplinary, and we are interested in the potential contributions of biomedical technology to the study of delinquency. In Appendix II, we review some biomedical measures that might be used in criminological research and recommend that several of these measures be included in the proposed study. While remaining optimistic about the research potential of biomedical techniques, we note that their application to the crime problem remains undeveloped. We also note that many of these technologies are expensive to use and present technical and logistical difficulties in large-scale implementation. For these reasons, we recommend that supplementary studies be undertaken in which biomedical measures are used on subsamples of cohort subjects. Among the measures that might be used in such studies are X-ray tests to identify concentrations of lead, neurological tests to identify problems with nervous system functioning, and biochemical analysis of cord blood that might identify toxins and other harmful substances that have been transmitted from the mother to the fetus.

Appendix II: Issues in the Use of Biomedical Measures

Many biomedical measures might be included in studies of delinquency and criminal behavior that reflect individuals' general health as well as the physiological and biochemical processes of the brain that regulate behavior. The relative importance of these measures in crime research has been inconsistent, and few measures have evoked the sustained interests or intensive efforts of investigators. Prevailing knowledge about brain-behavior relationships and available technologies has so far not provided great insight into how the body elicits and controls aggressive, hostile, and violent behavior. However, advances in behavior genetics, neurobiology, and molecular biology are generating renewed enthusiasm that important biological determinants of delinquent and criminal behavior may yet be discovered.

Biological risks for antisocial behavior are of two types: health-related factors that encompass congenital abnormalities and bodily diseases, and basic physiological and biochemical processes that support the activity of the brain. There is some evidence that violent individuals suffer worse health than their more conforming peers (Lewis et al. 1985). Possible sources of the difference include head injuries from accidents or abuse, infections involving the central nervous system, poor diet, and lead poisoning. In addition, recently recognized risks to normal growth and development have been inadequately studied in relation to outcomes we are interested in. Examples of these risks are prenatal exposure to psychoactive drugs, the survival of very low birth-weight infants, and exposure to nonnatural chemical agents in food.

These newer risks are both vexing and poorly understood. Although links to delinquency are not established, risks are none the less plausible. For example, the number of pregnant women using illicit drugs is reaching an alarming proportion, and use of cocaine, crack, and methamphetamine can result in more serious addictions than drugs (such as heroin) used at epidemic levels in the past. These newer drugs also have harmful consequences for the fetus, and withdrawal in newborns is difficult to treat. Very low birth weight (i.e., below 1,500 grams) is another biological hazard that seems out of reach of conventional medical approaches. Despite greater utilization of prenatal services and use of sophisticated technology in neonatal intensive care, the number of very low birth-weight babies has not reduced appreciably. In fact, the proportion of black women with very low birth-weight infants has increased over the last decade. Both prenatal exposure to drugs and very low birth weight have been linked to adverse behavioral and cognitive outcomes in children, boys being more severely affected than girls (Earls 1987).

Basic physiological and biochemical mechanisms involving genes, the brain, and behavior represent another set of biological risks. Genes probably operate in a variety of ways to influence behavior, but knowledge of the structural and dynamic properties of the human genome is primitive, and we are unable to forecast the mechanisms involved in producing behavioral characteristics that place individuals at risk for criminality. Nevertheless, we do know that genes specify a set of rules for creating the structure and organization of the brain and for regulating its functions. The challenge for neurobiology is to identify specific structures and functions in the brain that can be traced to a gene or group of genes. Once this goal is achieved, variations or errors in the genetic blueprint that produce structures that in turn regulate behaviors can be pinpointed. It is also important to point out that genetic factors are not responsible alone for the structural and functional development of the brain. Many epigenetic factors are involved, including the role of physical and social environments in the regulation of normal growth and development.

In preparation for a longitudinal study on delinquency and crime, it may be useful to consider two types of brain mechanisms that may be causally related to the behavioral traits that underpin delinquent and criminal outcomes. These mechanisms involve neurotransmitter substances, which may be under genetic control, and hormones, which are good examples of epigenetic mechanisms.

Neurotransmitters are substances secreted from nerve cells that transfer information from one cell to another. Networks of neurons sharing common neurotransmitters are formed in the brain, and manipulating these networks of cells (e.g., with drugs) permits study of how they relate to behavior. Presently, the neurotransmitter of greatest interest in studying impulsive and aggressive behavior is serotonin. Although other transmitter substances are almost certainly involved in the genesis of criminogenic behavior, serotonin has emerged as a leading candidate (Linnoila et al. 1983). The research is novel, however, so that it is very likely that other substances or combinations of substances will be found to be equally, if not more, important. Nevertheless, current research offers a valuable lead that should be pursued in animal and human research.

Metabolic products of serotonin, reflecting activity in the human central nervous system, can be measured in cerebrospinal fluid and in autopsy specimens. Indirect measures of serotonin activity in the brain can be made using blood, platelets, and urine samples. However, the correlation between direct measures of cerebrospinal fluid levels and indirect measures may be unacceptably low, thus arguing against use of indirect measures.

Adrenal androgens and testosterone also appear to influence impulsive and aggressive behavior. Unlike neurotransmitters, these substances do not appear to communicate directly between adjacent cells. The substances play two other roles. One, during the prenatal and early postnatal period, involves the development and organization of the specific brain structures regulating reproductive and possibly aggressive behavior. The second is activational. During puberty, when androgen levels surge, testosterone appears to play a fundamental role in mediating sexual and aggressive behavior (Susman et al. 1987). A bimodal distribution of testosterone occurs in the prenatal and early postnatal period. The first peak, occurring between 10 and 14 weeks after conception, coincides with a period of rapid neurogenesis. During this period testosterone probably exerts maximal influence on the organization of the central nervous system in males. It is less certain what effects are associated with the second peak in testosterone during the second to the eighth postnatal month, but it is likely that both prenatal and postnatal elevations in the production of testosterone are linked to distinctive structural and functional features of the male brain. It is equally likely that testosterone levels among males vary and contribute in part to variations in sexual and aggressive behavior in later life.

Because neither compelling theories nor clear scientific evidence exist to show how genes and the brain cause criminal behavior, choosing biomedical measures for the type of research project we propose has to be done with great care. Both the feasibility of measures and the advisability of methods have to be considered in relation to the likelihood of useful research results. Feasibility relates to the scientific credibility of a measure. If measurement is feasible, questions of the advisability of various methods for taking measurements must be addressed. Issues include costs, technical problems, and ethical acceptability of a given method.

To illustrate, consider the measurement of lead, serotonin, and testosterone, all reasonable candidates as biological measures in a study on crime and delinquency. Body accumulation of lead is a serious health risk, and measurement is considered a routine component of pediatric practice. There is no doubt that sufficiently high concentrations of lead in the body can cause seizures, mental retardation, and even death. Although there is no apparently useful role for lead in the body (implying that any amount of lead in the body is undesirable), there is uncertainty regarding the level at which accumulation of lead becomes medically unacceptable. The issue centers around behavioral and cognitive functions that might be impaired at concentrations of lead much lower than those associated with seizures and mental retardation. At stake are functions directly related to increased risk for conduct disorder and delinquency: lowered intelligence, reduced capacity for sustained attention, and impulsive behavior.

The issue is a major public health problem, given multiple sources of lead contamination in the environment and the particular susceptibility of children to harmful consequences. Moreover, programs to prevent lead exposure and techniques for treating children who have been exposed are widely available. Thus, the feasibility and advisability of including measures of lead in our study is quite high, even though present evidence indicates only weak causal effects when other confounding variables are controlled (Fergusson et al. 1988a, 1988b).

The feasibility of measuring serotonin and testosterone are more challenging to consider, because links to behavior are less well established. The most accurate measurement of serotonin uses cerebrospinal fluid obtained by inserting a needle into the lumbar area of the spine. The lack of firm evidence connecting low serotonin levels to impulsive behavior makes this an unacceptable procedure in all except individuals at very high risk of destructive behavior. Noninvasive methods of measuring serotonin in the central nervous system are being developed. In the meantime, a case can be made to measure serotonin from specimens of whole blood and platelets, especially if collecting blood specimens can be justified for reasons more directly related to healthcare.

Problems associated with measuring testosterone have been simplified by the development of a noninvasive method that gauges hormone concentrations in the saliva. This method lends itself to use with subjects of all ages, including infants, and could be used in the course of repeated measurements with minimal physical risks. Because measuring salivary concentrations of testosterone is not very costly, the feasibility and advisability of including this measure in the proposed study becomes more interesting. A more detailed consideration of the measurement of testosterone is given in a subsequent section of this Appendix.

Measures of lead, serotonin, and testosterone represent special instances of a more general problem in selecting biomedical measures. Our purpose is to design research that promotes a better understanding of how biological and social factors combine to increase the vulnerability of individuals to sustained delinquent or criminal behavior. We are also interested in research that suggests ways of preventing such problems. With this in mind, we now map out the possible range of biomedical measures and survey the costs, technical problems, and scientific relevance of particularly good candidates.

Rather than provide a detailed review of the literature on biomedical measures that could be used in our research, an abbreviated solution to this task is offered. The accompanying table (Table A.1) summarizes a number of scientific and technical concerns involved in making informed choices for a broad range of biomedical measures. The final selection of measures should be based on consultations with physicians and scientists with special skills and knowledge. As a preliminary exercise, we provide a detailed discussion of technical issues involved in measuring testosterone in saliva. The purpose is not to establish grounds for deciding whether the measure should be included but to alert nonspecialists to complexities in what at first blush might appear to be a simple, straightforward procedure.

In the system of checks and balances needed to carry out the kind of interdisciplinary research we envision, it is just as essential that behavioral scientists make informed decisions about the biology of crime as it is for biologists to make intelligent decisions about measuring behavioral and social variables. Testosterone is a good example of a biological variable, because variation in levels has been shown to have a modestly high correlation with aggressive behavior (Olweus et al. 1980). However, one of the impediments to research in this area has been the need to justify collecting blood samples to determine hormone levels. If a hormone can be accurately measured in saliva and if these levels show the same values as levels determined from plasma, then research in this area could be accelerated.

TABLE A.1. Methodological issues in selecting biomedical measures.

Type of measure	How measured	When measured	Reliability	Costs	Technical problems
Prenatal					
Exposure to alcohol & drugs	Maternal report	Throughout pregnancy	Acceptable	Inexpensive	Minor
Fetal movements	Sonography	Throughout pregnancy	Acceptable	Inexpensive	Minor
Perinatal					
Gestational age	Physical exam	At birth	Acceptable	Inexpensive	Minor
Birth weight	Physical exam	At birth	Acceptable	Inexpensive	Minor
Apgar Score	Physical exam	At birth	Acceptable	Inexpensive	Minor
Postnatal					
Physical Growth					
Height	Physical exam	At regular 6 month intervals, to age 7, then annually	Acceptable	Inexpensive	Minor
Weight	Physical exam		Acceptable	Inexpensive	Minor
Head circumference	Physical exam		Acceptable	Inexpensive	Minor
Body Type	Physical exam		Acceptable	Inexpensive	Minor
Nutritional status	Physical exam		Acceptable	Inexpensive	Minor
Muscle Mass & strength	Physical exam		Acceptable	Inexpensive	Minor
Neurological					
Hearing	Physical exam	1 year	Acceptable	Inexpensive	Considerable training & quality control required
Vision	Physical exam	1 year	Acceptable	Inexpensive	
Hard signs	Physical exam	1 year	Acceptable	Inexpensive	
Soft signs	Physical exam	1 year	Modest training	Inexpensive	
Minor physical anomalies	Physical exam	At birth	Modest training	Inexpensive	
Head injury	Parent report & physical exam	Periodically throughout the study	Acceptable	Inexpensive	
Infections			Acceptable	Inexpensive	
Heavy metal exposure	Laboratory exam		Acceptable	$40–100	Requires excellent lab facility

TABLE A.1. Continued.

Type of measure	How measured	When measured	Reliability	Costs	Technical problems
Biochemical/Hormonal					
Adrenalin	Laboratory exam of	Any age	Depends on standards set at individual laboratories	$25–45	Requires excellent lab facility and consultants to interpret results and to detect patterns
Dopamine	blood and urine	Any age		$25–45	
Serotonin	samples	Any age		$25–45	
Cholesterol	Blood	Any age		$25–45	
Testosterone	Saliva & blood	At birth & at puberty		$25	
Cortisol	Saliva & blood	At birth & at puberty		$25	
Electrolytes	Saliva & blood	Under stressful circumstances			
Physiological					
Skin resistance	Polygraph	Age 3 yrs	Not acceptable	$50	Sensitive to temp., humidity, etc.
Heart rate	Polygraph	From birth	Acceptable	$25	Minor
Blood pressure	Polygraph	From birth	Acceptable	$25	Minor
Attention span & distractability	Personal computer	From age 4 months	Acceptable	$50–100	May be age dependent
EEG evoked potentials	Neurophysiology laboratory	From birth	Marginally acceptable	$100–200	Requires dedicated laboratory and sophisticated computer/electronic equipment
Other					
Speech samples	Reg intervals	From age 12 months	Acceptable	Inexpensive	Minor
Photographs & video-tapes	Reg intervals	Annually	Acceptable	Inexpensive	Minor
Mother–child	Reg intervals	12, 18, 30 months	Acceptable	Moderately expensive	Minor
Play session	Reg intervals	30, 36 months	Acceptable	Moderately expensive	Minor
Peer relationship	Reg intervals	36, 48, 60 months	Acceptable	Moderately expensive	Minor

Steroid Measurements in Saliva

The assay of steroids in saliva is a recent innovation with increasingly useful applications in the field of clinical endocrinology. This simple, noninvasive technique has also become attractive to psychologists interested in links between biological mechanisms and behavior in nonclinical populations. Of particular significance is the finding that salivary concentrations of adrenal and gonadal hormones appear to reflect the nonprotein-bound fraction of steroid concentrations found in the plasma (Katz and Shannon 1969; Johnson, Joplin, and Burrin 1987; Galard 1987). What follows is a discussion of some of the technical issues involved in assaying the male gonadal hormone, testosterone. Many of the same issues are involved in using samples of saliva to assay other steroid hormones of interest, such as cortisol (Vining and McGinley 1987).

It is generally accepted that testosterone is passively transported into the saliva without being significantly catabolized. It does not appear to be actively secreted from the salivary glands because it is unaffected by salivary flow rate and enzymatic degradation. It is unclear what, if any, physiological role testosterone has in these glands, although some animal studies suggest that the salivary glands function as target organs and may have some synthetic activity (Luisi et al. 1980). If that is the case, then interpretation of reference values becomes more difficult.

Currently, testosterone measured in the saliva is presumed to be unbound, thus representing the biologically active component of the total testosterone measured in the plasma. Only 2 percent of the testosterone in the plasma is unbound (Landsman et al. 1976), and the remainder is bound to Sex Hormone Binding Globulin (SHBG), which presumably makes the hormone less readily available to cells. Various diseases and drugs alter specific binding proteins in the plasma, making measurement of the total plasma steroid concentration laborious, costly, and difficult to interpret. For these reasons, salivary measurements may prove superior to the more conventional methods of measurement, particularly in research that aims to monitor normal growth and development in children. The correlation between plasma and salivary measures of testosterone ($r = 0.81$) as reported in adult males (Tames and Swift 1983) is sufficiently high to justify continued refinements of salivary measures.

Collection and Storage of Samples

Whole saliva (parotid, submandibular, sublingual fluid, plus gingival fluid) can be used for the analysis. Whole saliva, however, contains mucins produced by the submandibular and sublingual glands that can interfere with some technical aspects of assay analysis. The volume of saliva used in radioimmunoassay methods is 1 to 2 ml. The stimulation of saliva production can be achieved effectively in a number of simple ways. For example, spitting stimulates a saliva flow of 0.5 ml/min. Chewing paraffin wax, rubber bands, or unflavored gum stimulates a saliva flow rate of 1 to 3 ml/min. Placing acid lemon drops of 0.5 ml/l citric acid on the tongue will yield a saliva flow of 5 to 10 ml/min (Bacon et al.

1978). It is essential to avoid blood contamination in collecting samples in situations that involve bleeding of the gums, which can increase salivary testosterone levels significantly in adult males.

Samples can be collected by simply having a child spit into a collection container. With infants, a small syringe with a plastic tube attached to aspirate the saliva from the floor of the mouth can be used. Both of these techniques collect only whole saliva. A large diurnal variation in salivary testosterone levels in adult males has been reported with peak levels occurring in the morning (Swift 1984), and a twofold difference between morning and night values. It is essential to freeze samples at $-20°C$ in plastic vials. Salivary samples of progesterone have shown a decrease in assayable hormone when stored at room temperature for two days.

Analysis

There are at least three types of assays available to measure salivary testosterone: radioimmunoassays (RIA), enzymeimmunoassays (EIA), and solid phase immunoassay using time-resolved fluorescence. The most widely used technique is radioimmunoassay. Of the three types of assays, the solid phase technique has the advantage of requiring fewer steps and decreased exposure to radioactive materials. In terms of reliability of measurement, no one method has yet proven superior. Costs associated with the methods will vary depending on the amount of experience the laboratory has with the technique and on the number of specimens being analyzed. The approximate cost for measurement of testosterone using the RIA method ranges between $20 to $30 a sample.

The analysis and interpretation of salivary testosterone levels in infants and children is hindered by lack of reference data on plasma levels of the unbound hormone. To date, studies have been done on adult and adolescent males and females (Landsman et al. 1976; Gupta, Attanasio, and Raaf 1975). Plasma levels in adolescents have been correlated with the six stages of pubertal development as described by Tanner (Gupta, Attanasio, and Raaf 1975). Plasma-free testosterone levels in children from age 6 to 14 have also been published (Ducharme et al. 1976). The levels in males become many times higher during puberty than in females, as expected. The data also reveal that levels in females, while comparatively low, are measurable. Marked variation in the level of salivary testosterone has been shown for boys aged 9 to 17 years (Tames and Swift 1983). This wide range of variation may be correlated with differential timing in the onset of and transition through puberty and with differences in behavior. Price (1984) reported the correlation between salivary testosterone levels and pubertal staging.

Comments

The physiological role of testosterone in human saliva has not yet been thoroughly evaluated. It is unclear whether salivary glands function as target organs of the hormone or have any synthetic activity. Despite that limitation, it is clear that the possibility of using salivary samples to measure and monitor hormonal physiology is enticing for developmental studies. Safe and noninvasive sample collection could even be done at home, with parents taking responsibility for transporting specimens to the laboratory, where they can be stored at $-20°C$ for an indefinite amount of time prior to analysis.

Several criteria have to be met to establish the diagnostic value of testosterone measurements in the saliva of children. The assay method should be sensitive enough to measure the normal range of the hormone in the saliva, and cross-reactions should be ascertained. The method should also yield reproducible results. The relationship between plasma and salivary levels should be well established, and the effects of different storage methods delineated. Normal ranges for children of different ages, sexes, and stages of physical development should be established and the schedule of diurnal variation determined. Most of these criteria have already been met or should soon be satisfied. Thus, salivary measurement of testosterone is a promising biomedical variable to include in the proposed study for reasons that support scientific interests and meet logistical and ethical demands of research on human subjects.

The major point to be made is that biomedical measures, particularly those that are not part of routine laboratory practice, require considerable planning and careful preparation prior to inclusion in a study on behavioral development. Illustrating difficulties with hormone measures, as we have done, can help anticipate difficulties associated with other biomedical measures, though some problems will not necessarily be of the same nature.

Appendix III: Program on Human Development and Criminal Behavior—Participants

ONSET WORKING GROUP

Delbert S. Elliott	Colorado	Sociology
David P. Farrington (Chair)	Cambridge	Psychology, Criminology
J. David Hawkins	University of Washington	Social Work, Education
Denise B. Kandel	Columbia	Sociology, Drug Epidemiology
Malcolm W. Klein	Southern California	Sociology
Rolf Loeber	University of Pittsburgh, Western Psychiatric Institute	Developmental Psychology
Joan McCord	Temple	Sociology
David C. Rowe	Arizona	Behavioral Genetics
Richard E. Tremblay	Montreal	Developmental Psychology

DESISTANCE WORKING GROUP

Kenneth Adams	Castine Research Corporation	Criminology
M. Douglas Anglin	UCLA, Drug Abuse Research Group	Psychology
Arnold Barnett	M.I.T.	Statistics
Alfred Blumstein	Carnegie-Mellon	Operations Research
Robert Boruch	Northwestern	Statistics, Research Design
Peter Greenwood	RAND Corporation	Program Evaluation
Lloyd E. Ohlin (Chair)	Harvard Law School	Sociology
Albert J. Reiss, Jr.	Yale	Sociology
Lawrence Sherman	Maryland	Criminology

RESEARCH ORGANIZATION WORKING GROUP

Robert Boruch	Northwestern	Statistics, Research Design
Alfred Blumstein	Carnegie-Mellon	Operations Research
Albert J. Reiss, Jr. (Chair)	Yale	Sociology
Lee N. Robins	Washington University	Psychiatric Epidemiology
Michael Tonry	Castine Research Corporation	Law

RESEARCH DESIGN WORKING GROUP

Kenneth Adams	Castine Research Corporation	Criminology
Felton Earls (Cochair)	Harvard Public Health	Psychiatry
David P. Farrington (Cochair)	Cambridge	Psychology, Criminology
Lloyd E. Ohlin (Cochair)	Harvard Law School	Sociology
David C. Rowe	Arizona	Behavioral Genetics
Robert J. Sampson	Illinois	Sociology
Richard E. Tremblay	Montreal	Developmental Psychology

References

Achenbach, Thomas M., and Craig S. Edelbrock. 1983a. *Manual for the Child Behavior Checklist and Revised Child Behavior Profile.* Burlington, Vt.: Queen City Printers.
———. 1983b. *Manual for the Teacher's Report Form and Teacher Version of the Child Behavior Profile.* Burlington: University of Vermont.

Achenbach, Thomas M., Stephanie H. McConaughty, and C.T. Howell. 1987. "Child/Adolescent Behavioral and Emotional Problems: Implications of Cross-Informant Correlations for Situational Specificity." *Psychological Bulletin* 101:213–232.

Ainsworth, M., M. Blehar, E. Waters, and S. Wall. 1978. *Patterns of Attachment: A Psychological Study of the Strange Situation.* Hillsdale, N.J.: Erlbaum.

Akers, Ronald L., Marvin D. Krohn, Lonn Lanza-Kaduce, and Marcia Radosevich. 1985. *Deviant Behavior: A Social Learning Approach.* Belmont, Calif.: Wadsworth.

Allison, Paul. 1984. *Event History Analysis: Regression for Longitudinal Event Data.* Beverly Hills, Calif.: Sage.

American Psychiatric Association. 1987. *Diagnostic and Statistical Manual of Mental Disorders,* 3d ed., rev. Washington, D.C.: American Psychiatric Association.

Anglin, M. Douglas, and G. Speckart. 1986. "Narcotic Use, Property Crime and Dealing: Structural Dynamics Across the Addiction Career." *Journal of Quantitative Criminology* 2:355–375.

Bachman, Jerald G., Patrick M. O'Malley, and Jerome Johnston. 1978. *Youth in Transition,* vol. 6. Ann Arbor: University of Michigan, Institute for Social Research.

Bacon, C.J., J.C. Mucklow, A. Saunders, M.P. Rawlin, and J.K.G. Webb. 1978. "A Method of Obtaining Saliva Samples from Infants and Young Children." *British Journal of Clinical Pharmacology* 5:89–90.

Baltes, Paul B. 1968. "Longitudinal and Cross-Sectional Sequences in the Study of Age and Generation Effects." *Human Development* 11:145–171.

Bayley, Nancy. 1969. *Bayley Scales of Infant Development: Birth to Two Years.* New York: Psychological Corporation.

Bell, Richard Q. 1953. "Convergence: An Accelerated Longitudinal Approach." *Child Development* 24:145–152.
———. "An Experimental Test of the Accelerated Longitudinal Approach." *Child Development* 25:281–286.

Belsky, Jay, and M. Rovine. 1987. "Temperament and Attachment Security in the Strange Situation: An Empirical Rapprochement." *Child Development* 58:787–795.

Berrueta-Clement, John R., Lawrence J. Schweinhart, W. Steven Barnett, Ann S. Epstein, and David P. Weikart. 1984. *Changed Lives*. Ypsilanti, Mich.: High/Scope.

Berrueta-Clement, John R., Lawrence J. Schweinhart, W. Steven Barnett, and David P. Weikart. 1987. "The Effects of Early Educational Intervention on Crime and Delinquency in Adolescence and Early Adulthood." In *Prevention of Delinquent Behavior*, edited by John D. Burchard and Sarah N. Burchard. Newbury Park, Calif.: Sage.

Block, J.H. 1965. *The Child-rearing Practices Report (CRPR): A Set of Q Items for the Description of Parental Socialization Attitudes and Values*. Berkeley: University of California, Institute of Human Development.

Block, J., and J.H. Block. 1980. *The California Child Q-Set*. Palo Alto, Calif.: Consulting Psychologists Press.

Blumstein, Alfred, Jacqueline Cohen, and David P. Farrington. 1988. "Longitudinal and Criminal Career Research: Further Clarifications." *Criminology* 26:57–74.

Blumstein, Alfred, Jacqueline Cohen, Jeffrey A. Roth, and Christy A. Visher, Eds. 1986. *Criminal Careers and "Career Criminals."* 2 vols. Washington, D.C.: National Academy Press.

Blumstein, Alfred, David P. Farrington, and Soumyo Moitra. 1985. "Delinquency Careers: Innocents, Desisters, and Persisters." In *Crime and Justice: An Annual Review of Research*, vol. 6, edited by Michael Tonry and Norval Morris. Chicago: University of Chicago Press.

Bornstein, M.H., and M.D. Sigman. 1986. "Continuity in Mental Development from Infancy." *Child Development* 57:251–274.

Both, D., and L. Garduque. 1989. *Social Policy for Children and Families: Creating an Agenda*. Institute of Medicine, National Research Council. Washington, D.C.: National Academy Press.

Botvin, Gilbert J., and Anna Eng. 1982. "The Efficacy of a Multicomponent Approach to the Prevention of Cigarette Smoking." *Preventive Medicine* 11:199–211.

Bowlby, John. 1969. *Attachment and Loss*. New York: Basic.

Bradley, R.H., B.M. Caldwell, and S.L. Rock. 1988. "Environment and School Performance: A Ten-year Follow-up and Examination of Three Models of Environmental Action." *Child Development* 59:852–867.

Breckenridge, J. 1989. "Replicating Cluster Analysis: Method, Consistency, and Validity." *Multivariate Behavioral Research* 24:147–161.

Brunswick, Ann F., Cheryl R. Merzel, and Peter A. Messeri. 1985. "Drug Use Initiation Among Urban Black Youth: A Seven Year Follow-up of Developmental and Secular Influences." *Youth and Society* 17:189–216.

Buka, Stephen. 1989. "Longitudinal Research in Rhode Island: History and Opportunities." Report to the Research Design Working Group of the Program on Human Development and Criminal Behavior. Castine Research Corporation, Castine, Maine.

Bursik, Robert J., Jr. 1988. "Social Disorganization and Theories of Crime and Delinquency: Problems and Prospects." *Criminology* 26:519–551.

Buss, Arnold, and Robert Plomin. 1975. *A Temperament Theory of Personality Development*. New York: Wiley.

Byrne, James M., and Robert J. Sampson, eds. 1986. *The Social Ecology of Crime*. New York: Springer-Verlag.

Campbell, Donald T., and Julian C. Stanley. 1966. *Experimental and Quasi-Experimental Designs for Research*. Chicago: Rand McNally.

Carey, W.B., and S.C. McDevitt. 1978. "Revision of the Infant Temperament Questionnaire." *Pediatrics* 61:735–739.

Carlson, M., Felton Earls, and R. Todd. 1988. "The Importance of Regressive Changes in the Development of the Nervous System: Towards a Neurobiological Theory of Child Development." *Psychiatric Developments* 5:1–22.

Cattell, Raymond, B., M.D. Cattell, and E. Johns. 1984. *Manual and Norms for the High School Personality Questionnaire.* Champaign, Ill.: Institute for Personality and Ability Testing.

Clarke, Ronald V., and Derek B. Cornish. 1985. "Modeling Offenders' Decisions: A Framework for Research and Policy." In *Crime and Justice: An Annual Review of Research*, vol. 6, edited by Michael Tonry and Norval Morris. Chicago: University of Chicago Press.

Cloward, Richard A., and Lloyd E. Ohlin. 1960. *Delinquency and Opportunity.* Glencoe, Ill.: Free Press.

Cohen, Albert K. 1955. *Delinquent Boys.* Glencoe, Ill.: Free Press.

Cohen, B., P. Erickson, and A. Powell. 1984. "How Does Length of Recall Affect the Number of Physician Visits Reported?" Proceedings of the American Statistical Association, Social Statistics Section. Washington, D.C.: American Statistical Association.

Cohen, Jacqueline. 1986. "Research on Criminal Careers: Individual Frequency Rates and Offense Seriousness." In *Criminal Careers and "Career Criminals,"* vol. 1, edited by Alfred Blumstein, Jacqueline Cohen, Jeffrey A. Roth, and Christy A. Visher. Washington, D.C.: National Academy Press.

Cohen, Lawrence E., and Marcus Felson. 1979. "Social Change and Crime Trends: A Routine Activity Approach." *American Sociological Review* 44:588–608.

Cohen, Lawrence E., and Richard Machalek. 1988. "A General Theory of Expropriative Crime: An Evolutionary Ecological Approach." *American Journal of Sociology* 94:465–501.

Coie, John D., and G. Krehbiel. 1984. "Effects of Academic Tutoring on the Social Status of Low-Achieving, Socially Rejected Children." *Child Development* 55:1465–1478.

Conger, John J., and Walter C. Miller. 1966. *Personality, Social Class and Delinquency.* New York: Wiley.

Conner, Ross F. 1977. "Selecting a Control Group: An Analysis of the Randomization Process in Twelve Social Reform Programs." *Evaluation Quarterly* 1:195–244.

Consortium for Longitudinal Studies. 1983. *As the Twig is Bent . . . Lasting Effects of Preschool Programs.* Hillsdale, N.J.: Erlbaum.

Cook, Thomas D., and Donald T. Campbell. 1979. *Quasi-Experimentation.* Chicago: Rand McNally.

Damon, William. 1988. *The Moral Child: Nurturing Children's Natural Moral Growth.* New York: Free Press.

Douglas, James W.B. 1970. "Discussion." In *Psychiatric Epidemiology*, edited by Edward H. Hare and John K. Wing. London: Oxford University Press.

Ducharme, J.R., M.G. Forest, E. De Peretti, M. Sempe, R. Collu, and J. Bertrand. 1976. "Plasma Adrenal and Gonadal Steroids in Human Pubertal Development." *Journal of Clinical Endocrinology and Metabolism* 42:468–476.

Durkheim, Emile. 1897. *Suicide: A Study in Sociology.* Translated by J. Spaulding and G. Simpson. New York: Macmillan.

Earls, Felton. 1987. "Sex Differences in Psychiatric Disorders: Origins and Developmental Influences." *Psychiatric Developments* 5:1–23.

Eckland-Olson, Sheldon, John Lieb, and Louis Turner. 1984. "The Paradoxical Impact of Criminological Sanctions: Some Microstructural Findings." *Law and Society Review* 18:159–178.

Edwards, Allen L. 1959. *Edwards Personal Preference Schedule Manual*. New York: Psychological Corporation.

Elliott, Delbert S., David Huizinga, and Suzanne S. Ageton. 1985. *Explaining Delinquency and Drug Use*. Beverly Hills, Calif.: Sage.

Elliott, Delbert S., David Huizinga, and Scott Menard. 1989. *Multiple Problem Youth: Delinquency, Substance Use, and Mental Health Problems*. New York: Springer-Verlag.

Elliott, Delbert S., and Harwin L. Voss. 1974. *Delinquency and Dropout*. Lexington, Mass.: D.C. Heath.

Empey, LaMar T. 1978. *American Delinquency: Its Meaning and Construction*. Homewood, Ill.: Dorsey.

Empey, LaMar T., and Maynard L. Erickson. 1972. *The Provo Experiment*. Lexington, Mass.: D.C. Heath.

Empey, LaMar T., and Steven G. Lubeck. 1971. *The Silverlake Experiment*. Chicago: Aldine.

Erickson, Martha F., L. Alan Sroufe, and Byron Egeland. 1985. "The Relationship between Quality of Attachment and Behavior Problems in Preschool in a High-Risk Sample." In *Growing Points in Attachment Theory and Research*. Monographs of the Society of Research in Child Development, edited by I. Bretherton and E. Waters. Chicago: University of Chicago Press.

Evans, Richard I., Richard M. Rozelle, Scott E. Maxwell, Bettye E. Raines, Charles A. Dill, Tanya J. Guthrie, Allen H. Henderson, and Peter C. Hill. 1981. "Social Modeling Films to Deter Smoking in Adolescents: Results of a Three-Year Field Investigation." *Journal of Applied Psychology* 66:399–414.

Farrington, David P. 1977. "The Effects of Public Labelling." *British Journal of Criminology* 17:112–125.

———. 1983. "Randomized Experiments on Crime and Justice." In *Crime and Justice: An Annual Review of Research*, vol. 4, edited by Michael Tonry and Norval Morris. Chicago: University of Chicago Press.

———. 1985. "Predicting Self-Reported and Official Delinquency." In *Prediction in Criminology*, edited by David P. Farrington and Roger Tarling. Albany: State University of New York Press.

———. 1986. "Age and Crime." In *Crime and Justice: An Annual Review of Research*, vol. 7, edited by Michael Tonry and Norval Morris. Chicago: University of Chicago Press.

———. 1987. "Implications of Biological Findings for Criminological Research." In *The Causes of Crime*, edited by Sarnoff A. Mednick, Terrie E. Moffitt, and Susan A. Stack. Cambridge: Cambridge University Press.

———. 1988a. "Advancing Knowledge about Delinquency and Crime: The Need for a Coordinated Program of Longitudinal Research." *Behavioral Sciences and the Law* 6:307–331.

———. 1988b. "Studying Changes Within Individuals: The Causes of Offending." In *Studies of Psychosocial Risk*, edited by Michael Rutter. Cambridge: Cambridge University Press.

Farrington, David P., Bernard Gallagher, Lynda Morley, Raymond J. St Ledger, and Donald J. West. 1988. "Are There Any Successful Men from Criminogenic Backgrounds?" *Psychiatry* 51:116–130.

Farrington, David P., and Rolf Loeber. 1989. Relative Improvement Over Chance (RIOC) and Phi as Measures of Predictive Efficiency and Strength of Association in 2 × 2 Tables." *Journal of Quantitative Criminology* 5:201–213.

Farrington, David P., Rolf Loeber, Delbert S. Elliott, J. David Hawkins, Denise B. Kandel, Malcolm W. Klein, Joan McCord, David C. Rowe, and Richard E. Tremblay. 1990. "Advancing Knowledge about the Onset of Delinquency and Crime." In *Advances in Clinical Child Psychology*, vol. 13, edited by Benjamin B. Lahey and Alan E. Kazdin. New York: Plenum.

Farrington, David P., Rolf Loeber, and Welmoet B. Van Kammen. 1990. "Long-Term Criminal Outcomes of Hyperactivity-Impulsivity-Attention Deficit and Conduct Problems in Childhood." In *Straight and Devious Pathways from Childhood to Adulthood*, edited by Lee N. Robins and Michael Rutter. Cambridge: Cambridge University Press.

Farrington, David P., Lloyd E. Ohlin, and James Q. Wilson. 1986. *Understanding and Controlling Crime: Toward and New Research Strategy*. New York: Springer-Verlag.

Farrington, David P., Howard N. Snyder, and Terrence A. Finnegan. 1988. "Specialization in Juvenile Court Careers." *Criminology* 26:461–487.

Fergusson, David M., J.E. Fergusson, L.J. Horwood, and N.G. Kinzett. 1988a. "A Longitudinal Study of Dentine Lead Levels, Intelligence, School Performance and Behaviour. Part II. Dentine Lead and Cognitive Ability." *Journal of Child Psychology and Psychiatry* 29:793–809.

———. 1988b. "A Longitudinal Study of Dentine and Lead Levels, Intelligence, School Performance and Behaviour. Part III. Dentine Lead Levels and Attention/Activity." *Journal of Child Psychology and Psychiatry* 29:811–824.

Fischer, Claude. 1982. *To Dwell Among Friends: Personal Networks in Town and City*. Berkeley: University of California Press.

Fleiss, Joseph L. 1981. *Statistical Methods for Rates and Proportions* 2d ed. New York: Wiley.

Foulkes, M., and C. Davis. 1981. "An Index of Tracking for Longitudinal Data." *Biometrics* 37:439–446.

Fox, Nathan. 1989. "Psychophysiological Correlates of Emotional Reactivity During the First Year of Life." *Developmental Psychology* 25:364–372.

Fullard, W., S.C. McDevitt, and W.B. Carey. 1984. "Assessing Temperament in One- to Three-Year-Old Children." *Journal of Pediatric Psychology* 9:205–217.

Galard, R. 1987. "Salivary Testosterone Levels in Infertile Men." *International Journal of Andrology* 10:597–601.

Garrison, William T., and Felton Earls. 1987. *Temperament and Child Psychopathology*. Newbury Park, Calif.: Sage.

George, C., N. Kaplan, and Mary Main. 1984. "Attachment Interview for Adults." Unpublished manuscript. Berkeley: University of California.

Glaser, Daniel. 1979. "A Review of Crime Causation Theory and its Application." In *Crime and Justice: An Annual Review of Research*, vol. 1, edited by Norval Morris and Michael Tonry. Chicago: University of Chicago Press.

Glueck, Sheldon, and Eleanor T. Glueck. 1950. *Unraveling Juvenile Delinquency*. Cambridge, Mass.: Harvard University Press.

Goodman, Leo. 1961. "Statistical Methods for the Mover-Sayer Model." *Journal of the American Statistical Association* 56:841–868.

Gottfredson, Michael, and Travis Hirschi. 1987. "The Methodological Adequacy of Longitudinal Research on Crime." *Criminology* 25:581–614.

Gottfredson, Stephen D., and Ralph B. Taylor. 1986. "Person-Environment Interactions in the Prediction of Recidivism." In *The Social Ecology of Crime*, edited by James M. Byrne and Robert J. Sampson. New York: Springer-Verlag.

Gough, Harrison G. 1948. "A Sociological Theory of Sociopathy." *American Journal of Sociology* 53:359–366.

_____. 1975. *California Psychological Inventory Manual*. Palo Alto, Calif.: Consulting Psychologists Press.

Graham, J.R. 1987. *The MMPI: A Practical Guide* 2d ed. New York: Oxford University Press.

Granovetter, Mark S. 1973. "The Strength of Weak Ties." *American Journal of Sociology* 78:1360–1380.

Gupta, D., A. Attanasio, and S. Raaf. 1975. "Plasma Estrogen and Androgen Concentration in Children During Adolescence." *Journal of Clinical Endocrinology and Metabolism* 40:636–643.

Hamparian, Donna M., Richard Schuster, Simon Dinitz, and John P. Conrad. 1978. *The Violent Few: A Study of Dangerous Juvenile Offenders*. Lexington, Mass.: Lexington.

Harlow, Harry F., and M.K. Harlow. 1973. "Social Deprivation in Monkeys." In *Readings from the Scientific American: The Nature and Nurture of Behavior*. San Francisco: Freeman.

Harrell, T.H., and T.A. Lombardo. 1984. "Validation of an Automated 16PF Administration Procedure." *Journal of Personality Assessment* 48:638–642.

Hawkins, J. David, Howard J. Doueck, and Denise M. Lishner. 1988. "Changing Teaching Practices in Mainstream Classrooms to Improve Bonding and Behavior of Low Achievers." *American Educational Research Journal* 25:31–50.

Hawkins, J. David, and Joseph G. Weis. 1985. "The Social Development Model: An Integrated Approach to Delinquency Prevention." *Journal of Primary Prevention* 6:73–97.

Hay, David A. 1985. *Essentials of Behavior Genetics*. Oxford: Blackwell.

Heist, P., and G. Yonge. 1968. *Omnibus Personality Inventory Form F Manual*. New York: Psychological Corporation.

Hewitt, John K., Lindon J. Eaves, M.C. Neale, and J.M. Meyer. 1988. "Resolving Causes of Developmental Continuity or "Tracking." I. Longitudinal Twin Studies During Growth." *Behavior Genetics* 18:133–151.

Hewson, D., and A. Bennett. 1987. "Childbirth Research Data: Medical Records or Women's Reports?" *American Journal of Epidemiology* 125:484–491.

Hindelang, Michael J., Travis Hirschi, and Joseph G. Weis. 1981. *Measuring Delinquency*. Beverly Hills, Calif.: Sage.

Hirschi, Travis. 1969. *Causes of Delinquency*. Berkeley: University of California Press.

Howes, C. 1988. "Peer Interaction of Young Children." *Monographs of the Society for Research in Child Development*. Serial No. 217, Volume 53, Number 1. Chicago: University of Chicago Press.

Huizinga, David, and Delbert S. Elliott. 1986. "Reassessing the Reliability and Validity of Self-Report Delinquency Measures." *Journal of Quantitative Criminology* 2:293–327.

Huston, Ted. 1983. "The Typography of Marriage: A Longitudinal Study of Change in Husband and Wife Relationships Over the First Year." Address to the International Conference on Interpersonal Relationships, Madison, Wisc.

Jencks, Christopher. 1980. "Heredity, Environment, and Public Policy Reconsidered." *American Sociological Review* 45:723–736.

Johnson, S.G., G.F. Joplin, and J.M. Burrin. 1987. "Direct Assay for Testosterone in Saliva: Relationship with Direct Serum Free Testosterone Assay." *Clinical Chimica Acta* 163:309–318.

Kagan, Jerome. 1982. "Heart Rate and Heart Rate Variability as Signs of Temperamental Dimensions in Infants." In *Measuring Emotions in Infants and Children*, edited by C.E. Izard. New York: Cambridge University Press.

———. 1989. *Unstable Ideas: Temperament, Cognition and Self*. Cambridge, Mass.: Harvard University Press.

Kandel, Denise B., and Victoria H. Raveis. 1987. "Changes in Drug Behavior from Middle to Late Twenties: Initiation, Persistence, and Cessation of Use." *American Journal of Public Health* 77:607–611.

Katz, F.H., and I.L. Shannon. 1969. "Parotid Fluid Cortisol and Cortisone." *Journal of Clinical Investigation* 48:848–855.

Kazdin, Alan E. 1987. *Conduct Disorders in Children and Adolescence*. Newbury Park, Calif.: Sage.

Klein, Malcolm W., and Lois Y. Crawford. 1967. "Groups, Gangs and Cohesiveness." *Journal of Research in Crime and Delinquency* 4:63–75.

Knight, Barry J., and Donald J. West. 1975. "Temporary and Continuing Delinquency." *British Journal of Criminology* 15:43–50.

Kolvin, Israel, Roger F. Garside, A.R. Nicol, A. Macmillan, F. Wolstenholme, and I.M. Leitch. 1981. *Help Starts Here: The Maladjusted Child in the Ordinary School*. London: Tavistock.

Kolvin, Israel, Frederick J.W. Miller, Mary Fleeting, and Philip A. Kolvin. 1988. "Social and Parenting Factors Affecting Criminal-Offence Rates: Findings from the Newcastle Thousand Family Study (1947–1980)." *British Journal of Psychiatry* 152:80–90.

Labouvie, Erich W., and John R. Nesselroade. 1985. "Age, Period, and Cohort Analysis and the Study of Individual Development and Social Change." In *Individual Development and Social Change*, edited by John R. Nesselroade and Alexander Von Eye. Orlando, Fla.: Academic Press.

Ladd, G.W., and Stephen R. Asher. 1985. "Social Skill Training and Children's Peer Relations: Current Issues in Research and Practice." In *Handbook of Social Skills Training and Research*, edited by L.L. Abate and M.A. Milan. New York: Wiley.

Landsman, S.D., L.M. Sandford, B.E. Howland, and C. Dawes. 1976. "Testosterone in Human Saliva." *Experientia* 32:940–941.

Lehoczky, John. 1986. "Random Parameter Stochastic Process Models of Criminal Careers." In *Criminal Careers and "Career Criminals,"* vol. 2, edited by Alfred Blumstein, Jacqueline Cohen, Jeffrey A. Roth, and Christy A. Visher. Washington, D.C.: National Academy Press.

Lemert, Edwin M. 1972. *Human Deviance, Social Problems, and Social Control* 2d ed. Englewood Cliffs, N.J.: Prentice-Hall.

Lerner, Richard, M. Palermo, A. Spiro, and John Nesselroade. 1982. "Assessing the Dimensions of Temperamental Individuality Across the Life Span: The Dimensions of Temperament Survey (DOTS)." *Child Development* 53:149–159.

Lewis, Dorothy O., E. Moy, L.D. Jackson, R. Aaronson, N. Restifo, S. Serra, and A. Simos. 1985. "Biopsychosocial Characteristics of Children Who Later Murder." *American Journal of Psychiatry* 142:1161–1167.

Linnoila, Markku, Matti Virkkunen, M. Scheinin, A. Nuutila, R. Rimon, and Frederick K. Goodwin. 1983. "Low Cerebrospinal Fluid 5-Hydroxyindoleacetic Acid Concentration Differentiates Impulsive from Non-Impulsive Violent Behavior." *Life Science* 33:2609–2614.

Loeber, Rolf, and Carol Baicker-McKee. 1989. "The Changing Manifestations of Disruptive/Antisocial Behavior from Childhood to Early Adulthood: Evolution or Tautology?" Report to the Research Design Working Group of the Program on Human Development and Criminal Behavior. Castine Research Corporation, Castine, Maine.

Loeber, Rolf, and Thomas Dishion. 1983. "Early Predictors of Male Delinquency: A Review." *Psychological Bulletin* 94:68–99.

Loeber, Rolf, and Magda Stouthamer-Loeber. 1986. "Family Factors as Correlates and Predictors of Juvenile Conduct Problems and Delinquency." In *Crime and Justice: An Annual Review of Research*, vol. 7, edited by Michael Tonry and Norval Morris. Chicago: University of Chicago Press.

Loehlin, John C., Lee Willerman, and John M. Horn. 1988. "Human Behavior Genetics." *Annual Review of Psychology* 39:101–133.

Luisi, M., G.P. Bernini, A. Del Genovese, R. Burinelli, D. Barletta, M. Gasperi, and F. Fanchi. 1980. "Radioimmunoassay for Free Testosterone in Human Saliva." *Journal of Steroid Biochemistry* 12:513–516.

Magnusson, David, and Lars Bergman. 1988. "Individual and Variable-based Approaches to Longitudinal Research on Early Risk Factors." In *Studies of Psychosocial Risk: The Power of Longitudinal Data*, edited by Michael Rutter. Cambridge: Cambridge University Press.

Main, Mary, and J. Solomon. 1986. "Discovery of an Insecure/Disoriented Attachment Pattern." In *Affective Development in Infancy*, edited by M. Yogman and T.B. Brazelton. Norwood, N.J.: Ablex.

McArdle, Jack J. 1988. "Dynamic But Structural Equation Modeling of Repeated Measures Data." In *Handbook of Multivariate Experimental Psychology* 2d ed., edited by John R. Nesselroade and Raymond B. Cattell. New York: Plenum.

McArdle, Jack J., and Edward Anderson. 1989. "Latent Variable Growth Models for Research on Aging." In *The Handbook of the Psychology of Aging* 3d ed., edited by James E. Birren and K. Warner Schaie. New York: Van Nostrand Reinhold.

McArdle, Jack J., Edward Anderson, and Mark Aber. 1987. "Convergence Hypotheses Modeled and Tested with Linear Structural Equations." Proceedings of the 1987 Public Health Conference on Records and Statistics. U.S. Department of Health and Human Services, Hyattsville, MD. DHITS Pub. No. 88–1214, pp. 347–352.

McArdle, Jack J., and David Epstein. 1987. "Latent Growth Curves within Developmental Structural Equation Models." *Child Development* 58:110–133.

McCord, Joan. 1978. "A Thirty-Year Follow-Up of Treatment Effects." *American Psychologist* 33:284–289.

McMahan, C. 1981. "An Index of Tracking." *Biometrics* 37:447–455.

Meany, M.J., D.H. Aitken, C. Berkel, S. Bhatnagar, and R. Sapolsky. 1988. "Effects of Neonatal Handling on Age-related Impairments Associated with the Hippocampus." *Science* 239:766–768.

Megargee, Edwin I. 1977. *The California Psychological Inventory Handbook*. San Francisco: Jossey-Bass.

Menard, Scott, Delbert S. Elliott, and David Huizinga. 1988. "The Dynamics of Deviant Behavior." Progress report, October 1988. Boulder: University of Colorado, Institute of Behavioral Science.

Messner, Steven F., Marvin D. Krohn, and Alan E. Liska, eds. 1989. *Theoretical Integration in the Study of Deviance and Crime: Problems and Prospects*. Albany: State University of New York Press.

Moffitt, Terrie E., and Phil A. Silva. 1988. "Neuropsychological Deficit and Self-reported Delinquency in an Unselected Birth Cohort." *Journal of the American Academy of Child and Adolescent Psychiatry* 27:233–240.

Moos, Rudolf H., and B.S. Moos. 1981. *Family Environment Scale Manual.* Palo Alto, Calif.: Consulting Psychologists Press.

Morash, Merry, and Lila Rucker. 1989. "An Exploratory Study of the Connection of Mother's Age at Childbearing to her Children's Delinquency in Four Data Sets." *Crime and Delinquency* 35:45–93.

Myers, I.B. 1985. *Manual: The Myers-Briggs Type Indicator.* Palo Alto, Calif.: Consulting Psychologists Press.

Novy, Diane M., and Stephen Donohue. 1985. "The Relationship Between Adolescent Life Stress Events and Delinquent Conduct Including Conduct Indicating a Need for Supervision." *Adolescence* 20:313–321.

Offord, David R., M. Boyle, Peter Szatmari, N.I. Rae-Grant, P.S. Links, D.T. Cadman, J.A. Byles, J.W. Crawford, H.M. Blum, C. Byrne, H. Thomas, and C.A. Woodward. 1987. "Ontario Child Health Study: Six-month Prevalence of Disorder and Rates of Service Utilization." *Archives of General Psychiatry* 44:832–836.

Olweus, Dan, Ake Mattsson, Daisy Schalling, and Hans Low. 1980. "Testosterone, Aggression, Physical and Personality Dimensions in Normal Adolescent Males." *Psychosomatic Medicine* 42:253–269.

Osborn, Steven G. 1980. "Moving Home, Leaving London, and Delinquent Trends." *British Journal of Criminology* 20:54–61.

Otnow-Lewis, Dorothy, Richard Lovely, Catherine Yeager, and Donna Della Femina. 1989. "Toward a Theory of the Genesis of Violence: A Follow-up Study of Delinquents." *Journal of the American Academy of Child and Adolescent Psychiatry* 28:431–436.

Patterson, Gerald R. 1982. *Coercive Family Process.* Eugene, Ore.: Castalia.

Patterson, Gerald R., John B. Reid, R.R. Jones, and Rand E. Conger. 1975. *A Social Learning Approach to Family Intervention. Vol. I. Families With Aggressive Children.* Eugene, Ore.: Castalia.

Plomin, Robert. 1986. *Development, Genetics, and Psychology.* Hillsdale, N.J.: Erlbaum.

———. 1989. "Environment and Genes: Determinants of Behavior." *American Psychologist* 44:105–111.

Plomin, Robert, and Denise Daniels. 1987. "Why are Children in the Same Family so Different From One Another?" *Behavioral and Brain Sciences* 10:1–16.

Plomin, Robert, John C. DeFries, and David W. Fulker. 1988. *Nature and Nurture During Infancy and Early Childhood.* New York: Cambridge University Press.

Plomin, Robert, John C. DeFries, and Gerald E. McClearn. 1990. *Behavioral Genetics: A Primer* 2d ed. New York: Freeman.

Plomin, Robert, Gerald E. McClearn, N.J. Pedersen, John R. Nesselroade, and C.S. Bergman. 1988. "Genetic Influence on Childhood Family Environment Perceived Retrospectively from the Last Half of the Life Span." *Developmental Psychology* 24:738–745.

Porter, Beatrice, and K. Daniel O'Leary. 1980. "Marital Discord and Childhood Behavior Problems." *Journal of Abnormal Child Psychology* 8:287–295.

Price, D.A. 1984. "Salivary Hormone Levels in Infants and Children." *Frontiers of Oral Physiology* 5:51–68.

Reiss, Albert J., Jr. 1986. "Why Are Communities Important in Understanding Crime?" In *Communities and Crime*, edited by Albert J. Reiss, Jr. and Michael Tonry. Chicago: University of Chicago Press.

_____. 1988. "Co-offending and Criminal Careers." In *Crime and Justice: An Annual Review of Research*, vol. 10, edited by Michael Tonry and Norval Morris. Chicago: University of Chicago Press.

Robins, James. 1986. "A New Approach to Causal Inference in Mortality Studies with a Sustained Exposure Period—Applications to Control of the Healthy Worker Survivor Effect." *Mathematical Modelling* 7:1393–1512.

_____. 1987. "A Graphical Approach to the Identification and Estimation of Causal Parameters in Mortality Studies with Sustained Exposure Periods." *Journal of Chronic Diseases* 40:139–161.

Robins, James, and H. Morgenstern. 1987. "The Foundations of Confounding in Epidemiology." *Computers and Mathematics with Applications* 14:869–916.

Robins, Lee N. 1979. "Sturdy Childhood Predictors of Adult Outcomes: Replications from Longitudinal Studies." In *Stress and Mental Disorder*, edited by James E. Barrett, Robert M. Rose, and Gerald L. Klerman. New York: Raven.

_____. 1988. "Data Gathering and Data Analysis for Prospective and Retrospective Longitudinal Studies." In *Studies of Psychosocial Risk: The Power of Longitudinal Data*, edited by Michael Rutter. New York: Cambridge University Press.

Rogosa, David. 1980. "A Critique of Cross-lagged Correlation." *Psychological Bulletin* 88:245–258.

_____. 1988. "Myths About Longitudinal Research." In *Methodological Issues in Aging Research*, edited by K. Warner Schaie, R. Campbell, W. Meredith, and S. Rawlings. New York: Springer.

Rogosa, David, D. Brandt, and M. Zimowski. 1982. "A Growth Curve Approach to the Measurement of Change." *Psychological Bulletin* 92:726–748.

Rogosa, David, R. Floden, and John B. Willett. 1984. "Assessing the Stability of Teacher Behavior." *Journal of Educational Psychology* 6:1000–1027.

Rogosa, David, and John B. Willett. 1985. "Understanding Correlates of Change by Modeling Individual Differences in Growth." *Psychometrika* 50:203–228.

Rohner, R.P. 1984. *Handbook for the Study of Parental Acceptance and Rejection* rev. ed. Storrs: University of Connecticut, Center for the Study of Parental Acceptance and Rejection.

Rowe, David C. 1981. "Environmental and Genetic Influences on Dimensions of Perceived Parenting: A Twin Study." *Developmental Psychology* 17:203–208.

_____. 1983. "A Biometrical Analysis of Perceptions of Family Environment: A Study of Twin and Singleton Sibling Kinships." *Child Development* 54:416–423.

_____. 1987. "Resolving the Person-Situation Debate: Invitation to an Interdisciplinary Dialogue." *American Psychologist* 42:218–227.

Rowe, David C., and Chester L. Britt. 1989. "Developmental Explanations of Delinquent Behavior: Trait or Transmission?" Unpublished manuscript. University of Arizona, Department of Child Development and Family Relations.

Rowe, David C., and D. Wayne Osgood. 1984. "Heredity and Sociological Theories of Delinquency: A Reconsideration." *American Sociological Review* 49:526–540.

Rowe, David C., and Robert Plomin. 1981. "The Importance of Nonshared (E_1) Environmental Influences in Behavioral Development." *Developmental Psychology* 17:517–531.

Rubin, Donald B. 1989. *Multiple Imputation*. New York: Wiley.

Rubin, Kenneth H., and T. Daniel-Beirness. 1983. "Concurrent and Predictive Correlates of Sociometric Status in Kindergarten and Grade One Children." *Merrill-Palmer Quarterly* 29:337–352.

Runyan, William. 1980. "A Stage-State Analysis of the Life Course." *Journal of Personality and Social Psychology* 38:951–962.

Rutter, Michael. 1989. "Age as an Ambiguous Variable in Developmental Research: Some Epidemiological Considerations from Developmental Psychopathology." *International Journal of Behavioral Development* 12:1–34.

Rutter, Michael, and Henri Giller. 1983. *Juvenile Delinquency: Trends and Perspectives*. New York: Guilford Press.

Sampson, Robert J. 1987. "Urban Black Violence: The Effects of Male Joblessness and Family Disruption." *American Journal of Sociology* 93:348–382.

———. 1988 "Local Friendship Ties and Community Attachment in Mass Society: A Multilevel Systemic Model." *American Sociological Review* 53:766–779.

Sampson, Robert J., and W. Byron Groves. 1989. "Community Structure and Crime: Testing Social-Disorganization Theory." *American Journal of Sociology* 94:774–802.

Sarnecki, Jerzy. 1982. *Brottslighet ock Kamratrelationer: Studie av Ungbrottsligheten i en Svensk Kommun*. Stockholm: Brottsforebyggnderadet (National Council for Crime Prevention). Portions translated in 1984 by Denise Galarraga as *Criminality and Friend Relations: A Study of Juvenile Criminality in a Swedish Community*. Washington, D.C.: National Institute of Justice, National Criminal Justice Reference Service.

Scarr, Sandra, and K. McCarthey. 1983. "How People Make Their Own Environments: A Theory of Genotype-Environment Effects." *Child Development* 54:424–435.

Schaie, K. Warner. 1985. "A General Model for the Study of Developmental Problems." *Psychological Bulletin* 64:92–107.

———. 1977. "Quasi-Experimental Research Designs in the Psychology of Aging." In *Handbook of the Psychology of Aging*, edited by James E. Birren and K. Warner Schaie. New York: Van Nostrand Reinhold.

Schaie, K. Warner, and Paul B. Baltes. 1975. "On Sequential Strategies in Developmental Research." *Human Development* 18:384–390.

Schanberg, S., and T. Field. 1988. "Sensory Deprivation Stress and Supplemental Stimulation in the Rat Pup and Preterm Neonate." *Child Development* 58:1431–1447.

Schonfeld, I.S., David Shaffer, P. O'Connor, and S. Portnoy. 1988. "Conduct Disorder and Cognitive Functioning: Testing Three Causal Hypotheses." *Child Development* 59:993–1007.

Schwendinger, Herman, and Julia S. Schwendinger. 1985. *Adolescent Subcultures and Delinquency*. New York: Praeger.

Shannon, Lyle W. 1988. *Criminal Career Continuity: Its Social Context*. New York: Human Sciences Press.

Shaw, Clifford R., and Henry D. McKay. 1931. *Social Factors in Juvenile Delinquency*, vol. 2. Washington, D.C.: U.S. Government Printing Office.

———. 1942. *Juvenile Delinquency and Urban Areas*. Chicago: University of Chicago Press.

———. 1969. *Juvenile Delinquency and Urban Areas*. Rev. ed. Chicago: University of Chicago Press.

Shaw, Clifford R., F.M. Zorbaugh, Henry D. McKay, and L.S. Cottrell. 1929. *Delinquency Areas*. Chicago: University of Chicago Press.

Simcha-Fagan, Ora, and Joseph Schwartz. 1986. "Neighborhood and Delinquency: An Assessment of Contextual Effects." *Criminology* 24:667–703.

Singer, Simon I. 1986. "Victims of Serious Violence and Their Criminal Behavior: Subcultural Theory and Beyond." *Violence and Victims* 1:61–70.

Sroufe, L. Alan. 1979. "The Coherence of Individual Development: Early Care, Attachment and Subsequent Developmental Issues." *American Psychologist* 34:834–841.

⸻. 1985. "Attachment Classification from the Perspective of Infant-Caregiver Relationships and Infant Temperament." *Child Development* 56:1–14.

Stark, Rodney. 1987. "Deviant Places: A Theory of the Ecology of Crime." *Criminology* 25:893–909.

Straus, Murray A. 1979. "Measuring Intrafamily Conflict and Violence: The Conflict Tactics (CT) Scales." *Journal of Marriage and the Family* 41:75–88.

Susman, E.J., G. Inoff-Germain, E.D. Nottelmann, D.L. Loriaux, G.B. Cutler, and G.P. Chrousos. 1987. "Hormonal Influences on Aspects of Psychological Development During Adolescence." *Journal of Adolescent Health Care* 8:492–504.

Sutherland, Edwin H. 1939. *Principles of Criminology.* New York: Lippincott.

Sutherland, Edwin H., and Donald R. Cressey. 1974. *Criminology.* 9th ed. Philadelphia: Lippincott.

Suttles, Gerald D. 1968. *The Social Order of the Slum: Ethnicity and Territory in the Inner City.* Chicago: University of Chicago Press.

Swift, A.D. 1984. "Salivary Testosterone in Male Adolescents." *Frontiers of Oral Physiology* 5:69–79.

Tames, F.J., and A.D. Swift. 1983. "The Measurement of Salivary Testosterone." In *Immunoassays for Clinical Chemistry.* 2d ed., edited by F.J. Tames. London: Churchill-Livingstone.

Telch, Michael J., Joel D. Killen, Alfred L. McAlister, Cheryl L. Perry, and Nathan Maccoby. 1982. "Long-term Follow-up of a Pilot Project on Smoking Prevention with Adolescents." *Journal of Behavioral Medicine* 5:1–8.

Terman, Lewis, and Maud Merrill. 1973. *Stanford Binet Intelligence Scale: Manual for the Third Revision.* Boston: Houghton-Mifflin.

Thomas, Alexander, Stella Chess, H. Birch, M. Hertzig, and S. Korn. 1963. *Behavioral Individuality in Early Childhood.* New York: New York University Press.

Thornberry, Terence P. 1987. "Toward an Interactional Theory of Delinquency." *Criminology* 25:863–891.

Thornberry, Terence P., and Margaret Farnworth. 1982. "Social Correlates of Criminal Involvement: Further Evidence on the Relationship Between Social Status and Criminal Behavior." *American Sociological Review* 47:505–518.

Trasler, Gordon B. 1962. *The Explanation of Criminality.* London: Routledge & Kegan Paul.

Tremblay, Richard E., Marc LeBlanc, and Alex E. Schwartzman. 1988. "The Predictive Power of First Grade Peer and Teacher Ratings of Behavior: Sex Differences in Antisocial Behavior and Personality at Adolescence." *Journal of Abnormal Child Psychology* 16:571–583.

Tremblay, Richard E., Joan McCord, Pierre Charlebois, Claude Gagnon, Serge Larivee, and Helene Boileau. 1989. "Can Disruptive Boys be Helped to Become Competent?" Paper presented at the meeting of the Society for Life History Research, Montreal, June.

Vining, R.F., and R. McGinley. 1987. "The Measurement of Hormones in Saliva: Possibilities and Pitfalls." *Journal of Steroid Biochemistry* 27:81–94.

Waldo, Gordon P., and David Griswold. 1979. "Issues in the Measurement of Recidivism." In *The Rehabilitation of Criminal Offenders: Problems and Prospects*, edited by Lee Sechrest, Susan O. White, and Elizabeth D. Brown. Washington, D.C.: National Academy of Sciences.

Wallace, Rodrick. 1988. "A Synergism of Plagues: Planned Shrinkage, Contagious Housing Destruction, and AIDS in the Bronx." *Environmental Research* 47:1–33.

———. 1990. "Urban Desertification, Public Health, and Public Order: Planned Shrinkage, Violent Death, Substance Abuse, and AIDS in the Bronx." *Social Science and Medicine*, in press.

Wechsler, David. 1949. *Manual for the Wechsler Intelligence Scale for Children*. New York: Psychological Corporation.

———. 1955. *Manual for the Wechsler Adult Intelligence Scale*. New York: Psychological Corporation.

———. 1974. *Manual for the Wechsler Intelligence Scale for Children*. Rev. ed. New York: Psychological Corporation.

———. 1981. *WAIS-R Manual*. New York: Psychological Corporation.

Weiner, Neil. 1985. "Violent Recidivism Among the 1958 Philadelphia Birth Cohort Boys." Report to the National Institute of Justice, U.S. Department of Justice. Philadelphia: Sellin Center for Studies in Criminology and Criminal Law.

Weis, Joseph G. 1986. "Issues in the Measurement of Criminal Careers." In *Criminal Careers and "Career Criminals"*, vol. 2, edited by Alfred Blumstein, Jacqueline Cohen, Jeffrey A. Roth, and Christy A. Visher. Washington, D.C.: National Academy Press.

West, Donald J. 1982. *Delinquency: Its Roots, Careers, and Prospects*. London: Heinemann.

West, Donald J., and David P. Farrington. 1973. *Who Becomes Delinquent?* London: Heinemann.

———. 1977. *The Delinquent Way of Life*. London: Heinemann.

Widom, Cathy S. 1989. "The Cycle of Violence." *Science* 244:160–166.

Williams, Carolyn, and Craig Uchyama. 1989. "Assessment of Life Events During Adolescence: The Use of Self-report Inventories." *Adolescence* 24:95–118.

Wilson, James Q., and Richard J. Herrnstein. 1985. *Crime and Human Nature*. New York: Simon and Schuster.

Wolfgang, Marvin E., Robert M. Figlio, and Thorsten Sellin. 1972. *Delinquency in a Birth Cohort*. Chicago: University of Chicago Press.

Wolfgang, Marvin E., Terence P. Thornberry, and Robert M. Figlio. 1987. *From Boy to Man, From Delinquency to Crime*. Chicago: University of Chicago Press.

Woodhead, Martin. 1985. "Pre-school Education has Long-Term Effects: But Can They Be Generalized?" *Oxford Review of Education* 11:133–155.

Yamaguchi, Kazuo, and Denise B. Kandel. 1984. "Patterns of Drug Use from Adolescence to Young Adulthood. II. Sequences of Progression." *American Journal of Public Health* 74:668–672.

Research in Criminology